D1038360

LET MY PEOPLE IN

LET MY PEOPLE IN

A Lesbian Minister Tells of Her Struggles to Live Openly and Maintain Her Ministry

ROSE MARY DENMAN

WILLIAM MORROW AND COMPANY, INC.
New York

Grateful acknowledgment for lyrics to the song "Mean Old Woman Blues" is made to Rev. Susan Savell, Heartlight House Music, P.O. Box 253, Biddeford Pool, Maine 04006.

Library of Congress Cataloging-in-Publication Data

Denman, Rose Mary.
Let my people in : a lesbian minister tells of her struggles to live openly and maintain her ministry / Rose Mary Denman.
p. cm.
ISBN 0-688-08470-2
1. Denman, Rose Mary. 2. United Methodist Church (U.S.)—United States—Clergy—Biography. 3. Methodist Church—United States—Clergy—Biography. 4. Lesbian clergy—United States—Biography.
I. Title.
BX8495.D445A3 1990
287'.6'092—dc20
[B] 89-35009
CIP

Printed in the United States of America

First Edition

1 2 3 4 5 6 7 8 9 10

BOOK DESIGN BY KATHRYN PARISE

For Winnie,

my partner, lover, confidante, and friend,

who has encouraged me to stretch beyond myself

and stood beside me in the struggle toward wholeness

ACKNOWLEDGMENTS

Special thanks to the following:

John MacDougall, whose sense of humor, brilliant mind, and loving heart believed in my fight for justice enough to put his own career on the line.

Priscilla MacDougall, who with gentle spirit and calm approach kept all of us from fraying along the edges.

Elizabeth Cazden, whose dedication to justice and clear-sightedness gave John and me the tools we needed to see our work through and whose generosity gave us a fighting chance.

Tony and Susan Jarek-Glidden, friends and supporters for whom I have a great deal of respect and whom I trust to keep the torch of love and justice lit in the church.

Mary Lou Evans, my soul friend, who, because of her belief in every person's need to walk her own journey, walked with me as I journeyed outside the confines of the patriarchal church.

My son, Matthew, who always understood my need to fight and who has made me proud of him, as he has been proud of me.

David Phreaner, who is more than a ministerial colleague. He served as my pastor during trying times. His support, encouragement, listening ear, and administrative gifts were much appreciated.

Dick Harding, a twentieth-century blend of Joan of Arc and Francis of Assisi, a United Methodist colleague of whom I am proud and for whose love and support I will always be grateful.

Acknowledgments

Pat MacHugh, my friend and colleague, who loved, supported, and listened to me as I worked through my confusion and anger—and who never judged me, even as I sometimes judged myself.

Brenda Chambers, Carol Etzler, Kay Gardner, and Ellen Lukingbeal, women with a gift of music and a message to the world. Their generosity healed my soul.

Laura Gordon, who has helped Winnie and me sift through our experience and come out of it stronger as individuals and more committed to each other as a couple.

The countless people who wrote letters of support. Without them there would have been some very bleak days. It was often their kind and generous words that kept me going.

And especially my editor, Lisa Drew, who believed in my ability to tell the story and who was always available to lend support and encouragement.

MAY THE UNIVERSE BE GENTLE WITH EACH OF YOU.

PROLOGUE

Severing the fragile threads of self-identity and creating new ways to define myself have been a frightening and awesome experience. My sense is that it was unsettling not only for me but for those around me as well. My parents raised me to become a wife, mother, and homemaker, to bow silently to the men in my life, be they my father, my husband, or the parish priest. The nuns who were my teachers trained me to be docile, obedient, and self-effacing. To be like Mary, the mother of Jesus, was raised before me as the epitome of all that is womanly. The society of my youth dictated that I be content with molding myself into the combined image of June Cleaver and Margaret Anderson. Later the advent of the feminist movement encouraged me to add Superwoman and Bella Abzug to the list of models I should emulate. The Church expected me, as a serious Christian and clergywoman, to model my ministry after that of Jesus Christ, to be, as much as I would allow the grace of God to operate through me, all things to all people: patient in the midst of turmoil, loving in the wake of hatred, peaceful in the throes of injustice, and available to all who would seek my help.

For thirty-eight years I struggled to be all that I was called to be by my family, my teachers, the feminist movement, and the Church, and in the middle of working so hard to be what others had defined I would be, I lost myself. I didn't know that I was suffocating. I had no idea that there was another more real, vibrant, and alive Rose Mary hidden deep inside the costumes of loving daughter, obedient student, dutiful wife, and ever-serving pastor. The layers of false identities were so thick and so carefully constructed that they fooled everyone, including me, into thinking they were authentic. I had grown so accustomed to wearing the heavy mantle of superimposed personas that I believed I had become them.

Discovering my true identity didn't take place in one great big dramatic moment. It was a slow and sometimes painful process of pulling at a loose thread here, snipping away at a frayed edge there, and gradually peeling away one mummified layer after another. I suspect that there are still some old, musty, hand-me-down remnants stubbornly clinging to the past. After all, to paraphrase a well-known bumper sticker: ". . . the Universe isn't finished with me yet."

Most of my snipping and peeling happened slowly, over years of laughing and crying, working and playing, running away and rushing forward. Occasionally, though, a huge chunk of old costume would give way and fall into the journal of my past. It was the disintegration of one particular false identity that brought me to the day I chose to challenge all who had tried to make me who I was not, August 24, 1987, the day I defied the United Methodist Church and went on trial for being a self-avowed practicing lesbian.

CHAPTER 1

I was raised in a traditional Euro-American patriarchal Roman Catholic household. My parents were hardworking factory employees who struggled to give my younger brother and sister and me the very best that they could. Mom and Dad were often not able to provide more than the basic necessities for our family. We were not wealthy by anyone's standards, yet we were certainly rich in the life experiences that build memories.

My father was a strange and complicated man, an unpredictable mixture of love and heavy-handedness. His world was made up of good and bad, with no room for exploration and expansion. Either something was right, or it wasn't. Both his parents were from Portugal, and although Dad was born in this country, his mind-set was very Old World. His mother never did learn to speak English, so my father's first language was that of his parents' mother country, Portuguese. Dad and his brothers all started their first days of school as foreigners in their own land, unable to communicate with many of their classmates and teachers.

My mother is of a more generic breed, a blend of several ethnic backgrounds which were never really explored or celebrated by her family. Her father died while Mom was still a child, and Grandma was faced with the task of raising seven children alone in an era when being a single parent was not in vogue. My mother has never talked much about what her life was like as a child, but I think that it must have been especially difficult considering the times and circumstances.

My parents met soon after my father came home from World War II. As the story was handed down to us children, Mom and Dad were on the same bus on their way home from work. Mom dropped her thermos, and Dad picked it up for her. Before they reached their stop, my father asked my mother for a date and she accepted. After three short months of courtship my father proposed marriage.

Storytelling has always been important in my family. It has kept the memories alive, as from generation to generation the adults have told and retold old familiar tales to one another and to their children. Some of the stories that I remember about my childhood have become so much a part of me that I can't even be clear whether I recall them because they are a part of my own remembering process or I am simply recounting a part of family history that has been handed down to me over the years. Nevertheless, my mind is a catalog filled with memories and family stories. Most are not about big, important family events. They are about playful, funny times. Sometimes, though, they are painful and tell about the cruelty and narrowness that were inflicted by one family member on another or about a hardship endured.

The story of my parents' wedding is one of the family favorites, and it was told often as a demonstration to us children that Mom and Dad were more sophisticated and open-minded than their parents. In the 1940's, especially in New England, great pride was taken in one's ethnic heritage. More often than not, families of different national origins did not intermingle. That was apparently particularly true for my parents' families.

Except for the years that he spent in the Navy during the war, my father lived all of his childhood and early adult life in a Portuguese section of Rhode Island called East Providence. My grandfather's favorite question when being introduced to a stranger was: "What nationality are you?" My mother, on the other hand, came from a family that wasn't particularly interested in its ethnic history but that was quite sure that none of its members need bother being involved with people of certain European extractions. The English, Irish, and French were fine, but there was little tolerance for the darker-skinned Europeans.

My father had gone from living at home with his parents to fighting in the war back to living with his parents again. In the "old days" unmarried children lived with their parents regardless of their ages, and Dad, at the age of twenty-four, found himself once again living under the patriarchal rule of his father's house. Dad worked full time in a factory and made a whopping twenty-five cents an hour. Every Friday he was expected to hand his pay envelope to my grandmother, who in turn gave him two dollars' spending money. With all that cash for bus fare, movies, and treats, I can imagine what a whirlwind courtship my parents were able to enjoy!

I think that my parents' eagerness to marry so quickly was based upon two factors: the need for economic and personal autonomy and the fact that neither of their families was happy about their relationship. My grandfather was not at all pleased that my father was seeing a non-Catholic woman who wasn't Portuguese. My grandmother was adamant about the fact that her daughter was not going to marry one of those superstitious Catholics whose kids would probably "turn out Negro." I guess that back then being Portuguese was sometimes seen as the same as being black, and neither was viewed as an advantage.

My parents stood their ground in spite of their families' demands that they put an end to their foolishness and "stick to their own kind." They didn't elope; they simply chose to announce their wedding date to their families. They also made it perfectly clear that they were going to get married with or without their parents' blessing or approval.

I have a picture of my parents on their wedding day. My father's parents did not go to the wedding. The ceremony was held in the rectory because being a mixed marriage, it could not, at the time, take place in the sanctuary of a Roman Catholic church. My mother's oldest sister and their mother did attend, though from the picture neither my aunt nor my grandmother appears to have been in a particularly celebrative mood. After the ceremony both families gathered in an attempt to let bygones be bygones, and there was cake and coffee for all—a birthday cake, that is. It seems that with such short notice, the only help the local bakery could render was to sell my grandparents a cake that was already inscribed with "Happy Birthday." Mom converted several months later.

That is all any of us ever heard about my parents' wedding day. It is not, however, the end of the "wedding day story." The story has a sort of happy-ever-after ending in that my parents were always sure to add: "And when you were born, Rose Mary, your father called Grandma and told her to come over to see his 'black kid.' From that time on your grandmother was always very clear that Dad was her favorite son-in-law, and she's not been any trouble to us since."

I was an only child for the first three years of my life, and from the warm memories that I have, it must have been a very pleasant time for me. I've never really thought of myself as having been a particularly precocious child, but I'm told that when I was a toddler, my favorite activity was to get into the cupboard that held all the canned goods. Once there I proceeded to tear all the labels from the cans, an act which resulted in many surprise dinners. Apparently this didn't provide a lot of stress for my parents because every time they told the story there was a great deal of hearty laughter.

My clearest memory of those three years is of the two days that my mother went away to get my new baby brother. By that time my parents had moved from East Providence to Rumford, a small town about six miles away, where the famous Rumford baking powder used to be produced. We lived in a duplex owned by my father's parents, who lived in the other half of the house. I had always had my own bedroom, and the rule about never going into my parents' room had already been firmly established. None of us children was ever allowed to have Saturday morning cuddle time in our parents' bed, something that I always missed. The rule about invading the privacy of my parents' bedroom was suspended only once in my life, during those two days that my mother was in the hospital "getting my baby brother."

Robert was born on December 22, 1950. It was a middle-of-the-night delivery, so I wasn't even aware of my father's not having been home. I went to bed one night as an only child and woke up the next morning to be told that Mommy had taken a trip to the hospital and had gotten a new baby brother for me. I was beside myself with delight. I could hardly wait until my mother came home with my new toy! The next two days seemed endless to me. My father must have been lonely, too, because on the night of December 23, the day before my mother and brother came home from the hospital, he let me sleep in bed with him. Being given permission to climb into that great big Mommy and Daddy bed was a special treat, and I have always cherished the memory. My father smelled of shaving lotion and talked softly to me of how wonderful it would be to have my mother and new baby brother home with us the next day. As I drifted off to sleep listening to him, I was aware of how secure it felt to be cuddled by my father's big, strong arms. I remember feeling a little confused, too, because even though I missed my mother and wanted to see my new baby brother, I knew that this would be the only chance that I would have to be just with my father, and that felt sad.

My father's parents were both very important in my life, but for very different reasons. My father's mother had died when my father was six years old. My grandfather was left with three small boys to raise, the youngest being just over a year old. The woman I knew as my grandmother was, at the time, a widow with one son. Her marriage to my grandfather was strictly, and clearly, a matter of doing what seemed sensible and most convenient for all concerned. They were never close, and sometimes there was out-and-out warfare between them. My father loved his stepmother. To him she was Ma, and she was as much a mother to him and his two brothers as if she had given birth to them. To my brother and sister and me, she was our grandma, or Vavó in Portuguese.

Vavó was a short, round woman who loved us with the kind of love that could be fierce when the occasion arose. Except for those times when we all went to church together, to a family wedding or funeral, or on a Sunday drive, Vavó always wore an apron over her cotton housedress. She was the one who would come next door to our house to get the three of us children ready for school after my parents had left for work, and it was she who was there to greet us with cookies when we got home in the afternoon. She was always interested in what we had to tell her, and we learned early in life that not only would she keep any confidence we shared with her, but she would always take our concerns seriously. It's really important to have adults take your worries seriously when you are ten years old.

Money was often scarce in our house, and treats were not common, but Vavó always had a dish of candy in her living room or chocolates in the refrigerator. It was fun to go next door to visit her after the supper dishes were done and homework was completed. I would sit next to her on the couch, and we would watch television together. During a commercial break Vavó would look over at me with a grin and ask: "Would you like some candy, *querida*?" (*Querida* is Portuguese for "dear.") She'd go to the refrigerator or pantry and bring out some wonderful goody or an orange, which she would peel. Then she would hand the juicy, sweet sections to me, one at a time. Vavó and I shared many nights together in her living room, eating chocolates or oranges, watching television, and sharing secrets. She and I created many wonderful memories together.

One of the highest tributes that I can pay to the memory of my grandmother is to say that her love never came with any strings attached. She gave to all of us from a heart that seemed big enough to house the world. Hugs and kisses and praise came from her as easily as a stern look and reprimand, and all interactions came with complete acceptance of us for who we were. No matter how confusing life was, we knew that Vavó would help us see that everything could work out for the best if we just trusted in God. She was a controlling woman, but with a soft and gentle way about her. She let the "Baby Jesus" do all her dirty work for her. Whenever any of us children, most often my brother, did something that met with Vavó's disapproval, she told us how much we had hurt the "Baby Jesus." That was usually enough to make us mend our ways. After all, who wants to hurt any baby, let alone the "Baby Jesus?" Vavó and the "Baby Jesus" had such a strong thing going that when I was confirmed, I gave her a statue of the Infant of Prague, the closest thing to "Baby Jesus" that I could find.

While Vavó's love had no strings attached, my grandfather, Vavô, bartered his love and offered it both sparingly and often at a very high price. I remember few moments of warm and clear exchange of love between my grandfather and any member of our family. He was a harsh, demanding man, who understood his role in the family to be that of patriarch. No matter the age of his children, Vavô demanded that they all bow to his demands and self-proclaimed wisdom. This attitude extended to his grandchildren, and because we lived in the same building, my brother and sister and I were more exposed to Vavô's rule than any of our cousins were. There were many strong and abusive exchanges between the adult members of the house and my grandfather. Dad was usually in the thick of it in an attempt to establish what he viewed as his rightful place as the head of his own family. Vavó and my mother usually served as mediators, my mother attempting to calm my father, while Vavó was in her apartment seeking to work miracles by placating my grandfather. Peace was always fragile, and we all knew that the balance could be upset at any moment.

Vavô was considered pretty stingy with money, and it was no secret that Vavó had to execute some pretty slippery maneuvers in order to eke out any amount of extra cash. She got to be resourceful in the ways she accomplished this feat. Those were the days when milk, bread, and ice were still delivered to the door. There were also the laundryman and the local fish and vegetable vendors making their rounds through the neighborhood. Vavó would yell to my grandfather to give her money for the milkman. He would ask how much she needed. If the bill was $2.50, she would tell him that it was $3.50. After she had paid the milkman his $2.50, she would stuff the extra dollar into her apron pocket. This little ritual extended to the breadman, the iceman, the fishman, the vegetable man, and any other unsuspecting vendor who came to the door. Vavó kept her stash in an old pocketbook hidden in her dresser and used this money to buy things for herself that she didn't feel comfortable discussing with my grandfather, things like her underwear. Most often, though, she used her hidden financial resources to stake one of us kids to the price of an ice cream cone. She was also in the habit of stuffing quarters and, as we got older, dollar bills into our hands as we went off to school. She'd give us a hug as the school bus rounded the corner, push the money into our hands or pockets, and whisper:

"Here, *querida,* buy yourself something nice on the way home today." Usually that meant a stop at Jack's, a little variety store a few blocks from our house. Jack had glass cases filled with penny candy and racks of shiny, colorful comic books. Stopping at Jack's was fun, and when we got home, Vavó always smiled and said, "Show me what you bought today," and we giggled together, proud that once again we had conspired to trick Vavô into being the unsuspecting benefactor of our purchases.

Vavô liked people to think that he was perfect, or at least as perfect as a man was supposed to be. I guess that in his own way he was a believer, but he was not one to go to mass. My parents, however, were convinced that one of their basic duties to us children was to see to it that we had good Catholic upbringings. Every Sunday we piled into the family car and headed for St. Margaret's Church to attend eight o'clock children's mass.

One particular year my father decided it was his duty to see to it that both my grandparents went to Easter Sunday mass. This, obviously, included going to confession. My father started softening Vavô to the idea weeks in advance, and by the time Easter Saturday rolled around he had convinced my grandfather to go for it. There was one stipulation, though. My grandfather insisted that he would not go to our church for confession, because he wanted the security of being anonymous. Father Anthony, our parish priest, would surely recognize his voice. My father had the perfect solution. We all would drive into Providence and go to confession at the Franciscan monastery.

Because of the Easter season, the chapel was busy with the many who had come to "make their Easter duty," and we had to wait quite some time before we could receive the sacrament of penance. As our little clan walked out of the chapel onto the city street, my grandfather began to mutter about "those sneaky monks." It took awhile, but my father was finally able to get Vavô to tell him what had gotten him into such a foul mood. In order to make sure that he had complete anonymity, my grandfather had made his confession in Portuguese, pretending that he did not speak English. The false sense of security provided an opportunity for Vavô to make the best and most honest confession of his life. The trouble was that the monk understood and spoke perfect Portuguese! By the time my grandfather discovered that fact, it was too late, and he found himself in the embarrassing position of having been duped. Our family has always considered the occasion a demonstration of ultimate justice.

For the first four years of school, kindergarten through third grade, I attended the local public schools. It was during my kindergarten year that I had my first crush on a teacher, Miss Kelly. Miss Kelly was tall and graceful and beautiful, and she possessed a soft voice and gentle manner. She always smelled of lilacs. What I remember most is her silk shirtwaist dress with stripes in every color of the rainbow. It was the prettiest dress that I had ever seen, especially on Miss Kelly. I loved Miss Kelly and would daydream about what her house looked like and what she did when she wasn't my teacher. Most of all, I wanted to be just like her when I grew up and wear a soft silk rainbow dress. Leaving kindergarten and Miss Kelly was awful. Every chance I had, I would go into her room after school to say hello. It came as a real shock when Miss Kelly came back to school in the fall of my second-grade year and she had become Mrs. Anderson. I felt betrayed. It would be many years before I would be able to comprehend what that sense of betrayal really meant, but for the time it simply became one of my sweet and gentle childhood memories.

St. Margaret's opened a parish school for fourth-grade year. My parents discussed the family finances between themselves and decided that as difficult as it was going to be, it would be worth the sacrifice to send their children to Catholic school. They wanted us to have good educations, as well as solid backgrounds in the faith, so, in September 1957 I transferred to St. Margaret's. My brother went to the first-grade classroom.

Rumford, at the time I was growing up, was a town that was divided into two distinct sections by a golf course. On the north side of the golf course were the homes of upper-middle-class families, single-family houses that belonged to doctors, lawyers, and businessmen. On the south side, or, as those of our neighborhood referred to it, on the "other side of the golf course," where we lived, were the homes of lower-middle-class families, houses that had once been company-owned mill houses. These houses had been sold to individual families when the mill's heyday had come to an end.

My first day at St. Margaret's school was frightening. There were only five of us from the "other side of the golf course" in my class: the Daily twins, Jannet Peterson, Mike Sullivan, and I. The Daily twins and Mike Sullivan had one thing going for them: They were Irish, and being Irish was always a plus for anyone who went to St. Margaret's. I felt out of place and awkward. Those of us who were from the south side of town and had gone to public school had not yet learned to write in longhand. We were still printing our words and sentences. For the first time in my life I experienced what it was like to feel stupid. It was a feeling with which I became very familiar over the years I attended St. Margaret's.

The message to those of us from the other side of the golf course was that there was something wrong with us, something missing that made us different from the other students. During the first year of operation St. Margaret's did not have a uniform dress code. We were allowed to wear anything we chose, as long as boys wore pants, shirts, and ties. The girls wore dresses or skirts and blouses. Before going to school at St. Margaret's, I never gave much thought to how I dressed or even to how many dresses hung in my closet. Mom always made sure that what I wore was clean and pressed, and even if the hems were a bit short, I went to school looking neat and tidy. Being in the fourth grade at St. Margaret's changed all that. Suddenly I became painfully aware of how limited and drab my wardrobe was compared with the clothes of the other girls in my class. It seemed that they wore something different every day, and their dresses were always pretty. I never said anything to my parents, but secretly I began to realize and resent our financial limitations. They drew a line of distinction between me and the other members of our class, between my family and theirs.

My years at St. Margaret's were filled with contradictions. On one hand, I learned to become self-conscious about my ethnic heritage, to be ashamed of being Portuguese, and to be ashamed that my parents worked in a mill instead of an office. I learned the distinction between blue-collar and white-collar work and that some people felt there was something less desirable and less OK about being a "blue-collar" worker. On the other hand, I learned the joy and nurturing that can be experienced in the spiritual life. As much as the sisters who taught us contributed to my sense of inequality with others, they somehow also instilled in me a hunger for the spiritual life.

When I was in the sixth grade, I read a book about St. Francis of Assisi. He became the hero of my adolescence. Together, he and St. Clare, had rejected the comforts and gains of the "worldly life" for the joys of "Lady Poverty." Francis founded the order named after him and helped Clare establish the order for women which became known as the Poor Clares. There was something daring and romantic about the approach that Francis and Clare took to life. They made poverty seem not only all right but preferable. Being poor was viewed as being a major step toward being more spiritual, especially if the poverty was extreme in nature and voluntary. Somehow this worldview of Francis and Clare took my own sense of deprivation and lifted it to a level of honor. I had found a way to turn my shame in not having into a badge of spirituality and grace. I had discovered a way of making something that others called ugly into something that the Church called good and beautiful. The rich kids in school were stuck in a web of worldly pursuits. I would be holy and free of such trappings. I had discovered a really creative way to handle the sometimes not so subtle judgments and condemnations of those with whom I had to deal on a daily basis.

One of the major dilemmas that I encountered for the first time was that St. Francis, not St. Clare, was my role model. It was the priests of the Catholic Church, not the nuns, whose lives I envied. Later the feminist movement helped me discover that the prescribed roles for women were artificial and man-made, but for those years during which I was maturing to adulthood, I was programmed by the dictates of what were considered appropriate and acceptable aspirations for women.

I liked being female, but I didn't like having restrictions placed upon me simply for that reason. What was right for women, and what was not right, were determined by everything and everyone around me. Everyone else defined what I was, and I began to feel increasingly trapped by the artificial limitations of my gender. What made matters worse was that everyone seemed to agree upon what I could aspire to and what I could not. My parents, the Church, my friends and their families, the government, all society seemed to have decided what shape my life could take and the restrictions placed upon that shaping. As I grew into adolescence, I became even more frustrated, but in ways so subtle it was not until my thirties that I could name those frustrations.

Throughout grade school what I secretly wanted was to be a Franciscan priest. While other girls my age were playing rock and roll music and trying different shades of nail polish, I was busy blackmailing my sister and brother into going down to the basement of our house and playing mass. I was always the priest, of course, and we would use Necco wafers and grape Kool-Aid for communion. I wanted to grow up to say mass in a church and wear a brown robe and sandals like St. Francis. But God had made me a girl; that must have meant HE wanted me to be a nun, not a priest—or at least that's what I kept telling myself growing up.

Later, during high school, I was to identify with another hero, a more contemporary role model, another man, Thomas Merton. Merton was a Trappist monk in Kentucky, and I was first introduced to this mysterious and holy man through his autobiography, *The Seven Storey Mountain*. In this book I found stories of a real live flesh-and-blood man who had fears and ambitions and aspirations and successes, as well as doubts and failures. This was not like the books I had read about women in convents of times past, women whose lives sounded boring and uneventful. Merton's life was like my own. He had doubts. He oftentimes bristled under the authority of those who were placed over him, just as I found myself bristling in the same ways. He hated the heat and mosquitoes and loved the quiet and time to write and reflect. He didn't spend his days making holy bread or doing needlepoint, as cloistered women did. Instead, Merton worked in the fields and thought hard and long and deep about life and its meaning. That's what I wanted to do, too.

I never shared these thoughts and desires with anyone. I didn't want to hear people tell me that I was wrong to have such aspirations. I didn't want to hear people tell me that I couldn't be like Thomas Merton because I was a woman. Most important, I did not want people accusing me of not being feminine because I had these desires.

Being a girl in my family had other real limitations. Early in our lives it was made clear to all of us children that there wasn't enough money available for education beyond high school and that if any of us went to college, it would be my brother. My parents' contention was that my brother would need a college education in order to assume the responsibilities of a wife and children, while my sister and I would be taken care of by the men we would marry. When my brother dropped out of high school in my junior year, I nurtured hopes of being sent to college in his place. However, I overheard my parents saying that although it was a great disappointment that my brother had dropped out of school, it may also have been a blessing. They had no money saved for his college education and had been prepared to borrow all that they could to help him. Now they were relieved not to have to face such an additional burden. I knew then not to broach the subject with them.

As a young child I never gave much thought to whether or not I was pretty. I remember people in my neighborhood saying that I was and that when I wore my hair in banana curls swept up on the top of my head, I looked just like the "little Sunbeam Girl," whose picture was on the end wrapper of every loaf of Sunbeam bread. However, at St. Margaret's I began to suspect that I wasn't pretty at all, and as the years there passed, these thoughts, at first distant and only an occasional suspicion, became increasingly real until I was convinced I was unattractive. I seemed to have all the wrong attributes. I had thick almost black hair instead of the long blond tresses of many of my classmates. My eyes were green, not the envied blue that seemed to be a major determining factor for beauty. But most damning was that my body had begun to burst into curves and roundness long before the other girls' bodies changed, making me even more different from them. That difference was not seen as a plus, either by others in my class or by me.

I was a very thin youngster, and from the time I was about seven years old, I sported a frizzy home permanent. I was the product of parents who were not only ethnic identified but also children of the Depression and who thought it important that their children not only *be* well fed but *look* well fed. When, by the age of eight, I had not grown into the proportions that would reflect my parents' ability to feed their children well, they decided to take matters in hand and do whatever was necessary to "fatten me up." They hauled me off to the family doctor, who determined that what I needed was a diet that included goat's milk and a daily dose of cod-liver oil. For two years my parents made the weekly trek to a farmer who would sell them milk from his goats, and every afternoon my mother would stand in front of me in the kitchen with that god-awful cod-liver oil in one hand and a squirrel nut candy in the other. I can remember being cajoled, teased, punished, and spanked into taking that cod-liver oil. I can also remember the nights when I would be forced to sit at the kitchen table over a dish of liver or a bowl of cold and thickened pea soup for hours after the rest of the family had finished dinner. My mother was determined that I would eat everything on my plate whether I liked it or not, and she never gave up until I was suitably rounded out.

By the time I was in the seventh grade my school uniforms were ready to burst at the seams. To my parents this was a sign of success and healthiness. To me it was yet one more difference between the other girls at school and me, another reason for me to be ridiculed and left out. I felt lonely and isolated and learned to console myself by eating. I used food as a pain-killer, to feed the emptiness in my life. And the more I used food to nurture the hunger I felt, the more hungry I became. It was an emotional hunger, but I was too young and immature to understand that, so I continued to eat in an attempt to feed and fill the emptiness within me.

I began to feel more and more isolated and turned to the two sources of nurturing that had never let me down: food and God. Food neither judged me nor made demands of me. It was there for me whenever I wanted and needed warmth and security. God did judge, and God did make demands, yet woven into the judgment and demands were a love and an acceptance that told me that no matter how short I fell of His will for my life, as long as I tried, He would not abandon me. That was a guarantee that was offered by only two beings in my youth: God and my grandmother. The guarantee of love and acceptance offered by my grandmother had no strings and therefore never caused pain in my life. However, the guarantee offered by God, through the voice of the Church, brought much pain into my life, pain which was needless and certainly not inflicted by God.

Much later I realized that the nuns at St. Margaret's School had a basic belief by which they judged each student: One's socioeconomic status was in direct correlation with one's intelligence. Because I was from an ethnic, blue-collar home, I was judged to be dull-witted. Therefore, I was not encouraged to consider college for my future. I was treated as something of a necessary nuisance, a missionary project tolerated out of love for those who are not privileged with money, position, or intelligence. It is memories like these that are the driving force of my need and desire always to champion the underdog. I look into the faces and hearts of those being persecuted, and I see my own.

Children graduated from St. Margaret's in the ninth grade and from there went on either to public high school or to another parochial school. Ninth grade was the watershed for those who would go on to college. It was in the ninth grade that students took algebra and Latin. Without these two courses, no high school would admit a student into the college prep curriculum. It strikes me as strange that it was the Daily Twins, Mike Sullivan, and I who were the ones told that we would not be able to take Latin and algebra. Except for Jannet Peterson, a niece of one of the public school teachers, it was the kids from the other side of the golf course who were excused from these courses. We were sent to the school library to study. I think that the nuns saw this as a kindness. It was their way of preparing us for what they thought our world would include, a world of factories, babies, or perhaps secretarial positions, but certainly not college and the professions. The differences between us and the others in our class were sharpened, and so was the pain.

It was when we were in the ninth grade that the nuns decided it would be lovely if we had a dance. It would not be a dance held in the evening to which we could invite friends, but a dance held during the afternoon and just for our class. We were allowed to decorate the hall, to wear something of our choice other than our uniforms, and some of the mothers provided special punch and cookies. A few of the girls were chosen to see to the arrangements. All of those chosen were from the affluent side of the golf course. Our class had approximately thirty students. Eight of those students were boys. We were told that we all would be expected to dance, that no one would be left out.

On the day of the dance Ann, one of the rich girls, had everything arranged. She held tickets made from two different colors of paper in her hands. Each set of tickets was numbered. The idea was that the boys would get a ticket from one color, blue, while the girls would be given a ticket from the other color, pink. Those with matching numbers would dance with one another. Once all of the boys had been spoken for, girls would have to pair off with other girls. Ann made sure that all of her friends were paired off with boys. The rest of us were forced to pair off with each other. There was no room left to chance. It all was arranged, and when I realized this, I called it to the attention of our teacher. She said this was to protect us from having our feelings hurt by any nasty remarks the boys might make if they were forced to dance with us. It took many years for the sting of this incident, and others just as hurtful, to begin to heal. Even now I still wonder if that nun knows that her condescending attempt to protect us was a much more painful experience for us to endure than anything any of the boys could have said.

In spite of this ignorant and thoughtless cruelty, I still held those nuns in the highest esteem and wanted to be one of them. My parents' plan was that once we had received a solid foundation at St. Margaret's, we would continue our high school educations at the local public school. I lived in dread of leaving what I believed was the security of parochial school. I wanted to be a nun, and I needed to be near nuns. I did not want to go to public school, where life would be even less friendly. Yet my parents were adamant about my going there. They did not know I wanted to be a nun or how important it was to me that I go on to another parochial school.

Nuns were always respected in our family, but respecting them and having your child become one of them were two different things. Nuns sacrificed their lives for God. Nuns gave up the pleasures of life because that was what God had called them to do. They were the brides of Christ and therefore would never know the pleasures of marriage, homes of their own, or children. The life of a nun was viewed as a hard life, one no girl would choose unless she felt compelled by God to do so.

Because I knew how my parents felt about nuns, I didn't want to tell them that it was my intention to go into the convent until I absolutely had to. I knew once they were aware of my plan, they would treat me differently, and that was the last thing I wanted after my experience at school. I needed to have at least one place in my life where I fitted in, and for now my family was it.

I could anticipate my parents' response because of my distant cousin Eileen. Eileen was probably close to fifteen years older than I and, when she was young, had entered the convent. She stayed with the order for only a few months, but even fifteen years later, in spite of the fact that she was the only Eileen in the family, she was referred to as "Eileen, you know, the one who used to be in the convent." Somehow I knew that I didn't want to be referred to as "Rose Mary, you know, the one who wants to be a nun," so I kept my intentions to myself. It wasn't until I was faced with the sure fate of going to public high school that I finally decided that I had to tell my parents about my plans.

If I live to be one hundred, I'll never forget that night. The five of us were seated at the kitchen table having dinner. My heart was pounding. I gave my brother and sister the most authoritative look I could muster and said: "I need to talk with Mom and Dad about something important. Don't interrupt." Then I looked across the table at my parents and began by trying to tell them that I had looked into several of the Catholic high schools in the area and had found one that didn't cost much more than St. Margaret's. Perhaps if I started my argument by addressing their fear about expense first, I could get them to agree to sending me to Sacred Heart High School without telling them my real reason for wanting to go there.

My father laid his fork down on his plate, cleared his throat, and said: "Rose Mary, your mother and I have sent you kids to St. Margaret's because we wanted you to have a good Catholic background. They've given that to you. If you can give me one good reason why we shouldn't send you to East Providence High School, I'll listen."

I sat there feeling my heart racing and my face beginning to turn several shades of crimson. My throat constricted, and tears began to fill my eyes. There was no way that I was going to get out of this one unless I told my parents my real motives. I took a deep breath and blurted it out as fast as I could through the tears: "Because I want to be a nun."

There was a moment of deadening silence. Not even my brother dared snicker. My father looked at Mom, cleared his throat again, looked over at me, and very quietly said: "Fine. Then you'll go to Sacred Heart." We didn't discuss the issue again for several months. My parents may not have understood why I would choose to be a nun, but I think that they felt that it would have been sinful to try to counteract what might be God's will for my life and theirs.

There wasn't a lot of money in our household for extras, but my parents always did their best to make sure that Christmas was special. Portuguese families have some truly wonderful holiday traditions, many of them involving the Christmas season. We always had a big Christmas tree, and right after Thanksgiving my father would begin to build a manger in the living room. The manger was the focal point of our Christmas and the way we decorated the house, and Dad tried to come up with a new manger scene every year. One year it took one whole wall. It was built on the top of a long board resting on sawhorses and draped with white sheets. The backdrop was dark blue velvet onto which my father glued little stars, with one big one representing the star that led the Wise Men to the Christ Child. We had iron and clay figures of the Holy Family, some of which had belonged to my father's grandparents. There were camels, shepherds, cows, sheep, and donkeys. There were also palm trees. That particular year my father created mountains out of papier-mâché and even used a pump from an old aquarium to create a waterfall. It was lovely, and a reporter from the local paper came to our home to take pictures and to talk to my father about how he had built the scene. It was in the Sunday supplement, and we all were very proud of Dad and his handiwork. Some people who had seen the story even called our home to ask if they could come to see it. My father was excited about such response and always told the callers that they were welcome.

In our tradition food was, and still is, an important part of the holidays. If sweets and potato chips and nuts were scarce in our home any other time of the year, they were plentiful at Christmas. It was tradition that on Christmas Eve a card table laden with goodies would be set up in the living room. It would be replenished whenever necessary, and it was kept stocked until the day after New Year's. This was the time of year when the extended family would "make the rounds," visiting one another to wish everyone a Merry Christmas and Happy New Year. For those two weeks our house was always brimming over with aunts, uncles, grandparents, cousins, and friends. It was a time for feasting and laughter and especially music made by those family members who toted their instruments around with them on their pilgrimage from one house to another.

Music was always very important to our family, but especially at Christmas. Christmas Day was for the children, but Christmas Eve was definitely a time of celebration for the adults. It was the one night of the year when the three of us children were allowed to stay up late. At 11:00 P.M. we were all dressed up in our very best and headed out into the cold, dark, exciting night for midnight mass at St. Margaret's. I loved midnight mass. The altar was covered with exquisite white linens and surrounded by dozens of poinsettias. The organist seemed to pull out every stop in the pipes, and the sanctuary nearly quivered with the vibration. The choir miraculously was double its normal size, and the voices mysteriously drifted out from the balcony with a sweetness that made the excitement of the night heighten with anticipation. Midnight mass always began with a grand processional of every altar boy the parish could enlist, followed by Monsignor carrying a beautiful Christ Child, which he laid in the manger in the front of the sanctuary. Midnight mass on Christmas Eve at St. Margaret's was sweet and gentle, and it left our hearts warmed by the experience.

After mass our family returned home. We three children were rushed off to bed to await the secret arrival of Santa while my parents changed into warmer clothing to begin the celebration of the grandest Christmas tradition in our family: Christmas caroling. Vavó was drafted to the position of baby-sitter for the night. Dad got out his old concertina accordion while Mom grabbed the triangle. Not being musically inclined was no excuse for being left out of caroling; there were always triangles, tambourines, or maracas with which to keep the beat. Mom and Dad would head over to a cousin's house and sing at the front door in the darkness. By the time they reached the second or third stanza, lights went on from the inside, the door flew open, and there stood a sleepy but smiling family. When the music was finished, the carolers were invited to come into the house for hot drinks and snacks from the card table. The adults of the household changed into warm clothes and joined the caravan to the next house. This went on all night, and by the time everyone arrived at the last home there were twenty or more carolers to awaken the inhabitants from the holiday slumber. My parents usually got back to our home just before dawn and slipped into bed for an hour or so, only to be awakened by the three of us boisterously announcing that Santa had come.

One particular year my parents must have gotten carried away with the festivities of the evening because just around 7:00 A.M. my brother, sister, and I got up, went down to the living room, and to our amazement found nothing under the tree! Vavó tried to calm us down by telling us that Santa had phoned in the middle of the night to tell her that there were more children and homes to visit than he had anticipated, that he was running behind schedule, and that if we went back to bed, he would be under the tree with our gifts very soon. We were a little leery of this story, but we didn't want to take any chances either, so we did as we were told and went back to our rooms. It seemed awfully strange that Santa's arrival and that of my parents coincided with precision timing!

The only time Mom and Dad consulted us before making a decision was just before the Christmas I was in the tenth grade. They had, for years, found it easiest to save for Christmas by joining a Christmas Club at the local credit union. Every week my mother made the specified deposit, and by November there was enough money to buy gifts, the treats for our holiday guests, and our Christmas tree. In early November of that particular year Mom and Dad proposed something to us. They had come up with an idea about which they wanted to ask us. My father laid out the proposal very clearly and carefully. They had money for our usual Christmas celebration, but they thought that we might like to do something different that year. My father's youngest brother and his family lived in Baltimore, Maryland, and we had never been to visit them. My father's plan was that if we approved, we would take the Christmas Club money, and rather than buy gifts for the family, we would buy railroad tickets and take the train to Baltimore to spend the holidays with my aunt and uncle and their children. He wanted us to be sure to understand that if we agreed, there would be only enough money for the trip. We needed to realize that there would be only one small Christmas gift for each of us that year. It didn't take more than five minutes for the three of us to agree that going to Baltimore was a wonderful idea. We were so excited about taking a train so far away that we didn't care about the Christmas gifts. Besides, Uncle Gene and Aunt Helen were fun to be with, and their three children were close enough in age to us that we knew we would have a wonderful time.

The decision was made, and all of us, my parents included, were excited about the forthcoming visit. Dad called his brother to let them know we were coming, and the next few weeks were filled with anticipation.

But I had one major concern. I didn't want my parents to tell my aunt and uncle that I wanted to be a nun. When I awkwardly broached the subject to Mom and Dad, my father just could not understand why this was such an important issue for me. He kept saying: "But if you want to be a nun, you should be proud of it. Why shouldn't people know?"

Finally I blurted out: "Because, if you tell them, they will start to treat me differently."

My father said he still didn't understand, but he agreed not to tell his brother.

Being on the train was wonderful. It was fun to look out the window as we sped by the different towns and the countryside. It was fun to buy sandwiches and hot chocolate from the vendor who came at lunchtime. It was also fun to make believe that this was not a new experience for me, that I was quite accustomed to traveling so far away from home. Finally, just at dusk, we arrived in Baltimore. My uncle was there to meet us. Rather than take us directly back to his home, he drove around the city, which was much larger than anything I had ever seen before and was lit up with wonderful Christmas decorations. Carols were being played on loudspeakers from the department stores. Everyone was talking at once, and the excitement of the past weeks seemed to reach new heights.

When we arrived at Uncle Gene's house, there was another flurry of hugs and kisses, and our luggage was deposited in the rooms where we would each be sleeping. We were proud of the number and quality of the gifts that we had brought for our relatives, and there was more excitement as everyone watched Mom and Dad unload bags of wrapped packages, placing each under the tree. The whole time Uncle Gene and Aunt Helen exclaimed: "You shouldn't have gotten so much. It isn't necessary." None of us dared mention that Mom had purchased most of the gifts for approximately one-quarter their value. One of the men at the factory sold "hot" items, stolen merchandise. Whenever I tried to talk to my mother about the ethics of buying stolen property, her response was the same: "I have no idea where these things come from, and I don't even know if they are stolen. I can't be responsible for something I didn't do."

We had arrived in Baltimore on the night of December 23. The next day was filled with activities. There was still food to be prepared for that evening's and the next day's festivities. There were last-minute errands to be run. And especially, there were stories to be told and family news to relay as we spent hours around the dining-room table, talking together. At that point in my life Aunt Helen and Uncle Gene were the only people I knew who had a separate dining room. Everyone else I knew ate at a table in the kitchen. Being at my aunt and uncle's house made me feel that I did know some rich people, and they were even my relatives!

It was about midafternoon on Christmas Eve day when my father and uncle decided that they needed to go out alone together to do a few last-minute errands. They were gone for about three hours, and I noticed that my uncle seemed to treat me differently when he and my father got back from their little excursion from the way he had acted before they left. I began to suspect that my father had broken his promise to me and told my uncle I wanted to be a nun. This suspicion grew as I realized that all the jokes my uncle was telling were religious jokes. I wanted to ask my father about it, but during the whole visit we were never alone long enough. By ten thirty that evening we all were dressed for midnight mass. My father handed me a small wrapped package. When I protested, saying that we all had an agreement there would be only one gift for each of us, he said this was something special that he had bought for me that day while he and my uncle had been out. When I opened the gift, I found a lovely pair of glass rosary beads. My uncle was gazing at me with an "I understand" look on his face, and it was then that I became absolutely sure my father had told my secret. I was angry with Dad, but the damage had been done. I couldn't confront him there in my uncle's house. I couldn't confront him at all. In our family kids just don't call their parents short on anything. There was nothing I could do except swallow my anger and pretend that everything was normal.

I don't even remember my graduation from St. Margaret's, except the feeling of relief that I was leaving and the joy with which I anticipated my first days at Sacred Heart. I somehow knew this would give me a fresh start. None of the nuns or students would know me at Sacred Heart. Maybe I would be treated like the rest of the class. It was an all-girls school, so at least I wouldn't have to worry about how boys would respond to me. I just knew that this experience would be different. I had not one sad moment in my leave-taking of St. Margaret's. I was going on to a more egalitarian situation, I just knew it.

My first days at Sacred Heart were filled with lessons in reality. Sacred Heart was only one of the Catholic high schools in the area. It was also the least expensive. Bay View Academy was probably the most costly to attend, and several of the girls from St. Margaret's had chosen to go there. St. Xavier's High School was also an option and was moderately priced. My friend Lisa chose to follow in her older sister's footsteps and attend St. Xavier's. Sacred Heart was a parish school in Pawtucket, Rhode Island. It started with the first grade, and there were two buildings to the school. One building housed grades one through nine. The second held the high school classrooms. This separation of the high school students from the rest of the school helped us feel grown-up and special.

The girls in my class came from families pretty much like mine, and it was comforting not to have to feel that I had lost the game before I even began to compete. Many of our fathers and mothers worked in factories, and the few girls who came from more affluent homes were in the minority. They also didn't seem to flaunt what they had in the faces of those of us who had not. We lived a peaceful coexistence.

The nuns at Sacred Heart were from a different order from the Sisters of Mercy, who had been my teachers at St. Margaret's. They were the Sisters of St. Joseph, an order which I immediately decided was more representative of what I thought nuns should be. They responded equally to all of us in class, rich or poor, and I appreciated their gentleness tremendously.

I had two teachers in the tenth grade, my first year at Sacred Heart High School: Sister Emanuel Joseph, whom we lovingly referred to as Manny Joe, and Sister Patrick Anthony. Manny Joe was our homeroom teacher and taught all but one of our classes. Sister Patrick Anthony was our biology teacher, and I have never loved biology as much as I did the year that she was my teacher. When I think about her now, I realize that she was probably just barely twenty-five or so. She was a petite, sweet, angelic young woman who was always smiling, and there was a perpetual gleam in her eyes that conveyed a mixture of mischief and giggles just about to burst forth from a barely controlled demeanor. Manny Joe was nice enough most of the time, but sometimes she would throw temper tantrums that would have the class braced in fear. Sister Patrick Anthony was a dream. She was also the eleventh-grade teacher. Those of us in Manny Joe's tenth-grade class could hardly wait until we were in our junior year of high school so that we could have her for our full-time teacher.

Father Luke was the curate at Sacred Heart Parish. He was a tall, not terribly good-looking man, perhaps in his mid-thirties. I arrived at school early enough each morning to go to mass before walking across the parking lot to my classes. I relished those fifteen or twenty minutes in the sanctuary of the church during mass. Quite often I would be the only person in attendance, and the silence and solitude were splendid. I was in my own safe little world with Jesus, the lover of my soul. This was our special time together at the beginning of the day, a time when we would exchange words of love and promises. My promises were to love and serve him all my life, just like St. Francis and Thomas Merton. His promises were to love and cherish me as his child. These made me feel special and precious. With the gentle spirits of the sisters, the security that the school offered to me, and the opportunity to attend daily mass, my first year at Sacred Heart High School was relative bliss. Perfect bliss would come the following year, when Sister Patrick Anthony would be our teacher.

In the spring of my sophomore year there were only a few weeks left to suffer through Sister Manual Joseph's temper tantrums, which seemed to be increasing in frequency as well as intensity. One Monday morning we came to class and were told that we would not be going to biology class. Manny Joe seemed to be in a foul but quiet mood. None of us asked any questions, but we knew that something was up, especially when we realized that Sister Patrick Anthony was absent. Our first instinct was to think that she had had a terrible accident or that she had been struck down by some mysterious illness and was in the hospital. We didn't have biology on Tuesday either or any other day that week. Still, no one would tell us what had happened to Sister Patrick Anthony. The most Manny Joe would tell us was that Sister would not be back to finish out the year as our biology teacher. No further explanation was offered. I also noticed that Father Luke wasn't at mass any morning that week. We assumed he was on vacation.

On the Sunday afternoon following Sister Patrick Anthony's strange absence, my friend Nancy called. She was one of my classmates, and she and I had long since confided in each other our mutual intention to go into the convent after graduating from high school. Nancy and her mother lived in Sacred Heart Parish and were members of the church. Nancy's mother, along with a few other parents, had met with the school principal demanding to know what was going on with Sister Patrick Anthony. They told the principal that their daughters were alarmed and worried and that they deserved to know the truth. Nancy was nearly bursting to tell me the story, and she tantalized me by drawing out the description of the encounter between the parents and the school principal. Finally the nuns admitted that Sister Patrick Anthony had run away with Father Luke. They had been married over the previous weekend!

For some reason the news about Sister Patrick Anthony and Father Luke seemed to shock our parents more than it shocked us. Sister was beautiful. She was filled with joy and sweetness. Why shouldn't she be happy? Why shouldn't she have all the things that marriage could give her? I wonder why Nancy and I didn't stop to consider our own motives for wanting to enter the convent as we giggled and fantasized about what Sister Patrick Anthony and Father Luke were doing at that very moment. Instead, we spent the time asking other questions, questions like: "What do you think her real name is? She must be just gorgeous out of her habit! What did she ever see in Father Luke? She probably could have picked any man she wanted to, even a movie star! Do you think that they ever made love while Sister Patrick Anthony was still in the convent?" That last question was immediately thrown out of consideration. We decided that they had probably just kissed and talked a lot before they decided to run away together. To think anything more than that would have taken us into territory we were neither prepared to fantasize about nor to face. All we knew was that what Sister Patrick Anthony and Father Luke had done seemed awfully romantic to us, and it certainly made the spring an eventful one. On Monday morning the girls in our class were abuzz with the news. The sisters never said a word about it to us, on that day or ever.

Nancy and I lived quite a distance from each other and therefore didn't have an opportunity to spend a great deal of time together outside school except on weekends. The rest of the week we would while away hours on the phone, discussing not boys or makeup but the saints we had been reading about or the different religious orders we were considering.

Nancy's parents were divorced. At that time in my life Nancy was the only person I knew who lived in a single-parent household. I knew Nancy's mother, who was always there whenever I went to visit Nancy for the weekend. I had never met her father, but Nancy liked him and seemed to think of him as a sort of adventurer. Just before one particular weekend that we had been planning to spend together, Nancy called to say that unless I was willing to spend Saturday afternoon with her and her father, we would have to cancel our plans. I wasn't thrilled about having to share hours of our precious time together with her father but decided it would be better than staying home. Besides, Nancy sweetened the pot by saying that if I came, she would try to talk her father into taking us for a ride in his plane. I had never been in a plane before. I hastily agreed to go. I also decided not to tell my parents about the hoped-for first ride in an airplane. I was afraid they would tell me that I couldn't go.

I had brought my overnight bag to school on Friday so that Nancy and I could begin our weekend as soon as our last class was over. We spent Friday evening in our customary way, hours of snacking, giggling, complaining about how restrictive our parents were, and refining our plans and dreams about what being a nun would be like. I slept fitfully all night as I anticipated the ride that Nancy's father would be giving us in his plane the following afternoon. This was pretty old stuff to Nancy, but it was quite the adventure for me. I was not accustomed to doing anything without my parents' knowledge or permission, and the fact that this had been planned with neither served to make the whole event only that much more intriguing.

The next day was glorious. The sky was clear, and from the plane I felt that we could see forever. Nancy was in the back of the four-passenger single-engine Piper Cub. Because this was my first airplane ride, I was given the front seat next to her dad. We circled over Providence, and I was amazed at how much of the city we could see from our vantage point. Then Nancy's father took us out over my neighborhood. As I looked down over my house, I kept wondering what my parents would do if they'd known that I was several thousand feet from them at that very moment—close, but perhaps not in a direction that would have given them comfort.

We flew for about an hour, but what a glorious hour! For the first time in my life I began to realize just how narrow and sheltered my existence had been. There was a great big world out there, and I had experienced so little of it. I can remember thinking that in two years, when I entered the convent, my world would become ever so much smaller. I began to have a twinge of doubt but quickly dismissed it as a temptation. Later, when we were back in her bedroom talking, Nancy and I discussed the fact that the world had many temptations that would try to lure girls like us away from the vocations to which God had called us. We knew that our task was to fight these temptations in order to become worthy of our calling. Such is the stuff of which some young girls' dreams are made.

When I got home on Sunday afternoon, I told my parents about my wonderful ride on the plane and how Nancy's father had even let me handle the controls for a few minutes. Mom and Dad tried to act annoyed that I hadn't asked them if I could do such a thing, but they always were bad actors. They were actually impressed that I had had such an adventure. It made me feel grown-up and important to be the first in the family to have had the experience.

Most of my teenage growing experiences were pretty tame by anyone's standards, and most of those experiences were shared with the same two friends, Francine and Lisa. The three of us had been friends since kindergarten, and we remained close through adulthood. Francine wanted to be a nun, too, and it was with her that I went to the Franciscan monastery in Providence every week for mass. Our trips were always the same. I met Francine at the bus stop in front of her house every Saturday at 10:00 A.M. In my purse were the $5 or $6 that I had earned baby-sitting, and every week I spent it in the same way: 70 cents for the round-trip bus fare, 50 cents for the collection plate at mass, and $2.25 for lunch—a hot dog, french fries, and a Coke at a diner near the monastery. The rest of my earnings was used during the week for snacks at school.

Lisa never entertained the idea of becoming a nun, but she could usually be counted on to accompany Francine and me to the city for mass as long as we promised to go shopping with her for the rest of the afternoon. "Shopping" consisted of wandering up and down the aisles of department stores, admiring all the things that we saw but couldn't buy. Lisa's mother worked at one of the big department stores in Providence, and if Lisa saw something that she liked there, she could ask her mother to get it for her on her employees' discount the following week. Francine's mother didn't trust Francine to choose her own clothes, so she never bought anything on our trips into town either. I liked the things we saw, but most of them didn't come in size eighteen, and so most weeks we bought very little.

The real reason Francine and I went into Providence each week was to visit St. Francis Chapel. It was filled with hushed silence and reverence. The smell of beeswax hung thick in the air, and the halls were lit by rows and rows of burning candles glowing before the statues of the saints to whom petitions had been raised. We were captivated by the monks at the monastery. We envied them the brown robes and sandals of their order. They always smiled at us, and their smiles exuded a peace and holiness that we knew would be ours once we had joined an order, too. A fifteen-year-old girl could spend hours in dreams and fantasy at St. Francis Chapel.

Alone among the other worshipers, I was free to contemplate my future with Jesus, serving Him with other sisters who understood the love and closeness that I felt toward Him. I had read a theology book entitled *This Tremendous Lover*, a treatise on the person of Jesus Christ, particularly in relation to the sacrament of holy communion. I knew precisely what the author meant when he referred to Jesus as the lover of our souls. That's how I thought of Him. He was my lover, and I knew that the relationship would grow even deeper when I became a nun and could give my whole life to Him.

My plans were to join the Order of Poor Clares right after graduation. Throughout my four years of high school I had been writing to the reverend mother at the order's monastery in Lowell, Massachusetts. The Poor Clares are a cloistered order. The women who join this order typically take the usual vows of poverty, chastity, and obedience and a fourth vow of enclosure. Once the vow of enclosure is taken, a cloistered nun never leaves the confines of the monastery walls. She may not even attend her parent's funerals. That part bothered me, but then I concluded that it was all part of the sacrifice one makes for God. I knew this was what I wanted for my life, hardships and all.

Toward the end of my first year at Sacred Heart High School, Sister Emanuel Joseph told the class that she and another sister needed a ride to Lowell, Massachusetts. She asked if any of us thought our parents could take them. My hand shot up. I told Sister that I would ask my father. I was hoping that if he said yes, we would be able to visit the monastery of the Poor Clares while we were waiting for my teacher. That night my father agreed, and we planned the day as a family outing.

Saturday came, and I was both excited and scared. I wanted very much to meet the reverend mother at the monastery and to see the place where I would be living in a few years. On the other hand, I was afraid of what my parents' reaction might be when they discovered that the convent I was planning to join was cloistered. My fears were well grounded. We dropped Manny Joe and her companion off at their destination and headed for the Poor Clare monastery. Dad didn't like to go anywhere empty-handed, so first we stopped at a bakery, where he picked up boxes of doughnuts.

When we arrived at the monastery, we rang the bell. It seemed to take forever for someone to come to the door, and my father asked me if they knew that we were coming. He was wondering aloud if there was anyone home. My heart raced as my mind gave him a silent answer: "They are always home, Dad." Finally, one of the extern sisters came to let us in. An extern sister does not take a vow of enclosure and can therefore be the link of the monastery with the rest of the world. She greeted us, escorted us into one of the "parlors," and told us that Reverend Mother would be joining us soon. In one wall of the room was a large window covered with iron grating. There was a curtain drawn on the other side. I knew that Reverend Mother would be visiting with us from the other side of this grating. My parents did not.

After ten or fifteen minutes we could hear the sound of a door opening and closing. Footsteps grew closer, and finally the curtain was drawn aside. My father stood up and greeted Reverend Mother and the sister who was with her. Introductions were made all around. Finally, unable to comprehend what was going on, my father asked Reverend Mother when she was going to come into the parlor and visit with us. She looked at me, lifted an eyebrow, smiled at my father, and said: "Well, I see that Rose Mary hasn't told you very much about our order. Why don't you go into the parlor next to this one, Rose Mary, and visit with Sister while I talk with your parents?" I meekly obeyed, grateful that the reverend mother would be doing my dirty work for me. I think she knew that it would be easier for my father and mother to take in all that they needed to know if it came from her. After about half an hour we all came together again and had a good visit. Reverend Mother graciously accepted the gift of the doughnuts and assured my father that all the sisters would enjoy them for dessert later that night.

The part of that visit most prominent in my mind is of how, even though the room must have been seventy-five degrees, my father decided he needed to put on his jacket. He had been wearing a short-sleeved shirt, and when he noticed Reverend Mother staring at the bare-breasted hula girl tattoo on his forearm, he turned several increasing shades of red and donned his jacket as quickly as possible. Under the circumstances the whole visit was as comfortable as it could possibly have been. The ride home was subdued, and I was grateful for the chatter of Sister Emanuel Joseph and her companion.

In the Roman Catholic Church there is a long-standing historical tradition called spiritual direction. If one is serious about spiritual growth, it is advised that the person have a spiritual director, someone, usually a priest, with whom one shares one's spirit journey. In my junior year of high school I asked Father Rivers, a parish priest in the next town, to be my spiritual director. Each week I took a bus from school to his church and we visited for an hour. He heard my confession, and we talked about how my prayer life was progressing. He told me that he felt I had too effervescent a personality for the convent. I liked Father Rivers, but I thought that his comment about life in the convent being wrong for me was just one more temptation that God was allowing to test my resolve.

Nancy and I had spent a great deal of time during the summer speculating over who would be our junior year teacher now that Sister Patrick Anthony and Father Luke were married. We were less than thrilled to discover that Manny Joe had been assigned the junior class. Faced with the inevitable, we hoped that at least a summer rest had mellowed Manny Joe's personality a bit. It didn't take us long to discover that if anything, she had grown more irritable. The slightest thing set her off, and we realized we were in a no-win situation with her. If we didn't ask questions and then did poorly on a test, she went into a tantrum. If we did ask questions, she went into a tirade about how she had just explained the material thoroughly. Usually these outbursts were accompanied by flying erasers, which never actually hit any of us but managed to skim the air just over our heads. Some of the girls in the class were able to laugh about how crazy Manny Joe was getting. Others of us became increasingly nervous and terrified, unable to keep from internalizing what was happening to our teacher.

One evening in the late fall I came home from school nervous and upset. At the dinner table I burst into tears. My father wanted to know what had happened. I told him about Manny Joe and how she had had a particularly bad day. He was outraged that a sister would behave like that with her class and told me that I didn't have to take that from her, that I could transfer right into East Providence High School. To my amazement, I was actually relieved. I wanted to do it right away, the very next day, as a matter of fact. My father had other plans. He told me that I needed to face up to the situation, to make a clean break. Dad had called ahead to talk to the principal and tell her that we would be coming to the convent shortly. He briefly explained the situation and told her that we needed to talk with her.

Immediately following dinner the two of us got into the car and headed for the Sacred Heart convent. As we drove to Pawtucket, I wished that I had never raised the issue. I was not looking forward to talking to Manny Joe or the principal. I wasn't accustomed to telling a nun that she was wrong. I had always assumed that if something was going wrong between me and anyone, let alone a nun, it must be my fault. My parents had raised us to respect our elders. Between my father and grandfather, I had certainly witnessed enough temper tantrums to know that it was not my place to interfere in any way.

I had taken the brown paper covers off all my books, and as we pulled up in front of the convent, I loaded them in my arms. Taking a deep breath, I prepared for what I thought would probably be the worst moment of my life. Dad and I walked up the sidewalk together and rang the convent doorbell. One of the sisters answered almost immediately and ushered us into a parlor. Dad and I waited, and within minutes the principal was standing there before us. We had a very short conversation. My father was calm and cordial but firm in his resolve that his daughter did not deserve the abuse that had been taking place in the classroom. The principal was also very cordial. She apologized for Sister Emanuel Joseph's behavior and said that Sister had been having a difficult time of it recently. She suggested that I give it another try. Dad said that the decision was up to me. I tried to talk between tears and told them that I just didn't want to go back into that classroom. In my mind I knew that even if by some miracle, Manny Joe could come into the classroom the next day behaving like a saint, I would not have the courage to face her after having squealed on her. I actually felt guilty for having told my father about what she had been doing. We were probably at the convent for a total of fifteen minutes, but it felt like an eternity. As my father and I finally came out the front door and stood on the steps, I breathed in and let out a deep sigh. I didn't know what was ahead of me at East Providence High School, but at least this nightmare was over. I would miss Nancy and some of my other friends, but I would not miss the fear that had been part of my classroom experience for more than a year.

The next day I caught the bus that took all the neighborhood teenagers to the high school. My resolve began to weaken as I sat among a bunch of noisy teenagers I didn't know. When we reached the school, I headed straight for the administrative offices. I was directed into a small cubicle to talk to a guidance counselor about my class schedule. She seemed like a really nice woman. What surprised me most was her insistence that because I was transferring in from a parochial school, I be placed into the highest division of the business classes. At St. Margaret's and later at Sacred Heart, I was considered one of the slower students who needed extra help and work. I found it impossible to convince this woman that I would not be able to keep up with a high-division class. She remained firm, despite my protests. That day, and that encounter with the guidance counselor, were very important in my life. It was the first time in many years that anyone put trust and confidence in my academic abilities. I was to remember that experience as the beginning of my recovery from imputed low self-esteem. That day was the birth of a small seed of confidence within me, a seed which would slowly be nurtured by caring and encouragement from others.

It took quite a bit of doing to adjust to East Providence High School after nearly eight years of parochial education. I made mistakes that brought ripples of laughter from my classmates and grateful smiles from the teachers. I learned quickly that we weren't expected to stand by our desks whenever a teacher called on us in class. I still think that there is something inherently nice about young people showing that kind of respect for adults, though. I learned that it was frowned upon to draw a little cross at the top of every test or homework paper. It took me months to stop blushing every time we had gym class and I was expected to change my clothes in the presence of the other girls in the locker room.

But most of all, it was a wonderful and liberating experience to be one of hundreds of students who didn't take life so seriously.

Those first six months at East Providence High School gave me enough self-confidence to decide it was time to take a real risk. I knew that I had to pass only one course in order to have the credits to graduate. I also knew that I hated bookkeeping and shorthand. I told my guidance counselor that I wanted to take as many college prep classes as I could squeeze into my schedule. She discouraged me but finally gave in to my persistence. I was scheduled to take algebra I and geometry, college prep English, and history, and I also chose to continue my typing classes. She told me that geometry was not supposed to be taken until one had a background in algebra. I said that I needed to try.

Fortunately my senior year was a smashing success. I flourished in the college prep courses. They seemed logical, easy, and fun. What I learned during that transition has helped me draw some pretty basic conclusions. It should never be an automatic assumption that students who have difficulty in grade school and junior high must take business courses in high school. Business classes should not be a "holding tank" for students who have difficulties with other courses. They can be just as difficult as college prep courses. It takes a certain kind of mind to do either. It would be much wiser to test the students first to see where their abilities lie, if they think in the concrete or the abstract. Until, as an adult, I learned to balance my approach and to nurture my concrete thinking process, I found it easier to operate in the abstract. It was through luck, and perhaps a bit of fate, that I accidentally discovered this for myself by insisting on taking those college prep courses.

My senior year was wonderful. I had spent the summer before seriously dieting under my doctor's care. I had climbed up to the uncomfortable, and unattractive, weight of 190 pounds. It was embarrassing to have to get my clothes from the large women's stores, and size eighteens just did not come in the wonderful colors and styles that attracted a teenage girl's attention. My doctor knew that I didn't believe I could lose all that excess weight on my own, so he told me to see him every week, at which time he weighed me and handed me a little brown envelope of diet pills to help suppress my appetite. The doctor didn't give me a rigid diet to follow. He simply told me that I could have only twelve hundred calories each day. He also asked me to write down everything I ate in a notebook.

The diet worked beautifully. I learned to put the most amount of food in my daily diet as my calorie allowance would let me have. I ate tons of fruit, vegetables, fish, and chicken. The weight melted off all summer. By the time I went back to school I was 40 pounds lighter, and everyone was amazed at the difference. By Thanksgiving I was down to 130 pounds, and I felt wonderful. It wasn't until I had reached my goal weight that my doctor let me in on the secret of those magic diet pills. They were placebos, fakes. He had a huge jar of them in his cabinet and gave them to people like me, people who didn't have confidence in themselves and their ability to lose weight on their own. He congratulated me on my efforts and success. I had a new confidence in myself, and I liked the effect, both in my body and in my mind.

With my weight under control and my body looking sleek and healthy, I began to realize that I had taken on a whole new batch of problems: boys. In a size eighteen I never had to worry about how boys would respond to me. They didn't. If I was lucky and they were kind, I was almost invisible. If I was unlucky and they were not kind, I was the brunt of fat jokes and snide remarks. That all changed in my senior year, and I felt very ambiguous about the sudden attention I was getting from the boys in school. While, on one hand, I enjoyed the smiles and awkward conversations, on the other, I felt an anger welling up inside me. I liked the attention, but I also knew that I was the very same person thin as I had been fat. Why were the very people who wouldn't have given me the time of day a year ago, when I wore a size eighteen, now suddenly interested in my thoughts and feelings? These attitudes and responses don't change for adults; my weight has taken several drastic turns in either direction over my adult years, and I still find people's responses correlating to what size I wear.

In the winter of my senior year I was asked out on my very first date. Loui Amerasini, a boy in my English class, invited me to attend the Winter Festival Dance with him. Loui, Mario Alexander, Carl Swartz, and I usually shared first-period lunch together in the school cafeteria. We had become a group, and although we didn't see each other outside school, we had grown close. I never really thought of any of them as potential dates. They were simply my school buddies. About three weeks before the dance Loui asked: "You wouldn't want to go to the Winter Festival Dance with me, would you?"

I broke out into a wide grin and tried to sound casual, even though I could hardly contain my excitement: "Yes, I would."

That dance was not only my first real date but Loui's, too, the first among many that we shared during our senior year. Yet neither of us moved beyond the friendship bond we had. My parents loved Loui and encouraged me to think about him as a potential husband. He was smart. He was heading for college. He had a good future ahead of him. We obviously enjoyed each other's company. What more could I possibly want? I was never able to help my parents understand that even though I loved Loui, I was not in love with him. Even then I realized that was not enough.

Loui and I remained friends for many years. After high school, when I moved away, he occasionally sent funny cards and let me know how school was going for him. When I moved back to Rhode Island, we dated a couple of times and even attended his college reunion together. But by then I think we both realized that our relationship would always be something special between good friends. It was confusing for me because I didn't realize why I couldn't love Loui the way that I would have liked. I have no idea if it was as confusing for Loui.

CHAPTER 2

My graduation from East Providence High School in June 1965 was a great event for the whole family. I was the first person in my immediate family to earn a high school diploma. My parents were proud of my accomplishment, and they gave a party in my honor. Food, music, and relatives were plentiful, and there were enough pictures taken to make sure that every moment was captured for the family record. My grandparents attended, of course, and so did an assortment of aunts, uncles, and cousins.

When I was in junior high school, my parents had purchased a summer cottage in Warren, Rhode Island, a small town approximately twenty-five miles from Rumford. It is close to the famous Newport Beach, and our little community was located on the bay. Our house was only three blocks up the hill from the water, and my parents loved the cool breezes and salty air. Once I graduated from high school, they wanted to move to this new house permanently. While we were still using the cottage as a vacation getaway, my parents poured every available dollar into doing the work that was necessary to make it a permanent dwelling. A well was dug, a foundation put in, a dormer built atop the attic in order to make more bedroom space, and on weekends my father worked on the inside, nailing paneling and Sheetrock to the studs that divided one room from another. My parents were proud of their accomplishments and looked forward to the day when this little cottage, cared for by their hard work and dreams, would become our permanent home.

The three of us children dreaded that day. All our friends were in

Rumford, and none of us had access to transportation that would get us back on home turf for visits. Summers and weekends were boring enough. The mere thought of having that boredom become permanent when we moved to Warren for good was not comforting. Mom and Dad would not allow us to go the three blocks down the hill to the bay to cool off with a swim if they were not home. They wanted to know that we were safe while they were at work, so we had to stay in or around the house.

Being the oldest, I was in charge of my brother and sister when my parents were away. This had been the case since I was twelve years old. It was during those six years of baby-sitting for my siblings that I first began to understand what it is to have responsibility without the authority with which to carry out an assignment. During the school year it was my responsibility to make all the beds, start dinner, and do the breakfast dishes before my parents got home from work. With summer vacation came the additional responsibilities of doing most of the housework and making sure that my brother and sister didn't get into any mischief. Somehow, I was magically supposed to keep the house clean and my brother and sister out of trouble without acting like a mother.

In retrospect, some of what happened while my parents were at work and I was left in charge is funny. There were times when I would have liked to wring my brother's neck. He was usually my biggest problem. He always managed to make the skirmishes we had while my parents were at work look like my fault. One particular day I had been washing the kitchen floor on my hands and knees with a bucket of soapy water and a sponge. My mother didn't think that a mop did a thorough enough job, so scrubbing was the only method she would allow. There was soapy water everywhere, and my brother pranced through the kitchen with no thought of the dirt he was tracking in. I told him to use the front door or to stay outside until the floor was washed, waxed, and dried. His reply was that he would do as he pleased. Five minutes later he came waltzing through the kitchen again. I sprang to my feet, chased him through the house and out the back door. Once he was outside the house, I locked the front door, ran though the house and locked the back door, and yelled that he wouldn't be getting in until the floor was waxed and dry. Just as I had finished waxing the whole floor, my brother turned on the outside faucet and held the nozzle of the hose to the screen of the kitchen window. I had to mop it up, wash the floor again to get rid of the now-sticky wax, and then wax again. When my parents arrived home from work, my brother was only too anxious to report how I had locked him out of the house. Even after I explained what had happened, my parents admonished that there was no excuse for locking my brother out of the house and that I was never to do it again. No matter what happened between us I was always put at fault, either because I was the oldest and should have know how to handle the situation or because my brother was a boy, and after all, "boys do get into mischief from time to time."

Moving to Warren presented a problem to us children. My issue was that now that I had graduated from high school I wanted to get a job and begin earning some real money. Up to then my only money was what I made from baby-sitting. I had never earned more than twenty dollars a week, and by the time I was in high school my mother told me that I was earning enough to be responsible for all my clothes except expensive items like winter coats. For four years I had been either buying my own clothes or making them on a secondhand sewing machine that my parents had purchased for me from a neighbor.

My plans to enter the convent immediately following graduation had been put aside for the time being. I had continued in my resolve to begin postulancy with the Poor Clares as soon as I graduated, but three factors caused me to postpone my plans. The first was that label that stuck to my cousin Eileen. If this was not the life to which I was called, I would forevermore be known in my family as "Rose Mary, the one who used to be a nun." I also was afraid that once in the convent, if I did discover that it was not for me, I wouldn't have the courage to leave, for fear of looking like a failure to others. Finally, Father Rivers's words about my being too effervescent for convent life gnawed at me. I was afraid that he might be right. I knew that my easygoing nature and bravado lay very close to the surface and that the least tampering by some well-meaning superior would bring it all crumbling down around me. If that were to happen, I wasn't at all sure that I would ever be able to find that center of strength inside myself again.

And so there I was, eighteen years old, ready to get my first "real" job, and twenty-five miles from Providence. Warren and the other towns between it and Providence were relatively small. It would have been very difficult to find work in any of them. I didn't have a car or driver's license, so I was limited to a job in Providence, where my parents worked, or someplace en route. After a week of making out applications and going on interviews, I finally landed my first job. I was hired by a small construction company to work as a combination bookkeeper and secretary. My take-home pay was a whopping sixty-seven dollars a week, and I was ecstatic. My parents had to be at work by 7:00 A.M., but I wasn't due until 8:30. Every morning we left the house by 6:15, and they dropped me off at a coffee shop close to the office. I read or wrote letters for an hour and then walked the half mile to the building where I worked. In the afternoon my parents picked me up, and we drove back to Warren. My only time for friends was on the weekend. Some weekends even that wasn't possible, and I would stay at home and read, watch television, talk on the phone, and fantasize about how life would someday be different for me. Someday I would have an exciting life, a life filled with love, riches, and adventure.

By August, after having worked at the construction company for only three months, I knew that I had to break away or be stuck in the boredom forever. One Saturday, on one of my excursions to Providence with Lisa, we happened to pass the Air Force recruiting office. I decided to stop in and talk to one of the people there. Lisa told me that I was crazy and that she wasn't about to go inside. We agreed to meet at our usual restaurant for lunch. When I entered the recruiting station, a handsome, polished-from-head-to-toe sergeant greeted me and told me he was Sergeant Anderson. I had never met anyone like him before. He was good-looking, had a charming southern accent, and treated me like an adult woman. I was taken with him from the very first moment. He asked me questions about my education, my background, and the kinds of things that I liked to do. I told him that if I did go into the Air Force, I would like to work in the towers and be one of those people who give landing and takeoff instructions to pilots. He told me that that was called communications. He seemed to be genuinely interested in me as a person. He explained that the Air Force didn't take just anybody and that I would need to take several tests to determine both my aptitude and qualifications. I took the tests and was told the results would be ready in a week. I promised that I would return to the recruiting office the following Saturday. I didn't mention my little excursion to my parents. I instinctively knew that they, especially my father, would not be at all pleased with the prospects of my joining the United States Air Force. There would be time enough to tell them later if indeed, I did pass all the tests and decided to join.

The week seemed endless. Finally Saturday came, and I persuaded my father to give me a ride to Providence. I told him that Lisa and I needed to do some shopping, that I would be spending the night at her house, and that she could drive me home on Sunday evening. At the appointed hour I went to the recruiting office. Sergeant Anderson was waiting for me. He said that he was pleased to say that I had done very well on my tests and that it appeared that I had a real aptitude for communications. Then he asked me where I would like to be stationed. I thought of the most romantic place I could imagine, San Francisco. He said that he couldn't make any promises but that it looked as if I might get both my requests: to be trained in communications and to be stationed at Travis Air Force Base, which was one hour north of San Francisco. I told him that I wanted to enlist. San Francisco and the Air Force just had to be more exciting than living in Warren, Rhode Island, and working for a construction company!

The following Monday evening I told my parents about my plans, and my father went into a rage. "First you want to be a nun, and now you want to go into the Air Force. How much more opposite can you be?" He would not give his permission for me to enlist, which I needed because I was only eighteen. The next day I called Sergeant Anderson, who assured me that he was accustomed to dealing with parents who wanted to be overprotective of their daughters. He asked if he could come to our house the following evening.

Tuesday evening came, and Sergeant Anderson arrived right at seven. My parents were cordial, but I could tell from the set of my father's jaw that he was not about to be open-minded about anything the sergeant had to say.

While my father and Sergeant Anderson talked, my mother and I looked on silently. We knew that we would have no clout in the purely male encounter. As I sat across the room from the two men, my hopes began to sink. My father was beginning to allow his anger to surface, and I wondered just how far it would take him. Finally, after he had exhausted every argument in the court of courtesy, Dad pulled out an unexpected big gun. He looked Sergeant Anderson squarely in the face and said: "I don't want my daughter in the military because I know what women in the military are like. I was in the Navy in World War Two, and I had enough of them myself."

My heart skipped a beat, and I thought that the room was more still and silent than it had ever been before. Sergeant Anderson looked back at my father with all the confidence in the world and replied: "John, you raised your daughter. You gave her your values, good values. Neither the Air Force nor anyone else can take those away from her. It's time you trusted your daughter to be who you brought her up to be." Of the things that he could have said, that was the most powerful statement of all. My father said that he would sign the release giving his permission. He then asked my mother and me to bring the dessert that had been waiting in the next room.

As I followed my mother into the kitchen, I wondered how my father's statement about the women with whom he had been had affected her. She didn't seem to be the least bit shaken. As we poured coffee and cut pieces of cake, I looked over at her. Her face betrayed no anger or pain. I was confused because I wouldn't have expected this kind of calm reaction from my mother upon hearing that my father had had sexual experiences before their marriage. Dad had always been emphatic about the fact that his daughters would be virgins when they walked down the aisle. My mother had been a virgin when she had married my father, and I had assumed that my father was also. Would this news break up their marriage?

I simply had to know. Finally, taking in a deep breath, I looked at my mother and said: "Aren't you mad?"

"About what?" she asked.

"You know, what Dad said about what he did when he was in the Navy." I looked into my mother's eyes. I needed to know whether or not this easiness was real or simply a veneer that she was using for my sake. I wasn't even sure that she knew what I was asking her, and I was beginning to think that perhaps she was in a mild state of shock or something.

"What do you mean about what your father said?"

I was right! Mom was in shock. "You know," I responded. "About the women in the military. Weren't you surprised?"

My mother continued to stare at me with a look of semirecognition. Then, finally, a glimmer of understanding came over her face. The sides of her mouth turned up the littlest bit. "No."

That's it? That's the extent of your response when you find out that your husband slept around before you married him? Now I was the one who seemed in need of resuscitation.

"Mom, you mean that it doesn't bother you that Dad"—I faltered in my attempt to find the most delicate way to express my question—"had a sexual experience with someone before he married you?"

My mother shrugged her shoulders as she continued to get the last of the dessert ready to take into the living room. "Oh, Rose Mary, of course not. He's a man."

The rest of the visit with Sergeant Anderson was polite and subdued. As my father signed the consent papers, I relaxed. I realized that-for the first time I was the only one who had total control over the direction that my life would take. I felt powerful, and excited, and frightened. Before this, when something went wrong in my life, I could blame someone else, but deciding whether or not to join the Air Force was my decision only. If my choice proved to be a bad one, I would be the one to take the blame. If it turned out to have been a good choice, I would be credited for the decision. Living across the country seemed to be an awfully big step for me to take. Yet I knew that if I didn't, my alternatives would be limited. Working at the construction company until some man asked me to marry him was not what I wanted for my life. I needed more choices than that, and the Air Force offered those choices. My most immediate concern, however, was to find out why my mother wasn't upset with hearing about my father's sexual activities before they were married.

I saw my opportunity the next evening as my mother and I were doing the dinner dishes. Dad was outside in the yard, watering the lawn. My brother and sister were out with some friends. There were few enough opportunities when my mother and I could be alone together, so I decided to seize the moment. "Mom, you mean that you really are OK about Dad doing what he did when he was in the Navy?"

She paused a moment and looked at me. "Rose Mary, your father is a normal man. Men have different needs from women. He's been faithful to me ever since the day we were married. Of course, I didn't expect that he would be a virgin."

I felt confused and after a moment or two said: "But, Ma, Dad is always talking about how no daughter of his is going to walk down the aisle in a white dress unless it really stands for something. He makes it sound as though you're a really bad person if you have sex before you get married. Are you saying that the rule is different for men?"

My mother assured me that indeed, it was very different for men. She told me that they needed to "sow their wild oats" before they could be expected to settle down and get married. She reiterated that the sex drive is different for men from the way it is for women and that it is a shame when a woman isn't a virgin when she gets married.

Without hesitation I asked: "But, Mom, if every man feels that his son has the right to sow wild oats but that his daughter has to be a virgin when she gets married, whose daughter is the man's son supposed to sow his wild oats with?"

My exasperated mother shrugged. "I don't know, Rose Mary. There are always girls who do that kind of thing. It's just that a good girl doesn't."

I wasn't satisfied with my mother's reasoning, but I also knew there was no point in pursuing the matter further. She had her own way of reasoning. I knew that it could never be mine. I would have to find one that fitted me for myself.

I continued to work at the construction company until a week before my induction into the Air Force in August. I would be going to Lackland Air Force Base in Amarillo, Texas, for twelve weeks of basic training. After basic training was completed, I would receive my orders and have a week at home with my family before reporting to my first assignment. As the time drew closer for me to go into Providence to be sworn in, I grew more and more excited. I created all sorts of fantasies about the adventures that I would have in San Francisco. I had heard stories about how awful basis training could be, but I knew that if I could just hang in there for those twelve weeks, I would go on to have all sorts of wonderful experiences.

Finally the day of my induction arrived. I put on my nicest dress, and my parents dropped me off in Providence. I was scheduled to be sworn in at ten that morning. After the induction Sergeant Anderson was going to take me out to lunch, my very first time out with a grown man! There were thirty or so inductees lined up in a large room who were asked to repeat the oath in front of several officers and the United States flag. After we all had taken our oaths, we were given airline tickets. We had two more weeks until we flew out to Texas.

The time went by slowly. I spent as much as I could visiting with friends. Lisa still thought that I was crazy, but she also admitted that she envied my deciding to get out of Rhode Island. She made me promise that I would write to her every week.

On the day of my departure we were all aflutter. Mom and Dad took the day off from work so that we could be together. I repacked what had been packed for days and added a few last-minute items. Finally we were ready to drive to the airport. This would be my first time on a commercial plane, and that alone had my heart racing with excitement.

There were lots of other young people at the airport who were also headed for basic training.

Saying good-bye to my parents was really hard. We hugged and cried. My father reminded me to write often and promised that he would do the same. My mother tucked a twenty-dollar bill into my hand and tried hard not to lose control completely. Every time I have left home or come back again after having been away for a long time, I have seen my mother's pain. She has never liked the idea of her children being so far away from her that it takes a plane ticket to retrieve them.

The flight was wonderful. One of the boys had brought boxes of doughnuts and passed them out to everyone. Another boy had brought his guitar and soon had the whole plane singing the folk songs that became a trademark of the sixties. Several boys got sick and were forced to use airsickness bags. I simply enjoyed the whole experience. I felt so grown-up and mature as I thought about how I was venturing forth farther than any of my friends or relatives ever had—the women anyway.

We landed in Amarillo at midnight and were met by a sergeant in green fatigues. He herded us into a group by shouting orders, and finally we were on a bus heading for the base. By the time we arrived and were dropped off at our assigned barracks, we all were too exhausted to be excited. All any of us wanted was a nice comfortable bed and about ten hours of uninterrupted sleep. We got the nice comfortable bed, but we didn't get the ten hours of sleep. Our training instructor informed us that because it was our first night on base and we had arrived so late, we would be allowed to sleep in. That was the good news. The bad news was that instead of getting up at the usual 5:00 A.M., we would be given two extra hours and wouldn't be required to turn out for roll call until 7:00! The Air Force was treating us by giving us a whole five hours to sleep!

The next morning we were awakened by what sounded like a cowbell being rung up and down the halls of the barracks. We were told to dress, make our beds, shower, dress, and form a line outside on the sidewalk in front of the building within half an hour. I have never moved quite so fast in my life, but we all made it. Of course, some of us still had wet hair, but we were there. A tall, beautiful woman stood in front of us and told us that her name was Airman Reins and that she would be our TI (training instructor) during our twelve weeks of basic training. I fell in love immediately, although at that time in my life I would not have called it love. She was six feet tall and had flaming red hair. She was also the best-groomed woman I had ever seen. Her shoes gleamed. Her uniform didn't have a single crease. Her hair was short and impeccably coiffed. Her makeup was sparse but tasteful, and most of all, she smelled wonderful. About two weeks after I had been in basic training, I finally got up the nerve to ask her the name of her perfume. It was Jade East men's cologne.

The first item on the agenda for the day was breakfast, and our TI tried to get us into some semblance of order by having us form two columns. Then we were marched to the dining room, called the chow hall. Breakfast was delicious and plentiful, and we all ate heartily as we introduced ourselves and wondered aloud what we could expect for the next three months. Most of us agreed that we had really lucked out in getting Airman Reins as our TI.

After breakfast we were marched to another building that was filled with classrooms. It wouldn't take long for us to figure out that in the military there are several very basic rules:

1. Do what you're told and don't ask questions.
2. If it's less than five miles away, no matter if there are one hundred buses available, you'll be marched to your destination.
3. Cleanliness isn't next go godliness; it *is* godliness.

The classrooms became familiar territory to us. In the sixties women in the Air Force did not receive the same basic training as the men. We were given courses in grooming, makeup, posture, and how to interact with men in public places. The instructors even went so far as to show us how to hand our lighters or matches to men when we were out on dates so that they could light our cigarettes. I enjoyed these courses and viewed them as a way to smooth out some of my rough edges. It never dawned on me that learning how to have a man open doors for me or light my cigarette was only serving to deepen the sexism that was already so much a part of my life and experience. As far as I was concerned, the women who taught these classes were helping us turn ourselves into real ladies, and I was all for it.

The first week of basic training was full. Most of us had brought makeup and rollers to curl our hair every night. In the sixties most of the girls wore a very pale pink shade of lipstick, sometimes almost white, and we all did our hair up in huge bristly rollers that made it impossible to get a decent night's sleep unless we slept on our faces. The first order of business was to go to the PX. We were told that we needed to purchase ditty bags to serve as our purses during basic training. A ditty bag is a small cylindrical-shaped canvas bag with a zipper. Airman Reins gave us a shopping list of things we were required to buy along with our ditty bags: a plastic cup, a pill case in which each of us would keep salt pills, regulation sanitary napkins (whatever they were), and a lipstick of our choice. When some of us tried to inform her that we already had lipsticks, she simply restated her initial order. When we entered the PX and began to paw through the various shades of lipstick, we discovered the reason for our TI's order. No matter what the label said, the inside always contained the same color, bright fire engine red! At first we felt as though our lips were the only things that could be seen on us from miles away. After a couple of weeks it just didn't seem to matter any more. We all knew that as soon as we completed basic training, we would go back to the shades we each liked best.

During that first week of basic training we were measured for our uniforms. We would be issued two suits of winter dress uniforms, two suits of summer dress uniforms, and three light blue skirts and blouses that would be our fatigue uniforms during basic training. We were also issued two pairs of dark blue cotton fatigue pants. Until our uniforms were ready, we had to wear civilian clothes. A week later, when our fatigues were ready for us, we were thrilled. Now we would fit right in with the others. We wouldn't stick out as the new recruits anymore.

On the day that we were finally issued our fatigues, we were given a class on how to care for them, wash them, starch them with full-strength liquid starch, and hang them out to dry. Ironing those stiff skirts and blouses was a great challenge, and we were not shown how to do it. We were simply told that they were to be ironed so that not one wrinkle remained. A single wrinkle could mean not passing inspection and, therefore, not being granted privileges. The clothes had to be wrinkle-free and stand upright on the floor without assistance. We spent every moment of our "free" time in the evening spit-shining our shoes and working to create skirts and blouses that could stand up.

Our barracks received a white glove inspection once each week, and preparing for it was a major project. The floors had to be waxed and buffed until you could see your reflection in them. Our beds were supposed to be made so snugly that our TI would be able to bounce a quarter off them. Our closets were to be so ordered that all the hangers were an equal distance from one another. For each infraction we would receive a gig. Any more than the allowed number of gigs resulted in losing privileges. At first we were stumped when we received gigs for having "unauthorized objects" in our closets or drawers. When we discovered that most often these unauthorized objects were a stray hair on a roller and a piece of dandruff on a brush, we came to a logical and creative solution. We bought new combs, brushes, and rollers, put them in their appropriate places, and didn't touch them again until we graduated from basic training. The combs, brushes, and rollers we did use, we hauled out every night and stored away in our suitcases just before inspection. None of us had any trouble with gigs because of unauthorized objects again.

I loved basic training. I loved being rewarded with off-base passes for having my belongings clean and in order. I liked having my life ordered. I liked knowing what was expected of me at all times. I flourished in the demand for physical fitness. We were required to do calisthenics every day, and I think that the marching from one place to another, which could add up to ten miles or more, also did a great deal to contribute to my overall sense of well-being. I had never been very athletic as a child, and those first two weeks of basic training, with all its physical activity, left my body aching where I didn't know it could. But gradually, as the days and weeks wore on, I began to feel more and more fit. My body felt alive. It increased in strength and endurance. I thought that Airman Reins was my guardian angel, and I would have jumped through hoops of fire for her. Even when all the other girls in the barracks were lamenting the rigorous schedule and counting the days until graduation, I was living in dread of the day. By the end of the second month I had decided that my goal was to become a training instructor so that I could teach basic training just like Airman Reins.

In the ninth week of the twelve-week program, Airman Reins called me into her office. She told me that I was being held back one week from graduation because she felt that I needed the extra time to acclimate myself to the demands of the program. I wasn't concerned about the decision until I realized it meant I would have to move into another barracks and have a different training instructor. I was going to lose Airman Reins! I tried to sound calm and rational as I asked her if I could please stay with her group, that I would be willing to put in an extra week or even work harder if I could just stay with my group. She was gentle but emphatic. I tried not to cry in her presence, but my tears surfaced nonetheless. I left her office and went to my room to pack my things. At the moment it felt as though that day would be the saddest in my life.

That extra week in this new class did prove to be good for me, and I was able to graduate with my class and go to my assignment, training as a communications specialist at Travis Air Force Base in northern California. I had been granted both my requests.

Following graduation from basic training, we all were given two weeks' leave before reporting to our new commander at Travis. We were excited about our futures and anxious to go home to see family and friends. We wanted them to see how much we had matured in the three months that we had been away. I wanted my parents to see that I was an adult and able to handle my life away from them. It was important to me that they understand I was becoming my own person and that I did not need to be defined by their standards and parameters.

The two weeks flew by. My father had come to accept my being in the Air Force and made a big splash out of the fact that his daughter was in uniform. He even dug out his old Navy uniform from World War II, which still fitted him, and we had our picture taken together. Grandparents, aunts, uncles, and cousins came to visit, and there was ample time for me to spend just with my friends. Loui had already started his freshman year at the University of Rhode Island, but we were able to go out on a date or two while I was home. He seemed to be enjoying his first days of college life as much as I was relishing my first experiences in the military.

My departure came all too quickly. Once again there was a teary good-bye with my family. We all knew it would be much more than three months before we would see each other again. I tried not to think about the fact that in four weeks I would be missing our family Christmas for the first time. I boarded the plane and took my seat by the window. As I looked out toward the terminal, I could see my parents standing close to each other. There were tears in my eyes and a tightness in my throat. While they had been very restrictive, and there were times I would have liked to put considerable distance between us, the only memories I could recall were warm, loving, and beautiful. They were memories of all the times my parents had protected me and given to me from the bottomless well of love they seemed to have for all their children. They were memories of how hard they had worked and the sacrifices they had made to provide for us. They were memories of family gatherings, trips to the ocean, and the music we had made together over the years. As the plane began to pull away, I tried to keep my parents in sight for as long as possible. Then, as we taxied down the runway in preparation for takeoff, I began turning my mind from the pain of separation toward the adventures that lay ahead for me in California. I was on my own now, and it was my responsibility to make my life work and to make it exciting. I needed to prove to my family, and to myself, that I could meet the challenge. Throughout the daylong flight I kept my thoughts on the future, my future. I had to succeed. I just had to.

We had arrived in San Francisco by early evening. It seemed to take forever to find my luggage and the bus that would get me to the base. By the time I arrived at my barracks it was getting late. Cots had been set up in the dayroom for the four new women who arrived that night. We would be assigned our rooms the next morning, when the barracks commander was back on duty. We introduced ourselves and then fell into a heavy sleep. We all were too exhausted from our traveling to spend much time wondering what our new lives on the base would be like. Tomorrow would bring many of the answers.

The morning brought a flurry of activities. We met briefly with the commander and first sergeant and were each given a booklet that outlined the basic rules and procedures for women living in the barracks. Then we were assigned to our rooms and given our keys. It was suggested that anything of particular value should be kept locked in our closets or in the first sergeant's office. I was rather taken aback by the precautions we were being asked to take. I couldn't imagine any of us stealing from one another, but I took the warning seriously and decided to lock my things in my closet.

I was assigned a room which I would be sharing with another young woman who had already left for work. While I unpacked and put away my things, I enjoyed the quiet and privacy. I was also keenly sensing feelings of loneliness and apprehension. I wished there were at least one person with whom I could sit and talk over a Coke. I wanted to share my feelings and fears with someone who was experiencing the same things. But except for us new arrivals, everyone was either sleeping or at work. None of the other new women appeared to be anxious. They seemed to be at ease with themselves and this new environment, to be confident of their ability to meet the new demands and expectations we all would be facing over the next days and weeks. Obviously I would not be sharing my fears with them. I did not want to be the only one who seemed not to be able to meet the challenge. I, too, would learn how to put up a good front, to the women in the barracks, to the people at work, to my friends and family, and especially to myself. It's all part of being grown-up and mature, isn't it?

Travis Air Force Base is something of a small city. Besides the living quarters for single and married personnel, the base houses its own hospital, churches, movie theater, several dining halls, a supermarket (referred to as a PX), and something of a department store (called a BX, or base exchange). My first meal on base was at the chow hall across the street from my barracks. I quickly realized that not all Air Force bases can boast about the quality or presentation of their food. This particular cook throve on the challenge not to waste a morsel of food. The leftover bacon from breakfast was crumbled into the green beans at dinner. Many of us often chose either to eat off base or to skip meals entirely. During my two and a half years at Travis I had a difficult time keeping my weight up to the minimum for my height. It was a joy for me to have someone tell me I needed to gain a few pounds.

My second day on base I awoke early. I was excited about my first day at work and wanted to be dressed and spit-shined for the occasion. I had no idea where the communications center was located, so I allowed myself the luxury of a taxi. As we drove around the base, I realized that we were going away from the control tower, not toward it. I mentioned it to the driver, who in exasperation pounded his foot onto the brake and turned around in his seat to face me. "Look, lady, you said you wanted me to take you to the Com Center, right? Well, that's where I'm taking you." We sped away as I slunk down in my seat. Patience did not appear to be one of the driver's more developed virtues.

We drove to the very border of the base, far from the humming center of things. He finally pulled up to a windowless building which was as far from the air terminal as one could get. On the door was a sign that said: BASE COMMUNICATIONS CENTER. The door was locked, so I rang the bell. A buzzer went off, and I gained access into a dingy hall with a sliding window along the left wall. A young man was seated at a desk behind the window. He confirmed that I was in the right place, and as he pressed a buzzer, I opened the door to the heart of the center. Immediately my ears were assaulted by twenty or more teletype machines and computers spilling out tapes as fast as their systems would allow.

I was introduced to the person in charge of the shift, Sergeant

Luke. Sergeant Luke was a short, almost round man, an ex-marine who had transferred into the Air Force. He had welcomed me and begun to give me a brief tour when I stopped him dead in his tracks by saying: "But, Sergeant Luke, there must be some mistake. I'm not supposed to be here."

"What do you mean you're not supposed to be here?"

I explained that I wanted to work in the tower and learn how to give takeoff and landing instructions to pilots. My recruiting officer had told me that the title for that job was called "communications specialist."

Sergeant Luke looked at me and broke out into a bellowing laugh. "Honey, you got taken. Your orders say that you have been assigned to communications, and this is the Com Center. Welcome to the United States Air Force."

That was the end of the discussion. There was nothing that either of us could do. Later I was to find out that at that time no women were assigned to be air traffic controllers. The military had decided that women were too high-strung and emotionally unstable, especially during their menstrual cycles, to be considered good risks for such a demanding job. After all, the lives of pilots and their crews were at stake. Happily, some of today's Air Force women are air traffic controllers.

With Sergeant Luke's help I settled into my new job. In many ways he became a surrogate father for me during my years at Travis. He gave me wonderful advice, straight from the hip with no mincing of words.

My first Christmas away from home was approaching fast, and I hadn't been on base long enough to make any good friends. The holidays loomed large and lonely before me, and I started to plot the most painless way to get through them. On Christmas Eve afternoon I got a phone call from one of the men who worked with me at the Com Center who asked if I had any plans for the evening. I didn't. He then asked if I would like him to drive me into town for midnight mass. He would go out for coffee while I was at church and pick me up afterward. I said I wouldn't go unless he went to mass with me. He thought that perhaps there might be some trouble if we went to mass together. He was black. I told him I didn't care about that if he didn't and anybody who didn't like it could go to hell. He laughed, and we arranged for him to pick me up at the barracks later that evening. We went to mass together, and although there were a few stares, no one made any nasty comments. After church we went out for a late supper. We had a few more dates together, and we really enjoyed each other's company. But we both were aware that in the sixties it would have been a frustrating, uphill battle for us to have gotten into a serious relationship. We stopped dating, but we remained good friends. I will always remember him fondly for his gentleness and the mutual respect we had for each other.

Women in the military are outnumbered by men at least twenty to one. Many women choose the military because the odds are so good. There was never a lack of dates, and most women could afford to be really selective. One problem was that most men assumed a roll in the sack was appropriate payment for a night on the town. I heard many arguments as to why I should fulfill a date's expectations. Most often it was something like "Come on, honey, I won't hurt you. You can't expect a man to buy a pair of shoes if he can't try them on first." It didn't occur to them that most women don't consider themselves merchandise. Probably the most difficult argument to handle came from the man who was on his way to Vietnam. It was true, no one knew whether or not he would come back to the States in one piece or even alive. But I always figured that my going to bed with one of them wouldn't change his odds, so that argument didn't work either.

My father had always been very clear that as far as he was concerned, no decent, self-respecting girl went to bed with a man before she was married. He was emphatic that his daughters would not walk down the aisle in a white gown unless it really stood for something. Between the nuns and my father's threats, I stood my ground and never had a sexual relationship with a man before my wedding night. One time I thought I was in love and was being worn down in my resolve by the man I was dating. Finally, out of desperation and the thought that perhaps my father was being too old-fashioned, I went to Sergeant Luke for advice. I told him about the situation and what my father had said. He looked at me the way a father looks at his daughter and said: "Honey, you listen to your daddy. I was in the Marines, and I had plenty of women before I got married. But when I met my wife, I said to myself, 'Luke, baby, you keep your zipper up, this is the woman you hope to marry. You don't mess around with her.'" I took Sergeant Luke's advice, and in that particular situation I'm glad I did.

During my two and a half years at Travis I continued to go to daily mass, as had been my custom since high school. I usually worked the night shift, so it was easy to walk over to the chapel and go to mass before heading back to my room to sleep. Father Pat was one of the three Roman Catholic priests who served as chaplains for the base. He was the most handsome man I had ever seen. He looked just like Richard Burton and had an Irish brogue that made him even more endearing. Father Pat and I quickly became friends, and occasionally we had pizza together. He knew that I had wanted to enter the convent and was still considering the idea. He, too, thought I had "too much personality" to be a nun. Obviously, back then it was not to a woman's advantage to have either a personality or a will of her own if she thought that she might have a vocation to be a nun. As the months passed, I began to fall in love with Father Pat. I never said anything to him or anyone else about it. Falling in love with a priest just isn't something one talks about. Neither is it a good idea to act upon such feelings.

One evening a visiting priest, Father Pat, and I went out to a restaurant for pizza and wine. The three of us talked, laughed, ate and drank for two hours, and after dinner went to Father Pat's house for more drinks. We had already had two bottles of wine, and at Father Pat's we polished off a bottle of bourbon. The visiting priest couldn't hold his liquor as well as we could, and he quietly fell asleep on the sofa. Father Pat and I continued to talk and drink into the night until I lost all my inhibitions and declared my love to him. Then I got sick. When I had sobered up enough to be able to walk, Father Pat suggested that he take me home. He gently ushered me into his car, drove me back to the barracks, and pointed me in the direction of the side entrance. I'm not sure just how I found my room or got into bed, but the next thing I knew it was after 11:00 A.M. and I had a splitting headache. I was also completely and utterly mortified when I remembered what I had done the night before.

I showered, dressed, and bought a Coke from the vending machine down the hall. The cold soda seemed to lessen the pounding in my head. I decided I might as well face the music and call Father Pat to apologize for my behavior the previous evening. He didn't seem the least bit angry, and instead, he asked if I felt good enough to go out for breakfast. I wasn't sure how much I could eat, but I wanted to talk with him. He picked me up by the barracks within half an hour. The first thing he did as we drove off base was take my hand. "I feel the same way," he said. That was the beginning of a wonderful one-year relationship between us.

Dating a priest is not an easy thing to do, especially on an Air Force base. Pat and I couldn't spend holidays together because one commander or other would always invite the clergy to his home for the festivities. We couldn't be seen together on base because our relationship would not have been tolerated. Most of the time we either drove fifty miles or more from the base to some obscure restaurant for dinner or stayed at his house. But it didn't matter to us. We were in love with each other. We were even talking about Pat's leaving the priesthood and our getting married. Life was wonderful. I was in love with the most handsome and gentle man I had ever met. I didn't care that I had to keep our relationship a secret. In fact, the need for secrecy seemed to make the relationship all that more enticing.

In retrospect, Pat and I had a really strange romance. Travis was the base that trafficked military personnel to and from Vietnam. Many nights he was called away to give the sacraments to soldiers who had been brought home in pieces. Those were the times when I saw Pat most alive and vibrant, times when he knew he was needed to offer comfort to others. To pass the time while he was gone, I would do the most domestic things for him I could think of: sorting out his bureau drawer or closet or making a surprise dessert for his return. We slept together often, and there were times when he would gently and shyly approach me about making love. But I always declined. I was afraid to take that last step toward physical intimacy. It was enough for me that we lie close to each other, that we hold and caress each other. There would be time enough for us to make love later, after we were married and out of the clutches of mortal sin.

During that whole year I only once felt guilty enough about our relationship to talk with someone. I decided to take a bus into town to a Franciscan monastery and go to confession. I needed to tell another priest, a person who I hoped could give some thoughtful guidance to me, about my love for Pat and his love for me. I was so afraid he would condemn us, but I needed to know if the two of us could have a relationship without also having to live with guilt and sin all our lives. As I knelt in the dark confessional, I could feel my heart pounding. Finally the little window was pushed aside, and the priest indicated that I could begin my confession. I tried to be as clear and honest as I could be. It was painful, but I needed to have some peace of mind. The priest listened quietly and only once or twice interrupted me to ask a question. When I had finished, I took a deep breath and waited for him to pass judgment. His response was warm, gentle, and loving. He suggested that perhaps both Pat and I needed a week or two apart in order to give ourselves time to think things through more clearly. He then said that if after we both had thought about our relationship, we still felt we wanted to marry, then we had his blessing and that Pat would know what to do about getting a dispensation from the priesthood. I never did know who the priest was, nor did I ever again feel the need to discuss the matter with anyone else but Pat. The next day I told Pat what I had done. He seemed to be deep in thought as I told him what the priest had said. We decided not to see each other for a week.

The seven days until I could see Pat again seemed endless. We didn't even talk to each other over the telephone during that time. Finally the week passed, and we met in his office in the chapel. We drove to his house together. I could sense that something was wrong. Pat seemed quiet and tense. We fixed coffee and took our cups into the living room. Pat sat on the opposite side of the couch from me rather than close by my side, as he usually did. Before he said a word, I knew that it was over between us. I wanted to cry but instead clenched my cup until my knuckles were white. I tried to look calm as I listened to him tell me about his mother and brothers back in Ireland. He was the youngest of five boys. His mother had always wanted one of her sons to be a priest. It was the very thing that would have brought honor and respect to their home more than anything else. Pat talked of how, as the years passed, he watched first one, and then another, of his brothers choose other vocations. He talked of how as each brother chose not to be a priest, he could sense his mother turning to him with her dream. At the age of fifteen he had left home to enter the seminary high school. He had never dated a girl, had never been rowdy with the other boys. He had simply chosen to live out his mother's hopes. He had never even taken the time to consider what his own hopes and dreams for his life might be. As he told me his story, I could feel his pain and emptiness. I could feel his despair. He had joined the Air Force because as a chaplain he had more freedom than he ever would have in a parish rectory living with other priests. He dreaded the day when he would have to retire from the Air Force. He saw that day as the end of his relative freedom and the beginning of a life sentence. Yet his mother was old, he told me. She could never bear to have him disgrace her and the rest of their family by leaving the priesthood. He could not bring himself to inflict this kind of pain on his mother. His hope was that when she died, he would feel free to choose for himself. Until then he would stay a priest.

It was finished. Pat and I would never be. His mother and the Church had torn us apart. I was confused and angry. I was also hurting for Pat. I could see the loneliness and isolation wrap around him like some kind of sickening cloak of honor. And yet I could only stand by and watch the man I loved crumble piece by little piece. My heart was breaking, for me and for him, and still, there was nothing that I could do to ease the pain for either of us.

I had never known the kind of pain I experienced those first days and weeks after Pat and I stopped seeing each other. I performed my daily tasks immersed in a thick protective fog that would not allow anyone or anything else to touch my heart. I felt fragile, and my sense was that if I allowed anyone to enter my pain, I would surely break into a million pieces. Gradually I began once again to nurture my social self. At first I made sure that I was involved only with groups of friends. I didn't want to be paired off with anyone. I didn't want to be vulnerable to someone again, not so soon. As the healing continued, I chose to date people whom I considered safe.

One day one of the men I was seeing asked me if I would like to accompany him to a Franciscan monastery to visit an old friend who had been in the Air Force, too, and who, after his enlistment was up, had decided to enter the order. Franciscans had always fascinated me, so I gladly accepted the opportunity to get off the base and out into the mountains. It was a beautiful day. The air was warm. The sun caused everything to gleam, and the leaves on the trees glistened like millions of shiny green crystals. As our car climbed higher and higher, there was a freshness in the air, and the peace that was all around us began to permeate the wall I had built around me. I was being renewed, and the lightness in my spirit brought with it a willingness to experience all that life had to offer. I was beginning to understand that life's beauty and grace can be experienced and appreciated only if we also know pain and sorrow. I was grateful that my pain was finally beginning to give birth to new joy and optimism.

We reached the monastery just before noon. My date's friend was called Brother William, and we found him dressed in a T-shirt and blue jeans. He was working with some of the other brothers on building a stone wall which would eventually outline a path around the stations of the cross. He was noticeably embarrassed that we had come while he was still in work clothes and covered with cement and was anxious for us to wait for him in the grove while he went inside, took a quick shower, and changed into his brown monastic robe. He invited us to join him and the community for lunch. Our visit with Brother William was pleasant, and I thoroughly enjoyed being immersed in such quiet and peaceful surroundings. Too soon it was time for us to go, and I left the monastery glad to have been there but never expecting to see Brother William again. Before we left, he asked if he could write to me.

Back at the base, life went on as usual. Travis was the first American soil to which men returned when their tours of duty in Vietnam were over. Some came home alive and at least physically well. Many were brought home in shell-shocked silence. The dead would at least be honored by their families, who would say their good-byes in private mourning. Others were brought back from the war broken in spirit and physically maimed. As much as so many would try to forget the senselessness of our military activity in Vietnam, these people would remember for the rest of their lives, and their very presence would confront us all.

The communications center operated full tilt during the war, and those of us who worked there were assigned to twelve-hour shifts. We worked six days on duty and two days off, rotating weekends. When we were on duty, we worked hard. When we were off for a weekend, we played just as hard. Most often we did our playing either at the beach or in San Francisco. I loved that city. It was always humming with activity, and as naive as I was about the burgeoning drug culture there, I saw San Francisco as a place that offered endless arenas for play.

One weekend four of us paired off as a double date, took to the road, and headed for that glorious city for an evening of fun and relaxation. We rode the cable cars, had dinner at Fisherman's Wharf, danced and drank at the Top of the Mark, and enjoyed ourselves to the fullest. At 2:00 A.M. we decided to go to one more spot and chose an all-night billiard parlor. I was reluctant to go. All that I knew of pool halls was what I had seen on television. They seemed dark and dingy places, full of rough-looking men. I didn't want to be the sour grape in our evening of festivities, so I decided to go along. I was certainly surprised by what I encountered. The walls on the inside of the billiard parlor were covered with red and gold fabric. Beside each pool table was a small round table covered with a spotless white linen tablecloth. Waiters in immaculate white shirts and black tails were delivering drinks and snacks to groups of people who were either playing pool or relaxing at their tables between games. Patrons were dressed in ball gowns and tuxedoes. Shiny chandeliers hung high above the room and cast a magical glow upon everything and everyone present. I was awed by the grace and splendor of the room. The four of us stayed until dawn before we were sleepy enough to head back for the base and a few hours of sleep. The whole evening had been perfect, and I could hardly wait to write home to tell my parents all about it.

My father had appreciated all the letters he had received from home when he was in the Navy. He said there were often days when they were the only glue that kept him together, especially when he had been at sea for weeks on end. True to his word, he wrote to me every week, sometimes twice. Often there would be a little something tucked into the envelope or Scotch taped to the letter itself: a small bit of pine; a crushed rose. They were precious to me, and I looked forward to reading all the little day-to-day news. I wrote to my parents equally often, telling them about work, the awful food in the chow hall, funny things that people had said. My life wasn't wild, but it was full. I was especially proud of the fact that I had started to take classes at the university. With my work schedule, I could handle only one course a semester, but I hoped in time I would be able to step up the pace and eventually earn a degree. My parents were happy for me and proud of my plans and accomplishments. About a week after our big evening in San Francisco, I wrote a long, detailed letter to them. A week went by, and I did not hear from them. Two weeks passed, and I began to worry. By the end of the third week I was concerned enough to call them. My mother answered the phone, and from the coolness in her voice I could tell that something was wrong. I asked her why neither she nor my father had written in such a long time. "Well, what do you expect?" was her reply.

I was baffled. "What do you mean by that?" I asked.

"Come on, Rose, you can't expect us to be happy with the kind of letter you sent to us. We can read between the lines. No self-respecting girl stays out all night. There's nothing decent that comes out of that kind of behavior. Your father and I aren't stupid, you know. How do you expect us to respond to a letter like that?"

I was dumbfounded into silence. Then the rage began to erupt. "There were no lines to read between, Ma. I had a wonderful time and wanted to tell you and Dad all about it. That's the trouble with you two: You keep looking for lines to read between when there are none. What do you want me to do, just tell you about the weather or work? Don't you want to know what I'm doing?"

"We know what you're doing. That's the problem. We never thought that you would do this kind of thing."

My mother and I argued back and forth until I could see there was no way to make her see that she and my father were jumping to conclusions that just weren't true. I ended the conversation as quickly as I could and stormed down to my room. I then wrote my feelings in a letter to them. Maybe if they had time to read what I had to say and to think about it, they would come to understand that I was not hiding anything from them. It did seem to smooth things over a bit between me and my parents, but I had learned my lesson. I never again wrote a letter to them in which I disclosed any activity from which they could draw false conclusions. It was a sad decision to have to make. It felt like just one more distancing between us.

About six weeks after I had been to the Franciscan monastery and met Brother William, I received a letter from him telling me how much he had enjoyed meeting me. It was quite a lengthy letter, and he wrote extensively about the joy and grace there were in marriage and children. The heat of Pat's and my relationship had cooled considerably, and the initial pain and awkwardness we both experienced after his decision to end our intimacy had finally subsided to the point that we could be friends. The letter from Brother William troubled me, and I shared it with Pat. He read the letter, handed it back to me, and said that he didn't see anything alarming in it at all. I disagreed and told him I thought Brother William's days in the monastery were numbered. His letter conveyed too much longing for what the monastery could not offer him. Pat insisted that I was reading too much into it. Two weeks later I received a phone call. "Rose Mary, it's Bob Denman. How are you?" My mind raced around through my memory bank. Bob Denman? I didn't know anyone named Bob Denman. My silence must have betrayed me. The man on the other end of the phone gave a nervous laugh. "It's Brother William. I left today."

CHAPTER 3

That phone call from Brother William become Bob Denman changed the course of my life. We talked for a few minutes about his decision to leave the order. He confirmed my suspicions that he wanted something more than the monastic life could offer—to be married and to have a family. He was now living with his mother in Los Angeles and planned to get a job in the next couple of weeks. He hoped that after a few months of working he could save enough money to rent his own apartment. He was eager to taste all that life had to offer. He told me that he was planning a trip to the base to visit friends in the next month and asked if I would like to go out with him when he came. I agreed to see him and went back to my room in a rather pensive mood. *What's wrong with me?* I thought. *First a priest and now an ex-monk. Can't you pick somebody normal for a change?*

Bob came to the base about three weeks later. He seemed happy with his decision to leave the monastery and excited about all the life choices before him. We spent three whole days together, mostly walking and talking. It seemed as if we could have talked on forever, there was so much we wanted to know about each other. After our three days we were sure we wanted to spend much more time together. I had nearly two months' leave accumulated. We decided that I would take two weeks at home with my family and then fly south to Los Angeles to spend a week with Bob and his mother. We were both excited about the thought of having one whole week together and promised to write or call each other as often as possible.

It had been two years since I had seen my family, and I was eager to be with them again. Because I was catching a military plane back to the East Coast and didn't know what day or time I would be arriving, I kept my visit a secret. When, after more than twenty-four hours of zigzagging across the country, I finally landed at the airport in Rhode Island, I called my father at work.

Within an hour my parents walked through the double doors of the airport lobby and walked right past me. I laughed and called out to them, "What's the matter? Have I been away so long that you don't even recognize your daughter anymore?" They turned around and stared at me for a moment. Full recognition finally came, and we ran toward one another with open arms. It was a warm and tearful reunion, and I think what surprised me most was how much my mother had aged over the past two years. Her face seemed worn, and her hair had grayed considerably. Most of us don't want to think about the fact that in all probability we will outlive our parents. It saddened me to realize just how mortal my parents were.

Even though I had lost considerable weight before going into the Air Force, during the two years away from home I had lost more than twenty additional pounds. I was lean and solid and in the best shape I had ever been. My parents were impressed, not only with my weight but also with the way I had chosen to do my hair and makeup. My father had never wanted me to go on a diet. He had always said that "if God intended for you to be thin, He would have made you thin." Yet, when I chose to lose the weight anyway, he was proud of me, as if he had had something to do with my achievement. He reacted that way to many of my choices over the years, first balking at them, lending no support through the process, and then, when all was accomplished, touting his prize for everyone to see. It was one of his behaviors that most baffled and irritated me.

The two weeks at home were fun, filled with the usual bounty of food, visits with relatives and friends, and sharing family stories. Before I knew it, it was time to catch the plane back to the West Coast. I didn't tell my parents about going to see Bob and his mother. I thought they would have been hurt that I had cut my visit with them. They took me to the airport, and we shared last-minute words of love and caution before it was time for me to board the plane. Again, we had no idea how long it would be before we would see one another, and the not knowing made us all the more precious to one another.

The flight between San Francisco and Los Angeles was short. A businessman seated next to me asked if he could buy me a drink. We chatted for a while, and then he asked me the purpose of my trip to L.A. Without hesitation I told him that I was going down to meet my future mother-in-law. I hadn't thought of it that way before, yet the words came easily, and as they did, something inside me knew that what I had just said was true. The realization brought a rush of fear and excitement.

Bob was grinning as he watched me walk up the passageway to the lobby of the airport. He was tanned and looked rested and happy. We hugged and said how much we had missed each other. He told me that his mother was eager to meet me and that she had prepared a festive meal for the three of us. I took in a deep breath and smiled at him. "OK, I'm ready, Bob. Let's get this show on the road."

He chuckled. "Oh, Ma's real nice. You'll like her."

I liked Margaret from the moment I met her. She had made space for me in her room, and Bob seemed pleased that his mother and I were hitting it off so well right from the very beginning. Margaret was a short, no-nonsense woman who had single-handedly raised her five children ever since she had divorced her husband when they were little. I respected her for her obvious ability to be strong and to do what had to be done. She had worked as a layout artist for years and was the first woman I had ever met who was a professional and a single parent. Bob was right, I did like his mother, very much.

Every moment Bob and I had together was precious to us. I don't even remember what we did, just that we spent most of our time talking and dreaming. On the third night Bob proposed and I accepted. We had spent six days together in all, yet we knew that we were in love and wanted to be married. Bob gave me a diamond ring, and I was surprised that he had one already. He admitted that it was a diamond that he had given to someone else a long time ago. I tried not to let my disappointment show. I knew that he would be hurt if he knew I didn't like the idea of having a ring originally intended for someone else. I told myself that I was being selfish, that it didn't matter, that it was my ring now. Later that evening we went home to tell his mother our news. She was happy for us and didn't seem to be the least bit surprised that we were engaged. The next morning at breakfast I called her Mom for the first time.

We called my parents after we had returned from Sunday mass. We told them we would be getting married in seven weeks at the base chapel. They were surprised about the sudden announcement and I think at first wondered if I was pregnant. We hung up with their promising to try to come to the wedding. There was so much to plan in such a short time, but we all were excited.

Bob's sister-in-law offered to let me borrow her wedding dress, which just fit me. I had always dreamed of a big wedding and a beautiful long white gown. Hers was short and not what I would have chosen; but money was scarce, and it didn't make sense to go into debt for a gown that would be worn for only a couple of hours. I gratefully accepted the loan and headed back to make preparations for our wedding.

The first item on the agenda was to secure the chapel and reception hall for the date we had chosen. When I called the chapel office, the secretary told me the date was free and Father Pat would be on duty that day. He also informed me it was mandatory for me to take the Pre-Cana, or premarital courses offered by Father Pat. The next series of classes was due to begin the following week. As I hung up the phone, I felt panicky. *Terrific, not only is Pat going to marry us, but now I have to sit in a classroom and listen to him tell the class what marriage is all about. How am I going to get through this one?* That evening I called Bob to let him know that the date had been cleared and that he needed to take the Pre-Cana courses at his home parish. I did not tell him about Pat.

When the first day of the course came, I was relieved that there were more than fifty people in the room. Once we all were assembled, the first thing Pat did was pass out the packets of materials we would be using throughout the course. I noticed that he was careful to hand a particular packet directly to me. As I opened it, a loose piece of paper dropped out. It was a note from Pat. "Please don't do this to me," it read. Tears came to my eyes, and there was a tearing in my heart. How could he try to dissuade me from marrying Bob when he had made it clear that there was no future for us? Two weeks later he approached me as I was leaving the classroom and again confronted me. My response was more telling than I realized at the time: "Pat, you're the only one who can put a stop to this wedding, and you know it." "I can't, Rose Mary, I just can't. Please don't do this to me." Pat's eyes were moist, and so were mine. There was a sad bond between us as we turned away from each other and walked out of the building.

Five weeks before the wedding I realized that I would be in the middle of my menstrual cycle on our honeymoon. While at the hospital for my blood test, I told the doctor about my dilemma, and he prescribed birth control pills. He told me that taking them through the first week after I was married would assure that I did not get my period during my honeymoon. He did not, however, warn me that taking the birth control pills would most likely cause a slight weight gain. Two weeks before the wedding my roommate and I were sitting around on our beds talking about the reception plans, and I decided to try on my borrowed wedding dress. To my horror the zipper wouldn't close. My roommate took hold of both sides of the back of the dress and pushed them together as much as she could while at the same time pulling up on the zipper. She kept insisting that I could inhale harder. I started to cry and ran for the bathroom scale down the hall. I had gained five pounds, apparently most of it in my bustline. Two weeks before the wedding, and the bride didn't have a dress! I had to be on shift at the com center in less than an hour, but before I left, I called Bob. He tried to be sympathetic and suggested that I might go into town the next day to try to rent one.

I cried intermittently all the way to work. When I arrived, I took one look at Sergeant Luke and burst into fresh tears. The first thing out of his mouth was: "Did that little bastard of a fiancé hurt you, honey?" Between sobs I tried to explain what had happened. He took matters firmly in hand. "Do you know how to sew?" he asked me. I told him that I did but that there wasn't enough time to get a dress made. He insisted there would be if he gave me some time off and I could find help from other "girls" at the barracks. Right on the spot he put someone else in charge of the shift and told me to get my purse and follow him. We got into his car, drove off base, and headed for the closest fabric store. Sergeant Luke didn't know a thing about fabric or patterns. He just stood by the door, looking as uncomfortable as a cat in a room full of rocking chairs. He told me to take my time but to find something that I really liked. "This is your wedding gown, girl. You be sure it's something special." Within an hour I had chosen the pattern, silk, and lace for my gown and we were heading back to the base.

For the next two weeks I spent every spare moment cutting, pinning, measuring, and sewing. Two of my friends in the barracks helped as much as they could. By the time my parents arrived, the day before the 3:00 P.M. wedding, the dress was completed. My roommate finished the silk underskirt two hours before the ceremony. I had a long white gown, and most important, it was mine.

It was a small wedding, but I was happy. Pat had insisted upon providing the flowers for the altar, and he wouldn't accept a check from us for his services either. During the mass Pat's eyes were moist. So were mine. As I knelt to receive communion, I was sure that if Pat were to say something to stop the wedding at that very moment and declare his love for me, I would have gone with him. In spite of the obvious, I still believed that I was doing the right thing to marry Bob. He was a sweet and gentle man. He was a good Catholic who loved God and the Church. I knew that he would be a good husband and father. I may not have been madly in love with him, but I did have many warm feelings toward him. That was enough. I knew that we would have a good life together. I never saw Pat again after the wedding.

Bob and I had a three-day honeymoon in the San Francisco area. It would be another two weeks before I was discharged from the Air Force. In the meantime, I still had to work at the com center and Bob had to get back to his job in Los Angeles. Our plan was that he would drive north to the base the weekend following my discharge so that we could use the car to transport all my belongings back to Los Angeles. The two weeks following the wedding seemed endless. After nearly three weeks I was able to call Bob and tell him that my discharge had gone through and that he could come to get me that Friday evening. We both were excited that we were finally going to be able to start our married life together. I was looking forward to our looking for our own apartment, to having a real kitchen in which to prepare meals for the two of us, and to getting a civilian job.

Bob came to the base late Friday night. By Saturday morning we had all my belongings crammed into the trunk and back seat and were heading south for Los Angeles, our new home. Soon after we were on the road, Bob said that he had a surprise for me. He had gone apartment hunting and found just the place for us. It was a lovely three-room furnished apartment that even had its own private patio. I felt a twinge of resentment, although I tried not to let it show. This would have been the first time I might have had a voice in choosing where I would live. The opportunity had been taken from me, and there was nothing I could do about it short of throwing a tantrum. We were newly married, just beginning our lives together. I didn't want to spoil it.

Our apartment turned out to be rather nice, and we settled into making it our home. I made new curtains for the dining alcove, and we bought inexpensive hangings for the wall. Two weeks after arriving in Los Angeles I landed my first job, locating missing luggage for Greyhound Express. Every morning my mother-in-law dropped me off at work on her way to her office. I enjoyed these mornings that we spent together, as well as the return trips in the afternoon. She was quickly becoming a second mother to me.

About two months after we were settled into our new lives together, Bob and I decided to have a dinner party. I was anxious to demonstrate my culinary skills to his mother as well as to his friend at work who was always lamenting the fact that his wife couldn't and wouldn't cook. We set the date for a Friday evening, and I spent hours working out the perfect menu. It would be my mother-in-law's birthday as well, so I planned a special cake in celebration of the event.

Neither Bob nor I got home from work until nearly five-thirty, and we had invited our guests to arrive at seven. The menu included roast beef, mashed potatoes, frozen peas and onions, and a bottle of wine. Bob set the table while I got the cake baked and the roast ready to go into the oven. I took the cake out of the pans too soon, and one of the layers broke in half. No problem, I knew that I could glue it back together with frosting. No one would be the wiser once I had frosted and decorated the cake. The roast was in the oven by six-thirty. We wanted to eat by seven-thirty. The cookbook said I needed to cook the meat for two and a half hours. I decided to push the temperature up to five hundred. That should have us eating in time.

The guests arrived, and everyone told us how nice the apartment looked. There were even a few chuckles about the fact that Bob was wearing an apron and helping me in the kitchen. We talked over a glass of wine, and at seven-thirty I announced that dinner was ready. Bob helped me carry the food out to the dinner table, all the time joking with his friend about how impressed he would be with my abilities in the kitchen. He then carved the meat, which, at least from the outside, looked as though it had been cooked to perfection. Unfortunately the roast was cooked down only to the first inch or so. Beyond that it was raw. By turning the meat over in the plate and carving only on the edges, we were able to serve everyone enough for a first helping. Bob's mother tried to rescue the moment by suggesting we put the rest of the roast in the oven to cook while we ate what was on our plates. Everyone tried to convince me that nothing was lost and that the rest of the meal looked absolutely wonderful. We all sat down to enjoy the food. Potatoes and vegetables were passed around, and I noticed Bob give me a strange look as he took a mouthful of peas. I tried mine, and they were still partially frozen! The dinner was ruined. I wanted to cry, especially when

Bob's friend commented that Bob shouldn't be too embarrassed because after all, his wife couldn't cook either.

Finally the excruciating dinner was over. I knew that I could at least partially redeem myself with the surprise cake. I went into the kitchen to light the candles, and when I gave him the signal, Bob turned out the lights and started singing "Happy Birthday." The cake was beautiful, and my mother-in-law was thrilled with the thoughtfulness of the surprise. As I put the cake down in front of her so that she could blow out the candles, the top layer, the one I had glued together with the frosting, began to separate. I plopped the cake down onto the table in front of her, put a hand on either side of the sagging layer, and mushed them together. Two frosting-covered hands flew to my face as I burst into tears. I'd never again convince anyone that I was a good cook!

Bob and I were so happy when, five months after the wedding, we discovered that we were going to have a baby. Bob had grown up on the East Coast, and soon after the good news, we decided to move back to Rhode Island. L.A. just didn't seem like the place to raise a family. By the fall of 1967 we were driving across country.

We lived with my parents for three weeks while Bob got settled into a new job and we looked for a place to live. We found a lovely five-room apartment in East Providence, and once moved in, we began the work of wallpapering and painting. We had no furniture of our own, and at the time there was no such thing as a furnished apartment. So we headed for the East Providence Furniture Company. I was excited about the idea of furnishing our own place and looked forward to choosing the furniture with Bob. We walked around the store for half an hour or so, looked at several showrooms, and before I knew it, Bob was telling the salesperson which living-room, bedroom, and kitchen sets we wanted to buy. Once again I was unable to tell Bob I was unhappy with his making family decisions without consulting me. I stood there mute and disbelieving. Maybe this was the way things were supposed to be. Besides, it wasn't awful furniture, just not what I would have chosen.

By the eighth month of my pregnancy we had adapted to our life in East Providence. Bob went off each morning to Davol, Inc., where my parents and half my extended family worked. Bob was in the bookkeeping department and seemed to enjoy it. I had never learned how to drive, so the fact that we had only one car didn't seem like an inconvenience. While Bob was at work, I spent my days sewing, cleaning, watching television, and cooking. Making wonderful meals for Bob was the major outlet I had for creative expression. We both were thin and sleek when we were married, but over the next few months we both had gained considerable weight. By the time our son, Matthew, was born, I had gained fifty pounds. Neither Bob nor I was happy with my weight gain. Bob, especially, seemed to become increasingly displeased.

Matthew was born on Palm Sunday evening, one week before our first anniversary. Being a new mom was the most wonderful thing that had ever happened to me, and Matthew was happy and easygoing, right from the very beginning. Bob was a good father, too. He enjoyed holding and playing with our son. I felt I was the luckiest woman in the world. I had a wonderful, hardworking husband who loved and cared for me and our baby. Money was tight, but that was the way things were for a newly married couple just starting a family. I knew that someday we would be less restricted by financial limitations. For now we had everything that we would possibly need or want.

Life was a little lonely for me. Once Bob went to work in the morning, I was home alone with Matthew. I didn't know any other young married women in the area. None of my old high school friends was married yet, and our lives were very different from theirs. But I was content to be home with the baby, and once Bob came home from work, the rest of the day was pleasantly full with preparing dinner, bathing Matthew and getting him ready for bed, and then sitting in the living room together watching television. During those first months the only times I left the house were on Friday evening to do the grocery shopping and on Sunday, when we went to my parents' in the afternoon after mass. At the time it seemed to me that we had a very full life.

A few months after Matthew was born, I took him to the pediatrician for a routine checkup. While in the waiting room, I got into conversation with another young mother. We discovered that we lived a very short distance from each other, and neither of us drove. Karen and I struck up an instant friendship. Every day either we would talk on the telephone, or one of us would walk her baby to the other's home. Soon we were socializing as couples.

Because both Bob and I were Catholic, had been raised in Catholic neighborhoods, and had attended parochial school, Skip and Karen were the first Protestants either of us had ever known. Before long they invited us to attend church with them. We both knew that the Catholic Church frowned upon our going to any other church. On the other hand, Skip and Karen were our friends, and we didn't want to offend them by refusing their invitation. We decided that going to church with them would do no harm.

That first Sunday was full of wonderful surprises. The things that pleased us, Protestants tend to take for granted: removing one's coat and hanging it up in a closet before the service; people busily and sometimes noisily greeting one another before worship begins; having a time for coffee, rolls, and conversation after the service rather than hightailing it for the door at the last amen. The fact that the sermon was the central point of the service was also a new experience for us. That it was eloquent was an added bonus. It addressed us in a very real way. The minister seemed to know what we needed to hear, and Bob and I were welcomed by the members of the church. The people there were a real community that sought to nurture its members. They were a family, and we wanted to be a part of it. That was our first Sunday with the congregation, and we continued to attend services there on a regular basis.

Several months after we began to attend Rounds Avenue Covenant Church, Bob and I decided to join the pastor's classes for those interested in becoming members. We had many questions to ask before actually joining the congregation. It would be a huge step for both of us. I needed to know what Protestants did with their sins without the sacrament of confession. Pastor explained to us that if he sinned against another person, he believed he needed to seek out that person. He felt it was far more difficult to face the offended party to ask forgiveness than to have the anonymity of the confessional and speak to a priest. When we thought about it, we agreed that it made sense. As the weeks in class progressed, we became more and more convinced that it was right for us to become members.

We joined during a Sunday service the next spring. My parents would not attend because they believed that we were leaving the "one true church." Later, after the service, we went to their house for Sunday dinner. My father was sitting at the kitchen table with tears in his eyes. He told us that he admired us for our courage to do what we thought was right, that he could see this was a good thing for us to have done. He wished he could do the same thing but said he had been a Roman Catholic for too long to change. As unfulfilled as he felt in the Catholic Church, he could not bring himself to search beyond its boundaries.

Bob, Matthew, and I seemed to flourish as a family. I enjoyed being a wife and mother, and Bob was an attentive husband and father. He worked hard, had only a drink or two occasionally, didn't gamble, wasn't abusive. I thought that he was a model husband and lavished a great deal of care and attention on him. I modeled myself after my mother and grandmother in how I cared for my husband. After all, he deserved it. He worked hard to provide for his family. The least I could do was to keep his house clean, make good hearty meals for him, and see to his needs. The first hint of potential disaster came from Bob's mother. She was visiting with us for a couple of weeks soon after Matthew was born. I was glad to see her again, and she and I spent hours talking while Bob was at work. One morning, toward the end of the first week, Margaret poured herself a second cup of coffee and asked me to sit down with her. She looked me square in the eye and said: "Look, Rose Mary, this is none of my business, so I'm going to say this only once. You've got to step on him. He's going to stray. I can see the signs. Stop doing so much for him. He's starting to take advantage of you." I tried to listen politely, but I knew that Margaret was wrong about her son. He was a good husband. We were fine. True to her word, she never did mention her misgivings again.

It's hard to believe that I ever had the attitudes about marriage or relationships between men and women I had back in the sixties. I was clearly the product of thinking fostered by my parents, the Church, and society. I bought it all and molded myself into the image of the contented little woman whose only role was to make life comfortable for her husband and child. This attitude crippled me as well as my husband. It cripples all of us.

Bob had never gotten his high school diploma. During our first year of marriage he decided to take the equivalency exam. I was thrilled. I had been thinking of going back to school for a few courses, but the old rules said that a woman should not have more education than her husband. I didn't see how I could go to college for more courses unless Bob chose to further his own education first. By the time we were into our second year of marriage, he had decided to take advantage of his company's program to pay for any courses that would help him in his work. He enrolled in an accounting course at Rhode Island College. It meant that he was not at home two nights a week, but we both knew that in time it would pay off with advancements and pay increases.

As the weeks went by, I began to notice changes in Bob. He was becoming distant, and our lovemaking was waning in both frequency and intensity. He seemed to be preoccupied much of the time, and I worried that perhaps the responsibilities of family, work, and school were too much for him. He kept telling me that everything was fine, that he just had a lot on his mind. I knew he was unhappy I hadn't lost any of the weight I had gained during my pregnancy with Matthew, and every night I would resolve that the next day would be different, that I would stick to my diet. By noon I would be opening a can of spaghetti or making a couple of peanut butter and jelly sandwiches. Bob didn't harp on me about my weight constantly, but there were always the occasional mean remarks that dug deep and hurt.

We had become good friends with a couple down the street from us who were our age and, like us, were raising a young family. Usually on Friday or Saturday night we had dinner with them or played cards. One night, just as we arrived, Bob gave me his sports jacket to put in the bedroom with my coat. He asked if I would get his cigarettes out of the jacket pocket, and when I reached in, I pulled out a box of condoms. I couldn't believe my eyes. We didn't use condoms. In fact, we were trying to have another baby. My heart was racing, and there was a huge pain in the pit of my stomach. I put the box back, found the cigarettes in the other pocket, and went back to join Bob and our friends in the other room. I waited until Bob had returned from taking the baby-sitter home before I confronted him. I threw the condoms in his face. I was confused, angry, and that pain in the pit of my stomach had caught fire. "How the hell do you explain this?" Bob just stood there, silently turning white. Finally he mumbled something about some of the men at work playing a joke on him. I didn't believe him, and I think he knew it. I didn't say anything more about the incident, but I was careful to check the pockets of his pants and jackets every day. Two months later I found a note from a woman with whom he worked. It talked about her pregnancy and subsequent abortion. In the midst of all the emotions that were stirring within me, a voice of calm practicality kicked into high gear. I made two quick decisions on behalf of self-preservation. I called my doctor and made an appointment to discuss birth control. Then I decided that I needed to talk to the wisest woman I knew, my grandmother.

Vavó had been diagnosed as having cancer a few months before and was growing increasingly weak. My parents had moved her into their home, and my mother had taken a leave of absence to care for her. That week, when we went to my parents' for our usual Sunday dinner, I went into my grandmother's room and told her what had been happening. She listened quietly. "Don't be a fool, *querida*. Tell him that you know what he is up to. Give him a second chance, but keep your eyes open. If he keeps doing what he's been doing, leave him and forget him. Life is too short for such misery. Don't do what I did. I should have left your grandfather years ago, but women just didn't do that back then. Now is different. You don't have to put up with that kind of man these days." I was grateful for my grandmother's words. She didn't try to fix anything. She knew that she couldn't. She just told me what she thought and then trusted me to make my own decisions. We never talked about the subject again. Vavó died a few weeks later, two days before my appointment with my doctor.

I heeded her advice and took control of the situation. I confronted Bob with what I knew. He didn't deny it but promised that he would end the relationship. I told him that I was going to use birth control because I didn't want to get pregnant until I knew that our marriage would be all right. I also insisted on counseling with our minister. He agreed to my demands. That was in February 1970. In June I discovered the affair had never stopped and the woman was pregnant again. Desperate, I called my brother-in-law, hoping that he could talk some sense into my husband. He tried, but Bob kept insisting that he was in love with the other woman. Shortly after they hung up, Margaret called. Her first words were: "Let me talk to that bastard, Rose Mary." That same night I packed a small bag for Matthew and myself and drove to my parents' house. Never had I been so grateful that I had finally gotten my driver's license.

Mom and Dad hadn't known a thing about the problems Bob and I were having. When I told them what had been going on, my father asked me one question: "Rose, do you still love him?" In spite of it all, I had to admit that I did. I never saw my father react as he did that night. He very quietly told me to put Matthew and my things back in the car and to follow him and my mother to our apartment. I was afraid that he would lose his temper, but he assured me that he knew how to talk to my husband "man to man."

When we reached our house, Bob seemed quiet and subdued. My father asked us all to sit down. He told Bob that he knew what it felt like to be tempted to stray, that he had had plenty of opportunities to have sex with other women. He said that whenever the occasion arose, he just reminded himself of what he had at home and how he didn't want to lose it. He told Bob that what he had been feeling was normal and that it was all right to have those feelings. It just wasn't all right to act on them. Bob listened and then thanked my father for his advice. He said that he did want to save our marriage and that he was willing to work at it. Mom and Dad left. I stayed. The hope had been rekindled. Two days later I received a phone call from the woman with whom Bob was having the affair. She told me that they really loved each other and asked me to give him up. Somewhere from deep inside myself I found the dignity and courage to respond: "You can have him, lady. I'm finished with him. But think about it. If he's cheated on me to have an affair with you, what makes you think that he won't cheat on you to have an affair with someone else?"

"That's the chance I'll have to take," she responded.

"You said it, honey, and that's one hell of a gamble."

Hanging up the phone, I let go of the last hope that our marriage could be salvaged. When Bob came home, I told him that we would be leaving that weekend, as soon as I'd packed. Matthew and I moved back to my parents' house on July Fourth, quite appropriate timing, I think.

Living with my parents was difficult. My father always believed that if you lived in his house, you played by his rules. I agree with the basic premise, and I feel the same way about my own home. It was the kinds of rules my father set that made me chafe under his domain. I was disillusioned and hurting when we moved in with my parents, yet one of the first things they said was that until the divorce was final, they would not tolerate my dating another man. I stared at my mother in disbelief. "What makes you think that I'm even remotely interested in dating, Ma?"

"We just want you to know where we stand, that's all."

We never discussed it again until my parents found themselves on the other side of the argument a couple of years later and began to encourage me to look for a new husband.

There were other rules, too. My parents would baby-sit for Matthew if I was working but would not take care of him if I had a social invitation. This was particularly frustrating because they would not allow me to hire a baby-sitter either. They told me that they didn't want strangers in their house. So, except for very few occasions, the next five years found me either not socializing at all or taking my son with me.

I found a job immediately. It had been four years since I had worked outside my home, and I felt out of touch and insecure, even after such a relatively short time. Now I stand in awe of the thousands of women who, after twenty or more years of being homemakers, find themselves in the same situation. My first job after separating from my husband was in the office of a lumber company. My friend Lisa had worked for the company since our graduation from high school and assured me that I would like it there. I hated it and lasted only two months. I found the work tedious. I also made very little money. The thought of doing that kind of work for the rest of my life added to my depression. I was beginning to realize that some decisions had to be made.

I left the lumber company in early September and spent a few days thinking through my situation. The way I saw it, I had five alternatives. I could:

1. Consider staying with my parents for the rest of my life.
2. Work two jobs in order to make enough money to support myself and my son.
3. Marry the first available man who was willing to support us.
4. Move out and go on welfare.
5. Make use of the GI Bill and get an education. This would allow me to earn enough to be independent and raise Matthew without assistance from my parents, another man, or the state.

I opted for school. It seemed to be the one alternative that made any sense.

Having made the decision, I went to see Pastor Hunt. I needed to know that the plan was workable. After I had told Pastor about my dilemma and how I had arrived at the decision to go to school, it took just a few more moments to zero in on one of the most important decisions of my life. Pastor asked me what my major would be. I had decided to be a high school English teacher. I had always enjoyed English more than any other subject in school. I had also decided that teaching would allow me to raise Matthew more easily because we would have the same schedule. I would be available to take care of him during summers and school vacations throughout the year. It seemed like the most workable solution. Pastor then gave me a great piece of advice. He said: "Rose Mary, don't ever choose a career based on what you think Matthew needs. I know it seems like a long way off, but before you know it, he will be all grown up and on his own. If you choose to teach only because you think it will be easier on him, you will find yourself with a vocation that has outlived its purpose. Let me ask you this one question. What would you do for a career if time, money, and circumstance were not at issue?"

Before I could realize it, I said with firm assurance: "I would be a minister."

Pastor looked me squarely in the eyes and replied: "Then do it!"

The next week I enrolled myself into Barrington College, a Christian school just eight miles from where I was living with my parents. I also found a young woman with a small son of her own who was willing to take care of Matthew during the day. The Friday before classes started I bought the books required for each course. I had not told my parents any of my plan. Later that afternoon I walked into the house laden down with Matthew, his bag of diapers and toys, and an armload of books. My father looked up at me from his chair in the kitchen. "What the hell are you up to now?"

I tried to sound as confident as I wished I felt. "I've enrolled at Barrington College, Dad. I start classes on Monday."

He looked at my mother, then at me, and took in a deep breath. "Rose, I'm telling you this for your own good. Don't do this. You've already had one big disappointment in your life. Don't set yourself up for another one. You can't make it through college. Listen, you have your high school diploma; that's more than any of the rest of us have done. Why don't you just come to work at Davol with your mother and me? You'll meet a nice Portuguese man and settle down again. People in our family just don't go to college. It's not in us. You won't make it, and I don't want to see you get hurt and disappointed again."

At that moment I mustered up more determination than I had ever possessed before. I grabbed my books off the kitchen table, headed for my room, and gave my reply over my shoulder as I bounded up the stairs. "I'm going to go to college starting Monday. I can too do it."

I stopped mid-flight at my father's next words: "I'm so sure you can't make it that if you do, I'll pay for your class ring the year before you're supposed to graduate. And if by some luck you do make it through, I'll throw you the biggest party you've ever seen."

I grinned at my father as I accepted his challenge. "Start saving your money, Dad." We never spoke about it again.

CHAPTER 4

My years at Barrington College were full of learning, new experiences, and discoveries. Most of the learning was pure delight. Some of it was hard and painful. All of it has proved to be of great value in my life. I will always be grateful for the wonderful people who made Barrington what it was. Unfortunately, like so many small private schools, Barrington closed its doors after graduating its final class in 1984. Some students and faculty chose to link up with Gordon College, Barrington's sister school in Massachusetts; but the spirit of openness that was so much a part of the fabric of Barrington is gone, and many of us still mourn the passing of our alma mater.

I majored in biblical studies and theology, and most of my elective credits were in these areas as well. Dr. William Buehler was the professor who had the most influence upon the formation of my biblical and theological roots. He was also the catalyst for what I like to call my awakening to feminism and liberation theology. Dr. Buehler—I still can't think of him as Bill—was a tall, rather lanky man. He had a way of lumbering across the small campus between his office and classroom in a style all his own, and often we students took advantage of these strolls to talk with him. He was an approachable man, even though he insisted that speaking before a colosseum full of people was less frightening to him than talking with one person. He was married and the father of eight children, who were by then in early adulthood. Dr. Buehler had been a pharmacist who had decided to go back to school for a Ph.D. in the New Testament. He had studied at the University of Basel in Switzerland. We were always reminded of that whenever he was required to wear academic garb. His wonderfully floppy hat was prominent among all the flat mortarboards worn by the other professors. During summer vacations Dr. Buehler and his family went back to California, where he still owned a pharmacy. For those three months he was a pharmacist again, his way of keeping in touch with his past.

My first course in the New Testament under Dr. Buehler was tough going. I quickly realized that I knew very little about the Bible and needed to use the index just to locate the various books he referred to in the course of one class period. Each class began the same way. We would be in our seats, and Dr. Buehler would come into the classroom with his enormous briefcase. He methodically placed it on a chair, pulled out his manila folder full of notes, opened it to the appropriate place, and then began his lecture. From the moment he opened those notes to the last word out of his mouth, Dr. Buehler rarely referred to his papers. Instead, he slowly paced the front of the lecture hall as word after eloquent word poured from his mouth. Occasionally I was so engrossed in what he was saying that I forgot to take notes. He made the people and stories in the Bible come alive for us. Jesus had always been important to me, but before these classes at Barrington he was a ghost of a figure, a Prince Charming who had received the endorsement of the Church. Dr. Buehler turned Jesus into a real flesh-and-blood human being. For the first time the significance of the humanity of Jesus became as important to me as his divinity. The most precious gift that Dr. Buehler gave any of us was his tolerance for others' ideas. He told us that if we disagreed with him and had good, strong, logical argument, we had earned the right to challenge him. He reminded us that neither he nor anyone else had all the answers. He challenged us to grow, to think for ourselves, and to have the courage to stand behind what we believed, regardless of whether or not it contradicted everything we were taught. He made it safe for us to test out some pretty outrageous self-designed theology. He never asked us simply to regurgitate information. He didn't think that was what learning and education were all about. He was a real teacher.

Barrington College had some pretty tough rules and guidelines for its students and faculty, but I never chafed under them because they were fair and for everyone without exception. Smoking, drinking, and dancing were not allowed on campus. Because I lived off campus, I had no problem with these codes, but I can imagine how some of the students who lived on campus may have wanted to take issue with the school about them. I was a smoker, so whenever I wanted a cigarette between classes, I had to walk the block or two off campus and smoke on the sidewalk. It was a nuisance sometimes, but I never thought it an unfair rule. Sometimes, when I would want to talk with Dr. Buehler or other professors, they would be kind enough to agree to go to an off-campus coffee shop so that I could relax and smoke. To my knowledge, none of the professors at Barrington smoked, but they didn't judge me for doing so.

The honor code was strictly enforced. If a student was found cheating, he or she was immediately dismissed from the school. Most of the teachers monitored their classes during exam periods, but Dr. Buehler did not. Before each exam he told us to sit in alternate seats and said that he did not plan to stay in the classroom during the exam and be a policeman. He reminded us that we all were adults, that this was an exam on biblical material, which in itself should preclude any kind of cheating, and that he trusted us too much to demean us by monitoring our behavior. Even those who might have given consideration to crib notes or glances at a neighbor's answers thought better of it after this man had spoken. Somehow cheating on a New Testament exam became the same thing as letting Dr. Buehler down. I never knew whether he realized the influence he had on the students in his classroom. I would rather think that he really did believe in the inherent goodness in all of us.

When I enrolled at Barrington College, I was afraid that my father was right, that I wouldn't be able to do the work, that in fact, I wasn't college material. The first semester was difficult. I had so much catching up to do and always felt that the other students had an edge over me. They were fresh out of high school. Most of them had had a great deal of exposure to the Bible previous to college. They had been college prep majors in high school and had long since been exposed to books and ideas that were foreign to me. I felt that I was running as fast as I could just to catch up with them. I completed my first semester with a C average. As far as I was concerned, it was a very successful beginning.

I began my second semester in September 1971 and managed to do much better. I was learning how to take notes in class, to study, and to enjoy writing the required papers. Dr. Buehler was still my favorite teacher, but I respected and admired several others: Dr. Marvin Wilson, who taught Old Testament and Hebrew studies; Terry Fullman, who gave theology new life and meaning; and especially Dr. Chuck Bowser. They all were special, and each in his own way had a part in enabling me to grow and flourish.

By my third semester at Barrington I was beginning to get into deep emotional trouble. I had never really grappled with how I felt about my divorce, and the self-protective bubble I had built around myself was starting to fray at the edges. One weekend Matthew was on one of his rare visits with his father, my parents were away with friends, and my sister was staying at the home of her fiancé's parents. I was thrilled with having the whole house to myself, a rare treat, indeed. On Saturday I slept late, did a few errands and some cleaning, talked with a couple of friends, and still managed to get quite a bit of studying done. It was a glorious day, and I was looking forward to yet another. I spent Sunday in very much the same way. I wasn't really interested in going out. I just basked in the luxury of being alone with my own thoughts. Bob was planning to take Matthew directly to his nursery school on Monday morning. My sister would be going to school from her fiancé's house, and my parents were extremely late in getting home. The daytime hours of Sunday were relaxed and enjoyable. By early evening I had begun to feel restless and wandered around the house, looking for something to occupy my mind. Nothing interested me. Gradually a feeling of panic began to come over me. I called various friends, but no one was home. By ten o'clock I was in a full panic. I didn't know what was happening, and I couldn't stop it. The feelings seemed to multiply until I was beyond panic and in totally unfamiliar and frightening territory. For the next two hours I sat curled up in a chair in the den with the phone in my hand, dialing the numbers of different friends in furious rotation. By midnight, when I was finally able to reach my friend Judy, I was crying so hard I couldn't even tell her who I was when she answered. I just kept sobbing into the telephone. Judy realized that whoever was crying on the other end of the line must be someone she knew. She was gentle and compassionate and encouraged me to take deep breaths. After fifteen minutes or so I had calmed down somewhat, and Judy began to assail me with hundreds of questions: "What's happened? Is Matthew all right? Are your parents there? Is anyone else there? Did something happen to you? Did something happen to Matthew or your parents?" I couldn't manage to respond to these and other questions with more than a yes or no. I couldn't explain what was happening to me. I didn't know what was happening. I was more frightened than I had ever been in my life. I kept thinking: *This is what it must be like to go crazy. I'm losing my grip. I have to get back in control. I don't want to end up in a mental hospital. I have to get back in control.*

Judy stayed on the telephone for another half hour. She kept trying to get me to tell her what was wrong. All I could say was that I felt sad and empty and scared, and I didn't know why. I asked if she would come over and talk with me. As confused as I was at the moment, one thing was clear: I did not want to be alone, even if it was well after midnight. She asked me to stay on the phone while she told her husband that she needed to go out. A few minutes later she returned and told me that her husband "wouldn't let her" come, that it was too late.

We spent another hour on the phone. A few minutes into our conversation I started to cry again. Judy listened to me, but mostly she talked and tried to calm me. At one point she even asked me if I thought I needed to call the hospital. The question sent me back to uncontrollable sobbing, and she quickly backed away from the suggestion. Before we hung up, at nearly 2:00 A.M., she made me promise that I would go to talk with Dr. Bowser, the school psychologist, first thing the next morning and that I would go directly to her house after I had seen him. After we said good-night, I went to bed and fell into an exhausted, druglike sleep. My parents had come home after I had gone to my room and by the time I got up, had already left for work. When I awoke, I felt drained and could tell that the panic was just below the fragile surface of my self-control. When I looked in the mirror, I was horrified to see my red and swollen eyes staring back at me. They were the eyes of a very troubled young woman.

At eight-thirty that morning I found myself sitting across from Dr. Bowser in his office. I couldn't tell him what was wrong because I had no idea. I began to cry almost immediately. He handed me a box of tissues and sat back as he patiently waited for the tears to subside. Bit by bit I tried to tell him what had happened the night before. Even though it made absolutely no sense to me, he seemed to be listening intently to what I was saying. Gradually, over the course of the next two hours, Dr. Bowser was able to piece a few things together. I told him that I had been separated for a little more than a year, that I was raising a three-and-a-half-year-old son, and that we were living with my parents. We talked about my classes and how they were going. We also talked about how I was working at two part-time jobs in an attempt to keep up with expenses. Finally, toward the end of our visit, Dr. Bowser gave me his verdict. No, I wasn't crazy. I had a lot of pressures in my life. I hadn't dealt with my feelings about the divorce at all. I was experiencing so many new things in my life that I quite simply had gone on overload. He told me that just two weeks before, Dr. Buehler had voiced concern about the fact that I seemed to be on the edge emotionally. The two of them had decided that if I didn't come to see Dr. Bowser on my own, Dr. Buehler would suggest that I do so. I was amazed. How had Dr. Buehler seen what I had not? I was grateful for his concern, and the thought brought fresh tears to my eyes.

Dr. Bowser and I talked on. He told me that I needed to reduce some of my responsibilities. I was trying to do too much, and I needed time to heal some of my postmarital wounds. I explained to him that I couldn't quit working. My parents had said that they would provide room and board for Matthew and me. The rest of my expenses were completely my responsibility. Because tuition at Barrington College was so steep, the GI Bill just covered it. Books and other costs had to come out of my own pocket. Matthew was in nursery school from eight until five. His tuition was fifty dollars a week. I also had car payments every month. Because of financial obligations, coupled with other expenses such as gas, insurance, and upkeep on the car, clothing for the two of us, and money needed for weekly trips to the Laundromat, there just was no way that I could stop working. Dr. Bowser understood and asked if I could approach my parents for help. My response was adamant. I didn't want to ask my parents for anything. If they had known what had gone on the night before, my father would have been the first to tell me that it was only proof that he was right, that I had no business going to college, that I was asking too much of myself. There was no way my parents were going to know that I was having trouble coping. There had to be another solution.

Finally Dr. Bowser outlined what he thought I must do. Because I needed to work, he said I should drop all but perhaps one course. I balked, but he insisted. I finally decided that I would stay in Dr. Buehler's class. Then he told me that I was to come in to see him regularly. I began to cry with relief. I had found a safe place, a safe person in whom I could confide. I left Dr. Bowser's office feeling as though a great burden had been lifted from me. I still felt empty and sad inside, but the sense of panic was gone. Maybe I would be all right after all.

For the next three months I saw Dr. Bowser three times each week. I didn't tell my parents that I had dropped most of my courses at school. I spent my nonworking hours in class, studying, sleeping, or writing in my journal. I couldn't believe how much sleep I needed. Dr. Bowser insisted it was good for me to be sleeping so much, and he encouraged me to continue writing in my journal. As the months went by, I became increasingly clear-minded and strong. By summer both Dr. Bowser and I agreed that I would see him only twice a week. I got a full-time job waitressing from four in the afternoon until one in the morning. Every weekday morning I got Matthew dressed and we headed for Newport Beach, where he spent hours building sand castles and playing in the water. I alternated between snoozes on the blanket while he was next to me or sitting in my lounge chair at the very edge of the water while he splashed away. Those were good months for both of us. Matthew was happy and by summer's end was bronzed like a little Greek god. I, too, had browned, but more important, I felt stronger and more sure of myself than I had in a very long time. By fall I felt ready to go back to a full load of classes. Dr. Bowser agreed. We also decided that I would see him just once each week.

Autumn proved to be a testing ground for both Barrington College and me. We both passed with flying colors. One of my courses that semester was on marriage and family. It was pretty basic, especially for those of us who had come to college after having had a few years of life experience beyond high school behind us. Our teacher was a part-time adjunct professor, hired to teach this one class. No one knew a great deal about him. Two or three weeks into the course he discovered that I was divorced and began asking me quite personal questions about my relationship with my ex-husband. He also pried for any residual feelings I might have since the divorce. I tried to be tactful while still maintaining my privacy. When the class was over, I left feeling as though I had handled a tough situation rather well and assumed that the matter was closed. A few days later I found a note in my school mailbox from the dean of faculty asking me to come to his office to see him at my earliest convenience. When I arrived, he told me that several students had been to his office to report what had happened in class. He asked me if it was true. I tried to tell him that it wasn't all that bad and that I had handled the situation. "You shouldn't have had to handle any such situation, Ms. Denman. I just want to know whether or not the accusations are true." I told the dean that they were accurate. The next day Dr. Buehler was in the marriage and family class and told us that he would be our teacher for the rest of the semester. No one asked any further questions. We never saw the adjunct again either. Barrington had high standards, for both faculty and students. The school played hardball with those standards, but it proved that it played fair, too. Unfortunately that claim cannot be made by many institutions, be they secular or religious.

The marriage and family course was fun once Dr. Buehler was teaching it. He interjected stories about his own family in his lectures, and as we students began to know him on a more personal level, our love and respect for him increased. On Friday Dr. Buehler would give a ten-question quiz on the reading material covered in class during the week. Our course grade was going to be the average of our weekly quizzes and two exams. Because it was such a basic course, I had never purchased the required books yet had always scored an A in the quizzes. The weekly tests always consisted of ten questions worth ten points each. We graded our own papers before handing them into Dr. Buehler. One Friday he asked five questions, then said: "I just couldn't think up five other questions, so, if you read a hundred percent of the assigned material this week, give yourself fifty points. If you read only half the material, give yourself twenty-five points. If you didn't read any of it, take fifty points off your quiz grade." I felt angry and stuck. I always got a hundred on the weekly quizzes. My midterm grade had been an A. I didn't want to jeopardize my course grade just because Dr. Buelher couldn't come up with another five questions. I gave myself the additional fifty points for having read all the material and passed in my test paper. What I had done gnawed at me over the next few days until I decided it wasn't worth the extra fifty points. The following week, as we were walking on campus together, I told him what I had done. He grinned and said: "It's my fault that I couldn't think of another five questions for the quiz. I won't penalize you for that. You'll still get the A for your grade. Confession's good for the soul, though, isn't it?" He turned and walked into the building where he was giving his next lecture. It was such a little exchange between us, yet I still get a warm feeling when I think of it.

The next few years flew by. I had my share of crushes on professors, including Dr. Buehler, but I knew them for what they were. I was hungry for role models and affirmation, and these people nurtured me. I got A's or B's in any courses having to do with theology or biblical studies; but the other courses gave me trouble, and I was happy to pass them. In all, I was pleased with the results of my efforts. When it came time to order our class rings, I triumphantly put the bill on the kitchen table in front of my father. Neither of us said a word. The next morning I found the exact amount of money needed next to the purchase order. My father had made good on his promise. I would be graduating the next year. Both my parents and I were actually beginning to believe it.

Halfway through the last semester of my senior year I received a pink slip for every course I was taking, which meant that I was flunking everything! I went to see Dr. Bowser. We had grown close over the years, and I had learned to turn to him whenever I was troubled. He took the pink slips from my hand, looked at them, and handed them back to me.

"What did you expect? This is your last chance to fail. If you don't do it now, you will have succeeded, and you're afraid of success, you don't know how to deal with it."

I couldn't believe he would talk to me that way. He knew how badly I wanted to succeed and how hard I had worked. Then a little light began to dawn.

"You're right. I'm hell-bent on failure. I've been conditioned for failure, but you've helped me to see that I don't have to fail if I don't want to. I can condition myself for success. That's what I'm going to do, too. I am afraid because I don't know if I'll fall on my face after I graduate, but I can't make myself fail just to prove a point. I'm going to do it. I really am going to graduate." Two and a half months later, when the semester was over, I had pulled all my failing grades up to B's and one C.

My parents never knew that I had come so close to not graduating. For weeks they had been planning my graduation party. Dad was proud of my accomplishments. A new deck was built off the back of the house. Nobody said that it was because I was graduating, but it did seem odd that the deck was finished just two weeks before the party. Mom planned, cooked, stored, and cooked some more. Our own freezer was so full that nothing else fitted in, so our neighbor let us use his. Two days before the graduation the already frantic pace picked up even more. Dad was constantly being sent out on errands to buy a little more of something. My aunt Helen and uncle Gene drove in from Baltimore, and they, too, were enlisted into the final preparations.

The day of the graduation was clear and beautiful. It was also hot and sticky. The men took to the backyard, where they put out the big aluminum tubs that would later be filled with ice and beer and soda. Rented tables and chairs were arranged under the pine grove. Charcoal and chopped wood were stuffed into the pit that would later cook all the clams, sausage, hot dogs, and hamburgers. Aunt Helen and my sister, Dolores, decorated the deck with crepe paper streamers in Barrington colors. The oven went on at dawn and continued to fill the already hot kitchen with higher temperatures while Mom baked stuffed scallops and quahogs. She prepared the batter for the hundreds of clam cakes that would be made later in the afternoon. Tray after tray of food appeared on every table, counter, or other available surface until there was just no more room. Finally, just as everything seemed to be ready, it was time to leave for the college.

Matthew chafed under the tie we insisted he wear. For a seven-year-old this was all pretty nonsensical. Matthew knew my graduation meant I had finished school at Barrington, but he didn't understand why it was such a big event. He wasn't at all sure that it was such an honor for his mother to be graduating at such an old age. One day, a couple of years earlier, after having picked him up at nursery school, he had asked me if I was stupid. He said he was asking because all his friends' parents had already graduated from school.

The graduation was long and hot and worth every bead of perspiration. I graduated in the bottom third of my class, but I was as proud as if I had been awarded the prize of being class valedictorian. I'd had a dream, and I had succeeded in making that dream come true. Throughout my years at Barrington I had never allowed myself to think about graduation. It was one course, one semester at a time. I had never thought about graduate school or seminary. It wasn't until my senior year that I began to make plans for more education.

I had started working in churches during my first year at Barrington College. My first job was as a youth director at an Episcopal church in Rumford, the town of my childhood. Father Alden Bessee was the priest at St. Michael and All Angels. I had never worked as a youth director before, and the experience was exhilarating. I wasn't more than ten years older than most of the teenagers in my charge, and I found that ministering to them was challenging and fun. They were always filled with questions about life, and as far as they were concerned, nothing was written in stone. It was a wealthy parish, and some of the kids tried to pull rank on me at first; but once I set them on their ears a time or two, we all settled in to a really close circle. Once I was trying to get the group rounded up and into the cars that would take us to the stables. We had planned a hayride, and there were blankets, guitars, and soda bottles everywhere. I told one particular young boy that he would be riding in my car. He looked at me in disgust as he eyed my Toyota.

"I don't ride in anything less than a Cadillac."

I stared him down. "Fine," I said. "Then I suggest that you get your buns home, pry your father out from under the Sunday paper, and tell him to give you a ride to the stables in his Cadillac."

The young boy clamped his mouth shut and meekly got into my car. We never discussed the incident again, and he later became one of my most ardent champions.

I had a lot of fun with those kids. We went to amusement parks, had pizza parties, raised money with bake sales and car washes, and took a ski trip or two. We also spent a lot of time just talking together. I was always very clear that I would not allow myself to be used as a glorified baby-sitter, taking the kids off their parents' hands. I was there to help those young people understand something about God and the Church. I was there to help them have a relationship with Jesus Christ. I took the task very seriously, and the kids knew it. When it was time to play, we played hard. When it was time to be still and try to know the voice of God speaking within us, we were all ready to do that, too. The kids got to the point that when I asked them what they wanted to do, they would say that they wanted to talk about the Bible. It was music to my ears.

Halfway through the year the parents started to get restless. They began to complain to Alden that their children were just getting too serious about "this religion thing." They were adamant that their kids were in church to have fun, not to get spiritual. Alden, whose daughter was a member of my youth group, decided to sit in on a few of our Sunday evening sessions. He was both shocked and delighted with what he saw. The kids were serious about wanting to know Jesus and wanting a deeper spiritual life. They also still enjoyed playing hard. These young people seemed to be quite healthy indeed; it was their parents who were confused. Alden suggested that I continue working with the group as I had been and leave dealing with the parents to him.

Eventually the parents and "concerned others" asked for a meeting. They continued to insist that it just wasn't normal for the children to be so interested in religion. Religion was for adults, they said. Fun and play were for the children. They were also concerned about there being so much talk about the Holy Spirit. One particular woman was furious and told everyone at the meeting that the Holy Spirit "just was not Episcopalian." Alden and I tried to stifle our chuckles, but he did manage to come back at the woman with the perfect response: "My dear woman, neither are the Father and Son." No real solutions came from that meeting. I finished out the year, but the board chose not to renew my contract. When I left St. Michaels, the teenagers went back to playing. Some of the parents, who had understood what I was doing, left the parish for another church where their children could play and learn, too. I lost touch with all of them. Alden and I remained friends for many years after I stopped working with him. He is a dear and wonderful man. He has gotten into his own share of trouble with parishioners who have thought that he didn't have both feet on the ground. As he once told me, "Rose Mary, St. Paul was thrown out of better churches than either you or I will ever be in."

During my sophomore year at Barrington I was hired as a youth leader for a Presbyterian church in Whitinsville, Massachusetts. The minister had come to Barrington College to interview students for the part-time position. The pay was sixty dollars for one evening's work. I was hired for the job. Every Friday I left Barrington at two in the afternoon and drove the hour and a half to the church. The program was designed so that all the youth of the church would be exposed to Christian teaching, music, and fun activities during the Friday session. Dinner was provided each week by parents who volunteered to cook and serve the meals. I was in charge of the high school group of approximately ten to twelve teenagers. I stayed in that position through graduation from Barrington, after which I rented a small cottage in the area and stayed on for an additional year. The kids there were wonderful, and some of them came to feel like my own. Bob Cook, the minister of the church, and I got along famously. We enjoyed a good working relationship during my first three years there. He and his family moved back to their homeland, Australia, soon after I had received my degree and moved to Whitinsville.

I always worked more than one job while in college. Because youth groups run only through the school year, I needed something else for the summer months. Two of the years I waitressed. One summer I served as the first woman to hold the position of Protestant chaplain at a Boy Scout camp. It was a live-in position, and Matthew spent the summer at the camp with me. He was housed in another area of the facility and given free rein to be involved in whatever area of camp life he chose. He earned several merit badges that summer, and we both enjoyed the leisurely pace. I was invited to return the following year but declined in order to accept a more challenging offer.

There were other jobs during the school year as well: preparing ex-felons in a halfway house for their high school equivalency exams, working in a factory as a hand collator, serving as a teacher's assistant in a Montessori nursery school, and cleaning private homes. Perhaps one of the most interesting jobs I had was the three years I worked as an administrative assistant to the rabbi of the Reform congregation in Barrington. I worked for him on Saturday and Sunday mornings, typing, answering the phones, ordering supplies for the Hebrew school run by the temple, and taking care of other general secretarial duties.

Rabbi Rob Schenkerman was a remarkable man, and it was both a pleasure and an honor to work for him. I had taken a course entitled "Modern Jewish History and Culture" at Barrington and had fallen in love with the stories of the Hebrew people. Rabbi Schenkerman and I came to an agreement. He would tutor me in Jewish history and theology, and in return I would play the little organ in the temple for Sabbath services. I didn't play very well, but I was the only available candidate. I accepted his proposal. Barrington also agreed to give me course credit for my work. I studied under the rabbi for two full semesters and have never done as much work or enjoyed it more than I did with him. He never assigned a reading list at the beginning of a semester but handed books to me by the armload every few weeks and said: "Here, darling, enjoy." And I did enjoy them, every one of them. Every week we spent an evening together in his home discussing what I had read, but first he set the atmosphere. In the winter we went into his living room and sat by the fire. He put a stack of classical records on the player, and his wife brought us a tray of fruit, cheese, and crackers. Often we sipped on glasses of chilled wine as we spent hours engrossed in discussion and friendly argument. Before I knew it, we had passed four or five hours together and it was time for me to go home.

I did an audiovisual presentation with slides as my final project for one of the courses. I arrived at the rabbi's house the night before the project was due, armed with all the slides I had produced, the music I had chosen, and the script I had written. Our task was simply to tape the script onto a cassette. I thought that we would have the job completed in a matter of an hour or two. The rabbi listened to me read the script. He liked it but wanted to discuss a few revisions. He also wanted us to work on my diction. I must have read and reread that script a hundred times during the course of the night. The rabbi was finally pleased with my speaking and approved the end result at 6:00 A.M. He insisted that he go with me to the school so that he could be there when I gave my presentation to the panel of six professors who would be grading my work. I had just enough time to rush home, shower and change, get Matthew to nursery school, and be at Barrington in time for the presentation. I must have been exhausted, but all I felt was excitement and anticipation. I knew that we had done really fine work together. I made my presentation, and when it was over, all my professors were very complimentary. Finally, the professor who was responsible for grading my project rose from his chair and gave me a great big hug. "I'm sorry that I can give you only an A for your grade, Rose Mary. Your presentation far surpassed any grade I could give." The rabbi and I looked across the room at each other and grinned. We both were feeling the satisfaction that comes with knowing that you have given something your very best.

When I graduated from Barrington College, I left that school with far more than a piece of paper stating that I had fulfilled the requirements for my diploma. My years there had made me rich in so many life experiences. I learned far more than anything I could ever have ever absorbed from a book. Real live flesh-and-blood people like Dr. Buehler, Chuck Bowser, and Rabbi Schenkerman taught me by their example. Dr. Buehler taught me the value of having a sensitive soul. Chuck Bowser enabled me to reach deep inside myself to find the inner core of strength that lies within each of us. And Rabbi Schenkerman helped me see the joy and pleasure that can come from study and learning. Each of them, in his own way, provided me with an education of quality and dignity, and I will always be grateful to them and honor them for that great gift.

CHAPTER 5

While attending Barrington College, I worked with the youth group at the Presbyterian church in Whitinsville. During the spring semester of my senior year Bob, the pastor, helped me find a little cottage in Northbridge, a town five miles away. Matthew and I used the cottage on weekends during the spring, and I spent the time papering and painting in preparation for our move there after graduation. Members of the youth group helped with the work, and we even planted a vegetable garden behind the house. By the time we moved in late May, the tender green shoots were already sprouted. We had ripe tomatoes, peas, and lettuce by July. I didn't have a full-time job but knew that some opportunity would arise before the money gifts I had received for graduation ran out.

No job was forthcoming. I had a good résumé; but the town was small, and the unemployment rate was high enough that entry-level jobs were not plentiful. I was planning to go to graduate school in the fall and needed a job that wasn't a career, just a way to make a living while I continued with my education.

By mid-July I was beginning to panic. The money had all but ran out. I put pride aside and went to the local welfare office. When it was my turn to be interviewed, I was met with the usual lack of interest and a long line of questions.

"Are you married?"

"No."

"Divorced?"

"Yes."

"Does your ex-husband provide child support?"

"Sporadically."

"Have you completed high school?"

"Yes."

"Do you have any trade school or college background?"

"Yes, I have a bachelor's degree."

The interviewer looked up at me. "Do you have any education beyond your college degree?"

"Yes, I have three courses toward my master's."

"God, you have more education than I do!"

Her tone and manner took on a new respect, and the remainder of the interview went smoothly. Her name was Trudy, and she told me that she would need to come out to our house to verify what I had told her before she could process our application. If everything checked out, we would be receiving help within the week. I had told her that we had a refrigerator but no stove. All our meals were being prepared with a hot plate, electric frying pan, and a toaster oven borrowed from my friend Lisa. If the social worker verified that we had no stove, I would receive a voucher for one. She was planning to come to the cottage within the next few days. I assured her I was looking for a job and didn't expect to need help for very long.

Two days later Trudy came to complete the investigation. Not half an hour after she arrived I received a phone call from the administrator of the local nursing home. He offered me the position of activities director at a salary that would provide a decent income for Matthew and me. When I hung up, I was so excited I ran right into the kitchen to tell Trudy. She congratulated me with a hearty handshake.

"When do you start your new job?"

"A week from Monday." It was only ten days away.

"When will you get your first paycheck?"

"Two weeks after I start the job."

"OK, as far as the department is concerned, you are eligible for welfare until you receive your first paycheck. That is just over three weeks from today. So I'm still going to give you a voucher for a stove and three weeks' worth of food stamps. You will also be receiving a check for a month's assistance. You need these things, and you have a right to them."

Tears began to surface. We did need the help, and Trudy was giving it to us. She had also helped me maintain my dignity throughout the process. She stayed for a half hour after the interview, and we exchanged information about our children. She, too, was a single parent and said she knew the struggle it could be to raise children alone. Before she left, we made arrangements to visit each other with our children. Over the course of the next months and years Trudy and I became good friends. We have kept in touch over the years in spite of various moves. Our children are grown now, and Trudy is in a new relationship. She and Bob have a new baby daughter. Once or twice a year we manage to visit each other. The need for state assistance is part of my life history now. So is the stove that Trudy helped me get. Our friendship has been the thing that has endured.

The job at the nursing home was just as much a part of my education as the classroom. I became more sensitive toward the dignity and needs of old people. I began to realize that consistently calling people "honey," rather than using their given names, robs them of their personhoods. Danny was a good administrator, and I often saw him taking even deeper cuts in profit than necessary in order to provide the residents with the little extras that made life pleasant for them. He didn't have to order shrimp and other fine foods to be included in the menu. He also didn't have to take the residents to restaurants for lunch outings. No state rules dictated that the nursing home had to provide special May Day breakfasts or St. Patrick's Day parties either. But Danny viewed them as necessary, so we had them.

I had always enjoyed the company of old people. Working at the Northbridge Nursing Home provided me with the opportunity to learn how to listen and to minister to their needs. It also helped me become more comfortable with the process of dying, which is very much a natural part of life. To be present with a resident during his or her last hours of life became a privilege as well as a learning experience. To see that there can be dignity in death, as in living, gave me valuable insights not only into my own life but into my ministry as well.

Our new lives in Whitinsville and Northbridge were shaping up nicely. I had hired one of the boys from the youth group to baby-sit for Matthew while I was at work. John was a mature young man, and he took his responsibility for Matthew's care seriously. The two of them spent the lazy summer days fishing, reading stories, and riding bicycles together. Money was still tight, and the bills didn't always get paid on time; but somehow they did get paid. I didn't mind. We were independent, living on our own, and I had my degree from Barrington College and was planning to add to the courses I had already begun to take on the master's level. It was hard work, and there was a lot more of it ahead before we could have the kind of life I wanted for us; but it would be worth it. The day would come when my father and the nuns from St. Margaret's would see that. Nobody was going to force limitations on my life.

Around mid-August I decided it was time to begin to do some entertaining. I had been dating Michael, whom I had met at Barrington, so I invited him to be our first dinner guest. He was to arrive about an hour after I got home from work. I started the dinner and asked Matthew to run the vacuum cleaner through the living room and his bedroom. About fifteen minutes later I heard him scream, and out of the corner of my eye I caught a glimpse of him being propelled across the room. He fell to the floor with a frightening thud and lay there motionless. I ran into his bedroom and looked at him in horror. He was unconscious, and there was a large hole burned through the side of his face!

I knew instantly that this was a life-threatening emergency. I turned off the stove, gathered Matthew into my arms, and ran out to the car. We lived three miles from the little town hospital, and I pushed the gas pedal to the floor as we sped down the winding country road. Matthew had regained consciousness but was disoriented and frightened. I hugged him close to me with my right arm as I held the steering wheel with the other. I pulled up to the emergency-room entrance, shut off the motor, and ran around to the other side of the car. I felt strangely calm and in complete control as I carried Matthew through the big double doors leading to the emergency room. Two staff members were standing nearby, and immediately directed us into the nearest examining room. One of the doctors looked at Matthew briefly and told me that he would need to be transported to the regional hospital ten miles away. The small-town facility just didn't have the equipment or staff needed to treat him. Matthew was in stable condition, and the doctor said that I could take him to the regional hospital but that it would be better if I didn't go alone. I thought of Michael, who must have arrived at our house by then. I hadn't turned off the lights or television when we rushed to the hospital. Dinner was still on the stove. I called, and Michael answered on the second ring. When I told him what had happened, he said that he knew where the hospital was and would pick us up right away.

A call had been placed by the staff at Whitinsville to the regional hospital to alert it. A pediatrician and a plastic surgeon were waiting for us when we arrived. For the first time since the accident Matthew and I were separated. The two doctors took him into an examining room while

Michael and I waited in the hall. We didn't say anything to each other. Michael just sat next to me and held me close. After more than an hour the doctors finally came out of the examining room. The pediatrician smiled.

"Your little boy will be just fine."

It took a moment for her words to penetrate. For the first time that evening my fears and feelings began to surface, and I began to cry with sheer relief. The doctor put her arms around me as she continued to speak.

"Your son has a serious electrical burn. The injury is very close to an artery near his mouth. We will need to keep him here for several days. It will be some time before we can complete all of the reconstruction work that will be necessary, but he will be fine. We administered an EEG, and there has been no brain damage. He's a very healthy little boy. He will be just fine."

We were allowed to see Matthew for a little while before we had to leave. He wasn't at all happy about staying in the hospital overnight. I promised him that I would be back to see him in the morning. Apparently he had tried to pull the vacuum cleaner plug out of the extension cord with his teeth. For the first time in the history of motherhood I held my tongue rather than give my son a lecture on the hazards of making that kind of mistake. I was too grateful that he would be all right to worry about lectures.

Before we left, the plastic surgeon warned us Matthew would look very different the next morning when we saw him. He told us that his face would probably be black and blue and that it would be very swollen. He cautioned us that it was important for us to try not to react to what we saw, that in order not to frighten him, Matthew would not be allowed to use a mirror until most of the discoloration and swelling were gone.

Michael and I drove back to Whitinsville in silence. When we got back to the cottage, he helped me put the kitchen in order. Then we went into the living room and sat quietly. He offered to spend the night, and I gratefully accepted. I didn't want to be alone. I had called my parents, and they were planning to drive to the hospital immediately after work the next day. I told them what the doctor had said about how Matthew would be looking, and they promised not to show any concern when they saw him.

The next morning Michael and I drove to the hospital early. I brought some of Matthew's favorite toys, and he was happy to have them. I was grateful to have been warned about how he would look. His face had more than doubled in size, and the whole left side was discolored. The skin around the hole near his mouth was white, and the exposed flesh was torn and mashed. I tried not to react to what I saw. Matthew wanted a mirror. He said that his face felt funny. He told us that it felt big. I was glad that at least it didn't seem to be hurting him too much. I was honest with him.

"Matthew, the doctor doesn't want you to look in a mirror right now."

"Why? Do I look awful?"

"You've had a bad accident, and your face is going to be swollen and a little black and blue for a while. But in a few days that will go away."

"Am I gonna have a scar, Ma? Am I gonna look weird?"

"Matthew, you're going to have to see the doctor a lot over the next few months, but he said that when he's finished with you, no one will be able to tell that you ever even had this accident. You need to trust me, and you need to trust the doctors. Can you do that for us?"

"Are you sure, Ma? I'll be OK? I won't look funny?"

"I'm sure, Matthew. You won't look funny."

With that, Matthew seemed to set his concerns aside. We had an honest relationship between us. I believe that children both deserve and can handle the truth. Because Matthew knew that, he believed me, and I was grateful for the special bond that we shared.

The next weeks and months were painful. Matthew dreaded the visits to the doctor's office, when he would be asked to lie very still while the doctor carved away at the dead skin tissue around his mouth. Life at home wasn't much fun for him either. His bicycle was off limits. We couldn't go to the beach or a pool. There was actually very little that he could do besides watch television, read, and eat. We also went to the park and movies or visited friends to break the monotony in his life. My once very active little eight-year-old was becoming sedentary. His eating began to go out of control. He couldn't eat food that required a great deal of chewing, but milk shakes, ice cream, puddings, Jell-O, potatoes, and other soft foods took on a new importance in his life. Within four months he had gained fifteen pounds and was no longer the tall, slim, healthy-looking youngster he had been. Matthew's mouth gradually healed, and by late fall there was only a small scar where the gaping hole had once been.

Once again, our lives took on a frenzied but manageable pace. We had moved out of the cottage and into a large apartment in the next town. The family on the first floor agreed to watch Matthew in the afternoon when he came home from school. He was happy to have their children as playmates, even though they got into the occasional scrap.

I was keeping a hectic schedule, working at the nursing home full time during the day, going to classes at Assumption College in Worcester two nights each week, and working at the Congregational church in Sutton, Massachusetts, on Sunday morning and evening. On the nights I was in class, Matthew had dinner with the family downstairs. I got home in time to read a bedtime story and tuck him into bed. Monday, Wednesday, and Friday evenings were ours to spend together. I taught him to play checkers and, later, chess, backgammon, and Monopoly. I used the evenings, after he was asleep, to study for my classes. Saturdays were a flurry of activities as the two of us did the grocery shopping and banking, went to the Laundromat, and cleaned the apartment. Our schedule was tight but as balanced as it could be under the circumstances. Friday night was date night for Matthew and me. We usually went to the restaurant of his choice—McDonald's, the Ground Round, or Pizza Hut—and then to a movie or bowling. Saturday night was my date night with Michael. Most often we stayed in the apartment and talked or watched television. On Sunday afternoons I carved out an hour or two to be alone, to decompress—time to clear my head and rest my bones with a long tub bath and lazy afternoon nap.

This kept up for the three years I spent at Assumption College. Most of my courses were in counseling. They were exciting and challenged me to reach deep inside myself for wisdom and understanding. I took every course possible from Rick Craig, who was the most colorful man I had ever met and certainly not the image of the learned ivory tower college professor. Rick wore corduroy pants and worn flannel shirts. He had long, wavy brown hair and an animated face that made people smile. I don't think that I ever saw Rick sit in a chair. The class usually gathered in a circle on the floor, or he perched cross-legged on his desk. He didn't lecture but talked to and with us. Rick had studied with Clark Moustakas, and many of our required books were written by this man whom Rick loved and admired so much.

I soaked up everything connected to those classes: the discussions;

the books that we read; even the assignments. As we read and talked, we learned about ourselves, about humankind—the way we learn and grow and relate to one another. They were never dull or boring classes, and they helped me understand that all the events and experiences in my life were a part of the fabric of the person I had become. These courses also helped me know that I—not the hands of fate and certainly not family custom and dictate—was in control of who I would become. There was new freedom in these discoveries. There was also a great sense of responsibility.

Being ordained a minister and shepherding a congregation had been my goal ever since the day I had met with my pastor and decided to enroll at Barrington College. Choosing to go to graduate school after leaving Barrington rather than enrolling in seminary had been a deliberate decision. To me, being a minister meant that I needed to be holy, to have the answers to difficult life questions, to be a polished, spiritual leader for my people. I wasn't any of those things. I needed more time to allow God to mold me into the kind of person who would exemplify all these qualities to others. Prayer became an increasingly central part of my daily life, and my prayer was always the same: "Father, please make me into a good minister. Make me your holy and worthy minister."

Just before completing my courses at Assumption, I visited Bangor Theological Seminary in Maine. My GI Bill had run out, and I had no money for school; but Matthew and I made the trip anyway. Bangor seemed worlds away from Worcester or Providence. I had never thought of myself as a metropolitan person, but Bangor is a very small city by comparison. I wasn't at all sure that this was a place in which I wanted to live for the next three years, even if I could manage to afford it.

I spent two days on the seminary campus, mostly auditing classes, meeting with professors, and talking with students. On the second day I met with the school bursar. She was a pleasant woman who didn't seem to be at all troubled by the fact that I had no money. She told me that most students were in the same situation. On the wall behind her was a large framed cartoon of five or six people sitting around a long table. They all were laughing hysterically. The caption read: "Dear Prospective Student: We, the members of the finance committee, are presently reviewing your financial application."

The bursar busied herself with her adding machine as she calculated how we could come up with the funds needed for my first year of seminary.

"Two thousand dollars in student loans, another fifteen hundred in grants, low-cost seminary housing, participating in the work-study program, a student position in one of the local churches—there, I think we have you in really fine shape. I see no reason why you can't begin classes in the fall."

I looked at her in disbelief. That was not the answer I had been anticipating. What was I going to do now? Three years of graduate school had gotten me no closer to being holy enough to be a minister, and here was this woman telling me that the details of money had been taken care of—all with a little work at her adding machine! I felt both trapped and exhilarated. Ordination was becoming more than a mere dream; it was becoming a real possibility. I completed the appropriate paper work before Matthew and I headed back to Massachusetts. My mind was reeling as I thought about all the changes that were going to occur in our lives over the next few months. By fall we would be moving to Bangor, Maine, of all places. I was actually going to be a seminary student.

The summer was busy with sorting and packing for our move north. We were living in a six-room apartment, and although most of our furniture consisted of odd castoffs from friends and family, it was difficult to decide what to take with us. I held yard sales and gave a few things away. Much of the rest went to the town dump. When I had pared our belongings down to a manageable number, we packed everything and loaded it into a rented U-Haul. On the day of our move I drove my car the eight hours to the seminary while friends from the church followed me in the truck.

I had been told that seminary housing was tight and the only thing available to us my first year was a small one-bedroom apartment on the second floor of one of the big old houses on campus. We hoped there would be a larger apartment available to us the following year. I had already decided that Matthew would have the bedroom while I slept on a sofa bed in the living room. However, it turned out that the whole apartment consisted of only two rooms. The kitchen, dining area, and living room were a compact affair shaped in a small L, with the bathroom having been carved out of one corner of what was once a lovely large bedroom. It was a charming apartment, and there was even a working fireplace. Fortunately the attic on the third floor was light and dry. Several other students in the building, also cramped for space, had set up study areas for themselves there. I laid claim to a far corner, and my desk, bookcases, and books were carried from the truck up the two flights into the attic. I sent my friends back to Massachusetts with a few items that just wouldn't fit into our apartment. By the time they left, Matthew and I were surrounded by boxes with hardly enough room to move. It took the next four days to make some semblance of order in our new surroundings.

Three of us moved into that tiny apartment: Matthew, myself, and a kitten named Smokey that Matthew had adopted through a neighbor earlier in the summer. Smokey was a frisky, adorable furry creature, if not the brightest feline I had ever encountered. He was being trained as an indoor cat since there was too much traffic in the street for us to trust him outdoors. Three days after we had moved onto the seminary campus, Smokey somehow managed to sneak out of the apartment. He was heading down the hall when Matthew caught sight of the open door. He ran for the hall, calling for Smokey, and the cat did what any self-respecting animal would do under the circumstances: He bolted for the stairs and kept running right out the front door. Matthew wasn't fast enough. He got to the front lawn just in time to see Smokey run into the street and be hit by a passing car. I reached his side as the car continued along its way. Smokey tried to get up but was dazed, and his leg had been badly injured. Matthew picked him up, held the kitten in his arms, and started to cry. I ran up the stairs to our apartment, got my purse and car keys, and we headed for the nearest veterinarian. After a thorough examination we were told that Smokey would be fine but that he had a badly broken leg. The doctor offered three alternatives: amputation, surgery, or allowing the leg to heal on its own. If we chose the last alternative, the cat would be dragging a useless leg behind him for the rest of his life. If we chose surgery, he would have at least partial mobility, but it would be costly. One look at Matthew helped me make the decision for surgery. Smokey would need to be in the hospital for five or six days.

The drive home was quiet. Matthew was worried about his kitten. I was worried about how I was going to pay the medical expenses. When we had arrived in Bangor on Saturday, I had seventy-five dollars to my name. After we had shopped for groceries, there was thirty dollars left. My tuition, fees, books, and rent were taken care of by the student loan and grants. My job through the work-study program wouldn't begin for another two weeks, so I wouldn't be paid for three. I had no idea how we were going to get groceries or gas for the car until then. Now, with the veterinarian expenses, we were really in a jam. As soon as we got home,

I walked across campus to the bursar's office. I hoped she would have a lead on a local job that I could start immediately. I had been to the employment office, and there was nothing available and flexible enough for both my class schedule and my need to be with Matthew. The bursar listened to my plight, but there was nothing she could do. For the second time in my life I put my pride in my pocket and went to the local welfare office. I was told that because I was a student, I was not eligible for welfare but that I could get a voucher for one week's worth of food at the local supermarket. I took the twenty-five-dollar voucher home, grateful for the help and praying that I would be able to make it and the thirty dollars stretch for the three weeks until I got my first paycheck. The next week I took the voucher and ten of my remaining thirty dollars and bought what I hoped would be enough to get us through. The bags I brought home were filled with macaroni and cheese, spaghetti and canned sauce, eggs, bread, peanut butter, and bologna. Fresh vegetables and fruit would have to wait until we were on more steady footing.

Within two weeks Matthew and I both had started school and were beginning to settle into our new lives at the seminary. I had a part-time position in the work-study program as a crisis counselor for Dial Help, a part of the Community Health and Counseling Services in the Bangor area. Like any work-study job, it didn't pay well, but it did at least give us enough income to keep food in the refrigerator, gas in the car, and coins in the Laundromat machines. This was definitely a no-frills time in our lives.

About a month after classes began, Dr. Cook, who was both the professor of pastoral care at the seminary and the person in charge of student placement in local churches, approached me about a job as a Christian education director at the United Methodist church in Orono, Maine. I wasn't thrilled about the prospect of working in education again, but I was eager to get into a more pastoral position. Dr. Cook encouraged me at least to have an interview with the church's committee. He told me that first-year students were never placed in pastoral positions. With this in mind I decided to accept the invitation for an interview.

The church was about ten miles from the seminary. Because of its close proximity to the University of Maine at Orono, it had more than its share of professors, department heads, and administrators among the membership. That scared me because in many ways Orono United Methodist Church was a Protestant version of the Roman Catholic church of my childhood, St. Margaret's—full of upper-middle-class overachievers. I had vowed never again knowingly to place myself in a situation where I would be looked down upon because of my ethnic, educational, or blue-collar background. I suspected that accepting a job with this church would be placing myself in exactly that kind of environment. Therefore, I purposely answered every question posed to me in a way that I hoped would convince the committee it should not hire me. I was emphatic that if hired, I would try to provide the congregation with the best exposure to Christian education possible but that I was not a baby-sitter. I made it clear that I would have fun with the youth group but that I would not be its social secretary. If what the committee wanted was someone to schedule pizza parties, ski trips, and dances, the parents had ample ability to do that. Because the position was part time, I would need to concentrate on the quality of leadership that I had to offer, not on frills. I also suggested that I might be too fundamental for their taste, that my understanding of theology was perhaps more narrow than they would like. I saved my best punch line for last: that I was charismatic, that I believed in the gifts of the Holy Spirit and our ability to manifest those gifts in our lives. Driving back to the seminary after the interview, I was convinced that I had talked myself out of a job. To my amazement I received a phone call from the pastor that very same evening. He and the committee had been favorably impressed with the interview and were offering me the job. Not knowing what else to do, I accepted. For the next three years of seminary I maintained both jobs: crisis counselor for the telephone hot line and the position at Orono United Methodist Church. They proved to be avenues for mutual nurturing and learning.

I was hired to work for twenty-five hours a week at the church in Orono, and my major duties were: recruiting and training Sunday schoolteachers, being a resource for them during the year, teaching the adult class, occasionally assisting the pastor during Sunday worship, preaching two sermons each year, and leading a Bible study for the retired women of the parish. I enjoyed my work there, especially the weekly Bible studies with "my ladies," which, during the first two years, were held at Hanna's house. Hanna was a regal lady in her eighties, and each week she had her dining-room table set with delicate cups and saucers and dessert plates so we could enjoy a light snack. During the spring of my second year at the church the pastor called to tell me Hanna had cancer and suggested we visit her. We decided that whichever of us she gravitated toward during the visit would serve as her primary pastor over the next months.

John and I went to see Hanna the next afternoon. I had been with people who were dying when I worked at the nursing home, and I wasn't afraid to talk with Hanna about her cancer. For the first half hour of our visit John engaged her in light conversation, and as time passed, I became increasingly uncomfortable. Finally I decided to jump in.

"Hanna, I understand that you have been to see your doctor."

"Yes, last week."

"Is everything all right, Hanna?"

"No, I'm sick."

"I'm sorry to hear that. Did the doctor tell you what it is you're sick with?"

"Yes, I have cancer."

I could feel John grow tense, but I kept my eyes on Hanna. My heart began to pound as I thought of what I needed to ask next. "Hanna, did the doctor say how bad your cancer is?"

"Yes, I'm dying."

It was out. Hanna had given us permission to talk openly about her cancer.

"I'm so sorry. Can you tell us how we can help you?"

"I guess I just need to talk about it."

"I understand. You can talk about it as much as you need to. But, Hanna, will you do something for me?"

"If I can."

"Will you talk with me about your thoughts and feelings? I don't know how to die, Hanna. Will you teach me?"

Soft tears surfaced on her delicate blue eyes. Mine were moist, too. "Yes, I'd like to talk to you about those things. I'd like that very much."

John began to breathe more easily. Hanna and I had created a new and special bond between us. The three of us sat quietly in her living room, and before we left, we decided that I would visit with Hanna once a week. Later the visits would be more frequent.

Hanna died the following fall. During the last month of her life she was in a nursing home, and I visited her several times a week. Much of the time we just sat quietly as I held her hand. The day before she died, as I sat beside her bed, Hanna asked me to hold her. I leaned over and put my arm under her head.

"No. I mean, really hold me."

She had grown frail and couldn't have weighed more than ninety pounds. I pushed my chair aside and sat on the edge of the bed. Slowly I moved Hanna until she was on my lap, with her head cradled in my arms. Her eyes closed, and she smiled. My eyes were moist as I bent my head forward and laid it against hers. I gently rocked her in my arms and thought my heart would burst with the love I felt for her. She had taught me a great deal about living as well as dying. She taught me that there can be dignity and triumph in both and that death does not have to be ugly or frightening. John and I conducted her funeral together. When it was time for me to give the eulogy, I cried—not for Hanna but for those of us who loved her and would miss her.

I think most ministers would agree that it is our interaction with people, both in and out of the parish, that makes us the ministers we become. At best, seminary informs our experiences. It is the skeleton, and our experiences with others provide the flesh and sinew.

As I have mentioned earlier, my educational progress through parochial schools was far from being an uplifting experience for me. The year and a half at East Providence High School had begun to help me see that perhaps I did have a good mind. But I went to Barrington College hardly convinced of my intellectual capabilities. All through college and graduate school I kept looking over my shoulder, convinced that somewhere along the line someone would find me out. Whenever I aced a course, I was convinced either that I had snowed the professor or that I had done well because it was a second-rate school after all. Little by little, but never quite completely, I had begun to consider that my mind was capable of thought and process, capable of contributing to society, especially the Church. Little by little I had begun to think that I really did have something to offer.

My years at Barrington College and Assumption College were wonderful experiences. When I finally decided to attend Bangor Theological Seminary, it was with a sense of wonder and anticipation. I looked forward to three more exciting years of discovery and learning. My first months there all but dashed those dreams. With few exceptions, I found Bangor Seminary a parched and barren wasteland. There was little encouragement of free-spirited questioning, investigation, or growth, but rather there was rabid consumption of party-line theology, more commonly known as orthodoxy. There was no room for the validation of the student's past faith or educational experience. In many ways my years at Bangor Seminary were filled with frustration and anger, which proved I had begun to believe in myself more than in days past, when I would have blindly accepted the callous judgments of those in authority. For the first time in my life I was beginning to question the competence of those who presumed to know my soul better than I, who presumed to dictate the whats, whys, and hows of spiritual life and relationship to God above individual experience with the divine.

Some of the best learning came not from the classroom but from long discussions in the student lounge. One afternoon, during one of these informal gatherings, I posed a question to the rest of the group: "Why is it that whenever we do something sinful, it's our fault, but whenever we do something good, it's to the glory of God? That certainly seems like an unbalanced division of accountability to me. If I'm going to take the rap for my failings, I should be able to take the credit for my triumphs." One of my fellow students came up with the canned answer we all had long since learned in Sunday school, but it sounded empty and meaningless. Nobody else had another answer, though, and the conversation drifted off to another topic. I wonder if that question continued to hound the rest of them as much as it hounded me for so long. It's a tricky one, and it was never addressed with any amount of serious inquiry in the classroom. Tradition, orthodoxy—that's what we learned.

Dr. Walter Cook was one of the few beacons of light in my life at seminary. He was a gray-haired, gentle Scotsman who, even in his late sixties, walked with a spring in his step and mischievous glint in his eye. He was the head of the pastoral care department at the seminary and taught the more practical, roll-up-your-sleeves courses that would, it was hoped, prepare us to respond in a gentle and pastoral way to our congregations. He taught us best by demonstrating those qualities in his responses to us as his students. More than a few of us turned to him with our own frustrations and turmoil. He wasn't rigid, and he gave the impression that he was willing to learn from any one of us. Because Dr. Cook treated us as his equals, we were willing to listen seriously to his wisdom.

One of the big issues on the seminary campus at the time was the use of inclusive language. Many of the professors were still accustomed to referring to all humankind as "mankind," and although we were told that God had no gender, there seemed to be a barrage of male terms when they referred to any of the three persons of the Trinity. Add to this the fact that all ministers were still referred to as "clergymen," and it was no surprise that we women on campus were becoming increasingly frustrated with being the invisible minority. Dr. Throckmorton, the New Testament professor, was the only teacher who used inclusive language.

One day I finally decided to approach Dr. Cook about his references to "Father God," "mankind," and "clergyman." Because he had demonstrated such gentleness in his interactions with students, I was able to confront him with equal sensitivity. When I explained how we women felt left out when he used such all-male language, he responded in a state of loving confusion: "But, lassie, you must know that I mean you, too, when I talk about clergymen." I sensed his sincerity and decided to do what I still do best: demonstrate my point with a story.

"Dr. Cook, let's do a fantasy for a moment. Let's pretend that in our Scriptures God has always been presented as She. Let's also pretend that society, rather than have a patriarchal history, has one that is centered upon the leadership of women. Because we have a matriarchal society, all of our spiritual, intellectual, scientific, and political leaders have always been women. Now, let's also pretend that the clergywomen, in their growing understanding of Mother Goddess and Her relationship to womankind, have decided to include a few well-chosen men in the ranks of ordained ministry, and you are one of those men. You come to the seminary and hear talk about how Goddess has no gender but is always referred to as 'Mother Goddess, She' and how all clergy are referred to as 'clergywomen.' When you balk at this language, as well as to being told that we mean you, too, when we talk about womankind, we pat you on the head and tell you that you are being overly sensitive, that you are nitpicking. How would you feel, Dr. Cook?"

He stared across the room at me, and his eyes grew misty. "Lassie, I'd feel so left out it would hurt. I've never thought about it that way. I'm sorry. You'll forgive an old man if I still slip, but I'm going to try from now on to be more sensitive in my use of language."

Oh, Dr. Cook still slipped up a lot. He still called ministers "clergymen" most of the time. But he truly did try, and his trying endeared him to us all the more. So, there were some tender moments at the seminary, some experiences that redeemed the otherwise pure frustration of it all. The seminary had instituted a policy for inclusive language, yet in direct contrast with the sincerity of Dr. Cook were the pure fear and rage exhibited by other professors when students challenged their sexist language. As the women grew stronger in their solidarity, these professors grew more entrenched in their unwillingness to change. During my senior year one of the professors had a heart attack. His wife blamed the women students for bringing it on by our persistence that her husband alter his sexist language in the classroom. The victims were made out to be guilty for accusing the oppressor rather than silently accepting their bondage. More painful was the fact that Dr. Zeigler, the one woman professor on the faculty at the time, was perhaps the greatest offender in sexist language and attitude. The one to whom we women should have been able to turn as a role model was, in reality, an embarrassment to us all.

Three particular professors—Dr. Cook; Dr. Andrew Grinnell, head of the Christian education department; and Dr. Burton Throckmorton—were the only faculty members who dared stray outside the stringent perimeters. Unlike Dr. Throckmorton, who because of his fame and stature in the academic world, seemed immune to the sharp and devouring teeth of the seminary bureaucracy, Andy Grinnell and Dr. Cook were considered dispensable.

Retirement was enforced whenever a member of the administration or faculty reached the age of seventy. During my second year of seminary, a year or two before his seventieth birthday, Dr. Cook was pressured into tendering his resignation under the guise of retirement. The seminary viewed him as ineffective because his courses were practical rather than full of the heady theology it respected most. I approached him to ask if my suspicions were true, and he confirmed them. When he saw my anger, he asked me to let it be; he didn't want to fight the system. I drew up a petition and gathered signatures from among the students and whichever faculty members I thought might be sympathetic. All but one student and several of the faculty signed the petition to keep Dr. Cook. None of us expected that it would do any good, but at least we let the administration know how strongly we felt about this injustice. We were given a few soggy platitudes, and at the end of the year Dr. Cook did retire. Many of us mourned his leaving and felt increasingly powerless to effect any change. Warm, vital, passionate people were being turned into docile, obedient robots. The Church would truly be pleased with the seminaries' handiwork.

Andy Grinnell was the next to go. He had tried to mold himself into the kind of professor the seminary would value, but it didn't work. His courses in Christian education were boring and stale. None of us was surprised when he was not granted tenure. Yet, when he had nothing left to lose during his last semester with the seminary, he offered a course in personal spiritual development. Ten of us signed up, and we met three times a week in Andy's living room.

What we witnessed was a radical transformation. This seemingly "dead" professor was raised to new life, and in that new life he flourished. So did we. We shared as equals together out of our pain and disappointment as well as out of our joy and hope for our future. We dared to be vulnerable with one another. We dared to address something we had never before been encouraged to share at the seminary: the strength of our faith and our struggle to be deepened in the spiritual life. We stood spiritually naked before one another, daring to let our love of Christ and our commitment to Him be seen. It may sound crazy to the general reader who assumes that preparation for ordination includes a great deal of prayer and introspection, but seminary, or at least my experience of Bangor Seminary, was that it was intellectual prowess and one's ability to do a good turn at theological gymnastics that earned respect and the coveted degree. Any sign of what was considered overconcern with one's spiritual life was viewed as so much fluff and unnecessary baggage. Those of us who saw the states of our souls as being of paramount importance were somehow made to feel like intellectual wimps. But the ten of us, along with Andy, felt the gentle flow of the spring thaw run through our souls. Before long the other students and faculty members heard that those of us participating in this course were actually enjoying it. Soon Dr. Glick, the president of the seminary, asked if he could meet with us, and we agreed to invite him to one of our final classes.

Dr. Glick arrived at Andy's house looking a bit nervous. For once we were the ones with the upper hand. We had something that he wanted, and we knew it. We spent the first few minutes drinking coffee and engaging in small talk. Finally Dr. Glick couldn't contain himself any longer. He looked around the room at all of us, took a deep breath, and blurted out his question: "What's so different about this course? What do we have to do to make all of our courses the kinds of courses the students rave about?" This was Andy's shining moment, and the ten of us were so proud of him. One by one we tried to help Dr. Glick understand that there was no way he could control what happened in our class. Each of us took turns describing the freedom and grace we had experienced in the course together. Finally I said: "Don't you see, Dr. Glick, you can't legislate integrity and spirituality? You can't tell people that they have to share a faith they don't possess. And most important, you have to see that Andy has always been this kind of teacher, but the school wouldn't honor him for that, so he buried the very thing that we all need most, the witness of his freedom and faith." Again nothing changed, except the eleven of us who had shared that semester together. Our faith had been given the freedom to express itself. We were grateful to Andy for that gift before his departure. He had gone into the course feeling like a failure as a teacher. We encouraged him to see that he was indeed gifted but that he needed to teach what he knew best and to be given the freedom to teach it in the way he knew best. It wasn't Christian education, but spiritual development, that he needed to teach. He went on to a new school, and I hope that there he has had the opportunity and encouragement to share what he shares best—himself.

Life in a seminary is financially, emotionally, and physically draining. Seminary students often take themselves too seriously, and if, when they realize this about themselves, there is even the tiniest bit of child left in them, they are apt to act out in some of the silliest ways. Stories about the antics of former students are part of the legacy that is passed on to each new class. We were told about the students who rented a cow from a local dairy farmer and somehow managed to get the critter on the school library's flat roof. The administration couldn't figure out a way to get it down and finally had to hire a crane and crew. There was also the time that several students took apart the Old Testament professor's Volkswagen, reassembled it in the main hall of the library, and then draped all the bookstacks with toilet paper. I'm not sure how true these stories are, but they served as catalysts for new and even more bizarre pranks.

One hot July evening, during the summer break from classes, another woman student and I spent several hours in her living room sharing piña coladas and stories of woe. I'm not much of a drinker, so it didn't take too many to get me giggling and silly. I've often been accused of being too serious, so this rare opportunity to cut loose was fun. As the evening wore on, Sharon and I decided that we needed to celebrate a holiday. We spent half an hour discussing one, and Christmas won, hands down. Sharon stumbled up into her attic and brought down a box of Christmas decorations. We obviously didn't have a tree, so we decided to decorate each other. We wrapped ourselves in gold and silver garlands and hung brightly colored ornaments from the garlands, our clothes, and our hair. Soon we were ready to go out caroling! We were sober enough to realize that we should probably restrict our festivities to the seminary campus. For thirty minutes or so we walked around the small campus, singing carols at various students' and professors' doors. Everyone giggled at the sight of us, and some even joined in the caroling.

Finally Sharon suggested that we sing in front of Dr. Zeigler's door. I had never known her to crack a smile about anything. I didn't think it was a very good idea, but Sharon kept insisting that I just didn't know Dr. Zeigler the way she did. She just knew that we would receive a hearty welcome. Finally I went along with the idea. Sharon and I walked past the chapel and stood in front of Dr. Zeigler's house. I was already getting sober enough to feel a little bit foolish. We had sung the first few lines of "Silent Night" when the front light went on. I continued singing until the door was flung open and Dr. Zeigler stood staring at me with a completely unamused look in her eyes and her hands on her hips. My voice faltered. ". . . all is c-a-l-m, all is b-r-i-g-h-t." I couldn't hear Sharon's voice. I was singing alone! I looked sheepishly at Dr. Zeigler, then slowly glanced around in search of Sharon. I caught sight of a piece of silver garland caught in one of the bushes. She had made a hasty retreat and was signaling me not to call attention to her hiding place. Dr. Zeigler continued to stare at me and then quietly, in her baritone voice, which could freeze a pond in summer, said: "I've shot people for less than this, Ms. Denman. I suggest that you go home." I was no longer smiling; the giddiness and humor of the evening were completely gone. Dr. Zeigler turned, slammed her front door closed, and turned off her porch light. I stood in the darkness feeling foolish and angry. A night of harmless, simple fun had been ruined.

Graduation from seminary was a bittersweet experience: sweet because I felt that I had beaten the system by managing to graduate without losing myself in the process; bitter because I felt that I had been robbed of what could, and should, have been a wonderful learning and growing experience. For more than a few of us, graduating from seminary meant nothing more than that we had earned our "union card," our right to be ordained.

CHAPTER 6

During my last months of seminary I had been involved in the prescribed meetings and completing the required forms to be considered for ordination by the Maine Annual Conference of the United Methodist Church. Everything had gone well, and I had been approved for Deacon's Orders, a time of probation for all new ministers. The date for ordination had been set for the last day of the Annual Conference, Sunday, June 14, 1981.

The weeks between graduation from seminary and ordination were busy. I had been appointed to serve two small parishes in mid-Maine: North Anson and Madison United Methodist churches. I spent the time before ordination trying to recuperate from classes and exams, working full time, and packing for our move. Matthew dreaded the idea of living in North Anson, a town of fewer than a thousand residents. Even at his young age, he had begun to become quite the little mercenary. He couldn't understand why I would choose to invest so much time and energy and spend so much money to prepare for a career that would never be really lucrative. He was fond of reminding me that had I studied to be a doctor or lawyer, I would have been able to look forward to being "rich." To Matthew, financial gain was the only sane reason to continue education. To this day he maintains that belief and has found working with computers to be a rewarding field. He will probably always enjoy his work and make lots of money, too, therefore pleasing both of us.

My parents drove up from Rhode Island for the ordination with my aunt and uncle from Baltimore. Other aunts, uncles, cousins, and friends also made the trip. My friend Howard had offered his log cabin home for the party afterward, and women from the Orono United Methodist Church offered to make and serve a buffet dinner. It was an exciting day to anticipate and more exciting to experience.

Every year a special choir is formed for the purpose of singing at the ordination service. Some of the best voices in the conference join together under the direction of a talented choir director. The church in Farmington, where the ordination was held, houses a fine pipe organ, and the music during the service was pure ecstasy. All of us about to be ordained met in the building across the street. The ministers whom we had chosen to be our presenters for ordination were with us, helping us to vest, giving us hugs and last-minute words of welcome, and trying to keep us as calm as possible. What had taken seven or more years to achieve was commemorated in one of the most important rituals and celebrations of our lives, and our joy and excitement were mixed with fear and awe. The big question in all our minds was whether or not we could measure up to what we believed were the denomination's, God's, and our own expectations of ourselves.

The ceremony itself—who said what, what hymns were sung, what the bishop's sermon was all about—is all a blur to me, but I do remember the total and certain feeling that I had been called by God to be ordained and to minister the Christian Gospel to others. All of my life the person of Jesus Christ had been the center of my attention. The strength and perseverance to go on through years of balancing school and work and raising Matthew had come from my faith in Jesus as the one to whom I was indebted for eternal life, the one who I believed had called me to minister in His name. Now I would be a pastor and would nurture a congregation as I had always dreamed I would. When the ordination service was over, I really was a minister, His minister. I was ordained!

My first pastorate was a lesson in reality. I had always honored those who were my ministers. It never occurred to me I would be challenged at every turn, on every decision that I made as a pastor. The people of the church in Madison were a delight, and at times I thought it was they who kept me sane. It was a handful of parishioners at the church in North Anson who made me wish that I had been able to buy stock in Pepto-Bismol! I was criticized for wearing shorts while gardening on my days off. A parishioner might call to tell me that I had left my porch light on. The first time I wore my contact lenses in the pulpit, a woman stopped me on her way out of church to say that I shouldn't be so vain, that if I needed glasses to see, I should wear them. I was expected to be the minister and the minister's wife. Previous pastors had donated time working in the church's booth at the North New Portland Fair. Their wives had always donated pies. Because I was a single woman minister, somehow it seemed fair to these people that I do all the things that had customarily been done by both the pastors and their wives. After a while I began to realize why ministers hate to hear the sentence "We've always done it that way" from members of their congregations.

We settled into the parsonage and life in a small Maine town. During the day Matthew went to the local junior high school, and in the evenings he immersed himself in his computer or watching television. I busied myself with becoming acclimated to the tasks of ministry. As I worked ten- and twelve-hour days, six days a week. I quickly came to resent those people who asked, "So tell me, what do ministers do between Sundays? It must be nice to collect full-time pay for part-time work." There was always something to do, and often I found myself feeling overwhelmed. I wrote the weekly sermons and monthly newsletters; spent hours on the telephone recruiting church schoolteachers and committee members; visited with parishioners in their homes, over tea at the local restaurant, in the hospital or nursing home, and even in their offices. There were always weddings to plan as well as the three or four meetings with the couples beforehand. Ministers don't just walk into funeral parlors and do funerals. We visit with dying parishioners, sometimes for weeks before their deaths. We help our people through the anger and denial of what is happening to them. And when they die, we try to be there with their families, to bring comfort to those who have lost someone they love. We train church schoolteachers, lead Bible studies, prepare teenagers for confirmation, and run youth groups. We spend our evenings attending committee meetings, planning budgets, building strategies for fund raising, and answering the phone. The local church is not our only responsibility. We are expected to be active on the denominational level as well, to attend clergy meetings, conference board meetings, retreats, training events, and conferences on how not to get caught in burnout. In the midst of all this, we are also expected to stay informed about local and global events. A minister's life is a busy one, and no two days are ever the same. My first year as a pastor in North Anson and Madison was spent trying to learn how to balance all these responsibilities while at the same time fending off those parishioners who thought they knew how to do my job.

As the summer wore on, I began to do some digging through the old church files. What I discovered sent me into shock. I was the seventh minister in eight years. It appeared that this church was accustomed to chewing pastors up and spitting them out on a regular basis. I called my district superintendent (DS). I needed to know why the cabinet would send a newly ordained person to such a troubled church. The only answer I got from the DS was an affirmation that the North Anson Parish had a reputation of being difficult, but he knew I could handle the situation. Somehow his faith in my capabilities did not give me much comfort.

The months passed, and matters grew worse. At one point I announced to the congregation that a German colleague whom I had met the previous summer was coming through Maine on his way back to Germany. I told them he would be giving the sermon, and I hoped the congregation would welcome this minister with an open heart. Two days later one of the older women from the congregation came to my office to talk with me. She said she was delighted we would be having this minister visiting with us and wondered where he would be staying. The parsonage had four bedrooms. Matthew and I occupied two of them. I had assumed Gerhard would be staying with us. Isabelle smiled and said I was naive, that I didn't know how people would talk. She told me I needed to protect my reputation, and it would be much better if Gerhard stayed with a married couple down the street. I was affronted by her insinuations but chose to go along with her suggestion. My friend felt silly about all the fuss. After all, he was going back to Germany to see his fiancée after a year of having been away. There had never been anything between us, yet for the sake of those who might misinterpret, Gerhard stayed down the street.

Every parish has an Isabelle, and in most instances she is a harmless nuisance. Unfortunately all too many churches have at least one quite harmful member whose activities can lead to the downfall of the minister and the destruction of the congregation. This is especially true if the pastor is not a seasoned minister. In North Anson it was the choir director who was causing me the most grief and who had been the bane of previous ministers' existences. She did everything in her power to make my life miserable, and for the most part she was successful. If there is going to be any beauty and continuity in the Sunday service, the choir director and minister must work closely with each other. Usually the minister informs the choir director of the tone of the service and sermon theme, and the choir director chooses music which will enhance the overall effect. Sally would have none of this. She chose whatever music struck her fancy, regardless of the theme of the service or the season of the church year. This was most evident the Sunday I spoke on the Scripture "Not everyone who says 'Lord, Lord' will enter the kingdom of heaven. . . ." Immediately following my sermon Sally directed the choir in "When the Roll Is Called Up Yonder I'll Be There"!

The final straw came just after Easter. Tempers were getting hotter, and although I never lost my temper with a parishioner, I did my share of ranting and raving in the privacy of my home, often at Matthew's expense. I finally decided we needed the intervention of the district superintendent. Fortunately for me, we knew each other well. He was the minister under whom I had worked so well during my three years at Orono during seminary. John and I arranged for a meeting. Members of the congregation were invited to attend and were encouraged to understand that this would be a time for them to vent their complaints in a safe environment for all of us. John was to serve as mediator. About thirty people attended. I was not surprised that Sally never showed up.

John did his best to sort through the anger. One person complained that there had been too many pages in the Easter bulletin. John looked at me in confusion. He was trying to be fair. "You did staple the pages together, didn't you, Rose Mary?" I nodded that I had. The only other complaint voiced that evening was that I talked too much about Jesus Christ in my sermons and not enough about God. This time John's facial expression was a mixture of confusion and amusement. He tried to help the folks assembled to understand that sermons centered upon the person and teachings of Jesus Christ were expected. After all, we were a Christian denomination. For the first time, at this meeting, I began to understand one of the basic causes of conflict between these few members of the congregation and me. I had assumed that they understood what it is to be a Christian Church. They had been going on for years thinking that being a Christian meant belief in God but not necessarily in Jesus Christ. In conversations with my bishop, as well as with other colleagues after that meeting, I came to understand that for many United Methodists, the local church is an extension of their social lives. Belonging to the church somehow puts them into a higher status of acceptability and "good living." For many it is simply a matter of having grown up in the Church, yet never having examined what membership in the Body of Christ really means.

To be fair, there were many supporters at the meeting that night in North Anson, too. One particular woman brought tears to my eyes as she talked about my ministry with the congregation. She clearly and simply told us that until I came to North Anson, she had never really known Jesus, that I had made it possible for her to begin to have a relationship with Him. She said that she was grateful for my ministry, and I felt warmed by her gratitude.

John was stuck. I think that he had expected some really concrete issues upon which to focus in his role as mediator. Instead, he found that the major complaint was that I was doing my job as a Christian minister. John is a very gentle spirit and has never had the reputation of being a fighter of causes, but that night he surprised me with his response to those assembled at the meeting. He may have surprised himself as well. He told those present that he knew me well, that we had worked together for several years, and that he knew my ministry to be one of solid theology and strong integrity. He then looked around the room and said: "I hope the day will come when you all will look back and realize what you are throwing away in the ministry that Rose Mary is offering to you." With that he asked me to leave the room while he spoke to the group alone. I think he hoped that my absence would encourage information that was being withheld. I waited for him in the parsonage behind the church. When he walked in the door an hour later, he just shook his head. "I don't know, Rose Mary. They just don't seem to understand what you are trying to do here. I'm afraid I may not have been very much help. All I can tell you is to keep up the work you are doing and keep me posted."

Before John left, I once again broached the subject of my being appointed to another church at the Annual Conference in June. I didn't think I could handle another year of the kind of abuse I had been taking since I had arrived. His response was pretty emphatic. I wasn't doing a bad job. It would be the same for any minister appointed to this church as the pastor. He didn't think that I could get a new appointment. As he drove out of town, I felt cold and numb. Was this what being an ordained minister was all about? Is this what I had to look forward to for the rest of my working life? The possibility seemed bleak. It seemed that I would be in North Anson and Madison for at least another year.

June 1982 came, and so did the Maine Annual Conference. On the second day the bishop, George Bashore, approached me at lunch and asked if we could meet later in the afternoon. He gave no indication of the purpose of the meeting. When the agreed-upon time arrived, we sat together in a small room behind the main auditorium. He asked me to tell him what had been going on at North Anson. I tried to be fair, to both the members of the congregation and myself. There were some wonderful people there, people with whom I had begun to develop a close and loving relationship. Yet, when all hell started to break loose, they had been very direct. They were on my side, they said, but they would do nothing against those who were pushing and pulling at me. Their reason was quite simple. I would eventually leave, but they would be left to go on with life in their small New England town. They could not afford to have bad feelings between members of the congregation and themselves.

The bishop listened attentively and thoughtfully. When I finished, he looked at me and said: "No one should be treated this way. I'm going to appoint you to another church. They don't deserve to have a full-time minister. Perhaps if I send a student to them on a part-time basis for a while, they will realize what is happening to them." Just like that! I was free! The bishop gave me permission to leave the Annual Conference in order to go back to North Anson and draft a letter to the congregation. I was to leave it on the pulpit so that the lay leader could read it at the Sunday morning service. I told the bishop that I didn't want to do it that way with the people from Madison. They had been wonderful to me. We had had a small but good ministry together. I asked if I could call the lay leader of that church and tell her about the decision in person. The bishop agreed.

First I went to the parsonage in North Anson and drafted the letter. After depositing it on the pulpit, I called the lay leader from the Madison church and asked if it was all right for me to come by to talk with her. The minute I walked through the front door she threw her arms around me and began to cry.

"You left Annual Conference to come here to tell me that you're not going to be our minister anymore, haven't you?"

I nodded.

"Why, why do those people have to ruin it for us whenever we get a good minister? It's not fair. Just because we're the smaller church, we have to go along with everything that they say. It just isn't fair."

Marie and I sat close together on the couch. She and her husband were retired, yet she had worked harder for the survival of that little church in Madison than anyone. She was the glue that had held the congregation together for years. It hurt me to see her feeling so betrayed, yet I had no answers for her. Madison couldn't afford to have a full-time minister of its own. It needed to be linked with North Anson. Together they could raise the funds needed to support a minister. But unfortunately, as all too often happens when a smaller church is yoked with a larger one, Madison was paying for North Anson's problems, and there was nothing that I could do about it. Marie knew that, but it didn't make it any easier.

Two weeks later I gave my last sermon in those two little churches. Their responses to my leaving were as different as night and day. My little family at Madison had taken a collection, and after the service we had a small reception in the church parlor. Later that morning, at the service in North Anson, the lay leader came forward and pinned a corsage on my robe. I tried to smile and act as if I were happy they had given this gift to me, but as I continued with the service, it was as if the flowers were burning a hole right through to my heart. I was hurt and angry, and no corsage was going to make those feelings go away. It only served to remind me of the time when, as a teenager, I had gotten so angry with my father that I refused to speak to him for days. His way of making amends was to buy me a tennis racket. All I ever really wanted was for him to say that he was sorry. All I ever really wanted from the people of North Anson was for them to say that they were sorry, too. As soon as the service was over and I was back in the parsonage, I ran into the kitchen and threw the flowers behind the milk on the top shelf of the refrigerator. The sight and feel of their token gift made me feel sick and empty inside.

My year at North Anson had left me feeling drained. I was beginning to doubt the validity of my ministry, but I was also not willing to throw in the towel just because of one bad experience. There had been some good things that had come out of my time in that area. A wonderful friendship had developed between the superintendent of schools, Charlene Popham, and me. Charlene had joined the North Anson congregation during the winter, and she had the rare gift of being able to relate to me as both pastor and friend. When her sister died, her secretary called to tell me that Charlene had taken the first available flight but would be in touch with me later that evening. When she had had a particularly bad time with a board meeting, she would stop by the parsonage on her way home to sit over tea with me. In turn, I was not hesitant to share my own frustrations with Charlene. In many ways she was my mentor. Often, after services were over on Sunday, we drove to a lovely restaurant about forty minutes from town and spent two or three hours talking over lunch and a couple of soothing drinks. Charlene was, and still is, a woman of great inner strength. And even though she is now retired and living in Columbia, Maryland, I am grateful that we are still able to see each other once or twice each year. Our friendship is precious to me.

Another woman with whom I became friends during my year in North Anson was Winnie Weir. At the time Winnie was married to the United Methodist minister in Skowhegan. She owned and ran the Christian bookstore there, and I often stopped to buy supplies for the church. Over the weeks and months we grew close, and we maintained a strong relationship even after Matthew and I had moved away. For the next three years we were to nurture our friendship.

Three weeks after the Annual Conference ended, Matthew and I were heading for our new home and my new parish. Again I was appointed to a "two-point charge," two little churches in the towns of Howland and Alton. Because Howland was the larger of the two parishes, the parsonage was there. Alton was a half hour drive south, toward Old Town. The two congregations were very different from each other, but each had its strengths. Alton was a feisty little group of fifteen that grew to be about forty strong over our next two years together. Their greatest strengths were that they were a tight-knit family who cared for one another and that they just didn't know the meaning of failure. They always believed that if they really wanted something badly enough, they could make it happen. During my two years with them the people of the Alton United Methodist Church managed to put new siding on the church building, have new carpeting and a new ceiling installed in the sanctuary, and put a fresh coat of paint on anything that stood still. They also bought the old grange hall across the street so they could hold meetings, sales, and parties. They always kidded me about their lack of singing ability, yet they enjoyed those times when I brought my guitar to church and sang a song or two for them. They were always ready to try something new, and even when, in my clamor to see growth and progress, I initiated something that didn't work the way we all had hoped, they graciously allowed me to maintain my dignity, even with egg all over my face.

There were approximately 120 members in the Howland congregation. The little white church building housed a lovely sanctuary of dark brown and white wood. Stained-glass windows graced the two side walls, and during Sunday morning worship the sun danced through the many colors, streaming soft hues of red, green, and blue across the room. Henry, our organist, was somehow always able to make the service more special with thoughtfully chosen hymns, and our choir, although small in number, blended voice and spirit as one. There was no great turnaround of growth in Howland over my two years there, as there was in Alton. We usually filled the pews comfortably, except perhaps at Christmas and Easter, when ushers scampered around, looking for extra folding chairs. The people of Howland were hardworking and generous with their time and talents. Money always seemed to be a problem, though, and oftentimes we were late with our monthly apportionment payments to the conference, the plight of many a United Methodist church. Apportionments are the amount of monies collected from each local church which enables the conference to pay its bishop and district superintendents, maintain offices and committees, and support its mission. There was one major problem about the church in Howland being late with its apportionments. I was on what is called equitable salary. Every minister is guaranteed a minimum salary, which is based on the number of years in service to the denomination. At the time of appointment, if the parish is unable to meet the minimum salary, the conference comes to an agreement with the congregation to pay part of the salary. The part that the conference pays is called equitable salary. When I was appointed to Howland and Alton, the conference agreed to pay approximately two thousand dollars toward my salary in order to bring it up to minimum. When I arrived at this new charge, Howland was six months behind in its apportionment payments. After having been there one month, I did not receive my first equitable salary check from the conference. I waited another week or two: still nothing. Finally I called the conference treasurer. To my amazement and dismay, I was told that equitable salary checks were sent out only to those ministers whose churches were up-to-date on their apportionment payments, something the district superintendent had told neither the churches nor me.

I reported this at the next meeting of the finance committee meeting. We all were feeling frustrated and embarrassed. The committee decided to empty its accounts in an attempt to catch up on payments. By October, after I had been there a little more than three months, we were caught up. The finance committee was proud of its efforts, and I was glad that I would be receiving my equitable salary checks. Two weeks passed, and still no check from the confernece. Again I called the conference treasurer. Yes, he had received the checks from the church, but he then explained to me that I would not be receiving any of the equitable salary money from the summer months. It seemed that if a church was late with its apportionment payments to the conference, its pastor would forfeit those months' equitable salary payment. It could not be considered retroactive.

Again I went to the finance committee and told the members about the rules relayed to me by the treasurer. They sat around the table staring at me in disbelief. Everyone had worked so hard to catch up on these payments, and now they were being told that their minister would be penalized by not being paid equitable salary whenever they were late with their payments.

Things became worse after that. The people in the Howland congregation seemed to lose their will to fight. The minister before me had been a lay pastor and therefore had commanded a lower salary than I. When I had come to them in July 1982, I was an ordained deacon, and therefore, a salary hike was required. At the annual meeting in June 1982, the conference had voted to raise the minimum salary, effective in January 1983. By the time January had rolled around, Howland had decided upon a different strategy. Any additional funds that it was able to raise went to the raise in my salary, not to apportionments. That way they could be assured that I would not be penalized any further. In June 1983 I was ordained an Elder, meaning that my probationary time with the denomination had been completed. It is something like receiving tenure. With Elder's Orders came another salary increase, and Howland carried the full burden of the increase rather than allow the conference to take its percentage share. At the annual meeting of 1983 the conference had voted a hike in Elders' minimum salaries, effective January 1984, and once again, Howland chose to carry the full burden.

Four salary increases in two years was more than the church could handle, and in spite of these increases, I was still earning very little money. I had also received very few equitable salary checks from the conference in that time. The new fiscal year started in January, and each

January Howland would decide to try to keep up with the apportionment payments. The winters are cold in Maine, and oil is costly. By March or April the finance committee would realize that the oil bills were getting out of hand and would decide to pay them first. The apportionment payments would be set aside. So each year I would receive two or three months' worth of equitable salary before the congregation got behind and never really caught up again. It was a vicious circle.

In early spring of 1984 I began discussions with my district superintendent about the possibility of being moved. We talked about the fact that Howland could not keep up with my raises. I didn't think that it had been a wise move for the conference to have appointed me to that particular charge. One look at its financial situation, coupled with the realization that there would be at least three raises for the church to handle during the first two years alone, should have been enough for the cabinet not to appoint a deacon there. All dignity had been stripped from the congregation. There was no room for it to vote merit raises when it couldn't even keep up with the minimum salary raises. With the rules concerning equitable salary, the conference had chosen to make a watchdog out of the minister, penalizing him or her when the congregation could not meet its financial obligations to the conference. It was a losing battle from the beginning.

By April I was told that I would be moved at the next annual conference. I felt both sad and relieved. The relief came in knowing that I would finally be receiving a full salary. Even with the free housing that the parsonage provided, it was not enough money to raise a son and make car and student loan payments. We both had gone without necessities for so long that I needed to spend a great deal of money on clothes, shoes, coats, linens, and other basics. Both the church and I were going under financially. We needed a break.

I felt sad at the prospect of leaving Howland and Alton. Alton had been a pure joy. Its percentage of the salary responsibilities had been small enough that it had been able to keep current with its responsibilities. It had never been behind in its apportionment payments, and as the congregation grew, it was able to meet the increasing demands in its part of my salary increases. Howland, on the other hand, had been crippled from the very beginning. There were many good and faithful people in the Howland church. They tried very hard to meet their financial obligations, but the increases were just too much for them. They were surprised, and sad, when I announced that I would be leaving, but there was also relief, especially from the members of the finance committee upon whom the biggest burden had fallen. Yet they had grown wiser in our experience together and were determined not to allow the conference to appoint as their minister someone whose salary they could not fully support.

The spring of 1984 was a time of transition for the Howland and Alton churches and for me. I had been having a number of physical problems over the past three years, and my doctor and I decided we could no longer put off surgery. I was scheduled for a hysterectomy two weeks before Easter. The surgery went well, and I healed quickly. I was able to lead the Maundy Thursday and Good Friday services as well as the two Easter services. I was weak, but both the congregations and I were grateful that I was able to be there with them for those last Holy Week services together.

My friend Winnie Weir, the minister's wife in Skowhegan, had been having problems of her own. We had continued our friendship since my leaving the North Anson area, mostly by telephone and an occasional visit. She had long since confided in me that she was a lesbian. She had come to that realization when she was eighteen years old and still living with her family in New York. As a youngster she had always preferred the company of other girls, and she told me she always seemed to be having crushes on her gym teachers rather than on boys. One day her mother had accused her of being a homosexual. Winnie had no idea what that word meant, but from her mother's tone she knew that it must be something terrible. She looked up "homosexual" in the dictionary and, from what she read, decided that it was indeed not good and that she was not going to be one. She buried her feelings and set her mind to being what her parents expected. After graduating from high school, she was hired as the administrative assistant in a United Methodist church. She met Jim, and they began working together with the youth group at the church. They were married in 1966.

Jim had always wanted to be a minister, and Winnie began to live vicariously through his accomplishments. Less than two years later they were heading for the seminary in Bangor, Maine, with their few possessions in tow. Their son, Adam, was born four years later, while Jim was still in school. Winnie describes her marriage to Jim as one of few sexual encounters, but of strong and solid friendship. They truly respected each other and worked hard in whatever church Jim was appointed as minister. They saw his ministry as being "their" ministry, and Winnie was always active in the life of the congregation: acting as choir director, working with youth groups, teaching church school, and even preaching in Jim's place occasionally. It was a good life for both of them and for Adam.

Winnie had told me that there had been two occasions during which she had had short affairs with other women, hardly affairs really, because not much that was sexual ever went on between them. Yet these encounters confirmed what she had known all along, that she was a lesbian.

By the time I was in my second year in Howland and Alton, Jim and Winnie had finally faced the fact that marriage had to be more than friendship. Jim had left the ministry and was trying to begin a second career. Winnie was realizing that although the marriage was a form of security for her in one way, in another way it was smothering both of them. By the spring of 1984 they had decided to separate.

My hysterectomy was in March. In late April I was told that I would be moving to a new appointment. I met with the joint pastor/parish relations committees of the Conway and Center Conway United Methodist churches in New Hampshire and was named their new pastor. Matthew and I were scheduled to move there in July, after the Annual Conference. My doctor had told me that I should not do any heavy lifting for several months, and we were planning to move to the parsonage in Conway by U-Haul. I needed help. Winnie also needed a place to live for the summer before she began her own studies in the seminary. We made an agreement. She would move in with us for the summer and, in exchange for room and board, would do most of the packing in Howland and the major unpacking in Conway. Parishioners had volunteered at both ends to load and unload the truck. She moved in with us in May.

We had a wonderful summer together. It was good to have the consistency of adult companionship again, and because she had been a minister's wife for so many years, Winnie served as a terrific sounding board as I began my new ministry with the congregations in Conway and Center Conway. My theological and spiritual journey had resulted in my being both biblically and theologically conservative. I was also charismatic. I fully believed in the evidence of the gifts of the Holy Spirit in the individual Christian's life. I believed in prayer meetings, Bible studies, speaking in tongues, and healing services. Winnie was a dear and close friend, yet because she was a lesbian, I could not support her decision to seek ordination. Somehow I was able to accept a layperson's being a homosexual, but not a minister. I told her that if she completed the seminary and got to the point of ordination, I would stand in her way. Our denomination had held a general conference during that summer and had made the ruling on the ordination of homosexuals clear: "No self-avowed, practicing homosexual would be accepted as a candidate, ordained into ministry, or appointed by the United Methodist Church" *(The Book of Discipline)*. At the time I agreed with the new ruling wholeheartedly and used it to support my own homophobia. In the face of that kind of thinking, it's amazing that Winnie continued to be my friend.

Yet Winnie and I got along beautifully, and I believed that the growing affection I had for her was pure friendship. The two congregations loved her and accepted her presence in my life with ease and graciousness. Invitations to dinner at the homes of parish members always included Winnie, and it reached the point that people expected to see both of us at special functions held in the church. While I was out working in the parish every day, Winnie was at home unpacking, cleaning, doing the laundry, and starting dinner. On my days off, or occasionally in the afternoon or evening, we would go out for a drive in the beautiful White Mountains, which were just outside our living-room window. We spent many evenings talking together at the kitchen table. Matthew turned to Winnie as well, flourishing in her ability to sit with him and listen to his concerns about life and growing to adulthood. Life in the parsonage was peaceful, nurturing, and full. Life with the two congregations was both a challenge and a joy. From the very beginning we seemed to fit one another perfectly as pastor and people.

Around the beginning of August I began to notice that Winnie had become increasingly quiet and introspective. As we sat in the living room one evening, I decided to broach the subject and asked if there was something on her mind. At first she said that she was just concerned about whether or not she would be able to keep up with the demands of seminary life. Finally she told me the truth. She was falling in love with me.

I remember feeling both fear and curiosity, and as a self-protective mechanism, I took on the role of minister as we talked about her feelings and mine. Although Winnie recognized the fact that she was falling in love with me, she was also aware that I was not a lesbian and had no intention of making me uncomfortable by pursuing a romantic relationship with me. I affirmed the fact that I was straight and that although

I did love her, I was not in love with her. We both knew that a physical relationship between us was impossible and didn't discuss the matter again that summer.

September came all too quickly, and I was deeply saddened as I watched Winnie begin preparations to leave for the seminary in Bangor. Finally the day of her departure arrived, and we piled her things into my car. We met Jim at the airport in Portland, Maine, where he was picking up their son, Adam, who was flying home from a visit with his grandmother. As we said good-bye at the airport terminal parking lot, we hugged each other and cried. I thought my heart would break, and as I drove the hour's drive back to Conway, I knew that I needed to do a great deal of thinking and praying. Something was wrong, something that I could not name. I knew that I was going to miss Winnie desperately, much more than one woman misses another woman who is "just" a friend. When I got back to the parsonage, I was greeted by a lovely vase of flowers on the kitchen table. Winnie had arranged with the local florist to have them delivered while I was gone.

Winnie and I talked on the telephone several times a week, sometimes every night. And in my spare time I began to read some of the books that she was telling me about, books that excited and challenged her. The seminary had hired several new professors since I had been graduated, and they seemed to be blowing fresh air into the place. Winnie talked excitedly about such writers as Mary Daly, Rosemary Ruether, John Boswell, and Jean Bolen. She was being exposed to some of the best and most current feminist theology and was learning about things that I had never even heard of. I bought these books, and as I read them, I began to feel a new sense of freedom blossoming, freedom to explore and to question and to doubt.

I also chose to do another kind of reading that fall. I didn't tell Winnie about those books. I needed to do that exploring and questioning on my own. As much as I dared, I bought books on lesbian identity at the local bookstore and read them from cover to cover, hoping to find that what the writers talked about certainly did not describe me. The books on feminist theology began to free me to ask questions I would never have dared ask before, questions about the person of Jesus Christ, the absence in our history of the contributions that women had made to the formation of religion, the fact that many of our Christian rites and rituals had been stolen from other peoples, some of them matriarchal, rites which had the life and vigor torn from them and then been claimed by the Church as its own. As I read these books and began to realize just how much the Church had lied, mostly by omission, I became angry. I was beginning to feel that I had been duped, that I had chosen to follow Christ not out of what I knew but out of conditioning and ignorance. As I continued my explorations, I became fearful. I prayed that God would help me not to lose my faith. I was comforted by the knowledge that if the Church's presentation of God and Jesus Christ was truth, God would help me to recognize it as truth. I tried to be mindful of St. Augustine's words that "All truth is God's truth." And as I became less afraid to examine my own theology as well as to explore others, I also became less afraid to ask myself the most threatening question of all: "Am I really a lesbian?"

Through the early fall, life as the minister of the Conway and Center Conway congregations was full and rewarding. I began to feel comfortable with the members as I visited them in their homes and worshipped with them on Sunday mornings. They were good, honest, down-to-earth people who worked hard, enjoyed one another, and had a genuine interest in the life and well-being of the church. We came to love one another quickly, and both congregations and I flourished in an atmosphere of mutual respect and caring. For the first time in my life as a minister, I felt really OK about admitting mistakes and failures. So did my congregations. We felt safe in being ourselves with one another, and no pretenses were necessary. As I continued to explore ministry with my congregation and to explore my own theology and sexual identity on my own, some wonderful things began to happen, not the least of which was the fact that for the first time in my life I was able to go on a sensible diet without the help of a doctor or make-believe diet pills. I had lost thirty pounds after my hysterectomy, and as the year progressed, I found myself losing more weight. I felt good about my work in the church. I felt good about my self-exploration through books, prayer, and a great deal of thinking. All these good feelings seemed to be spilling over onto my feelings about my body. I began to want to be good to my body, to nurture and care for it with the same care that I had always nurtured my soul.

By mid-fall I decided that I needed help with exploring my sexual identity. I began to see a therapist. We spent only six sessions together, but they were enough to help me to begin to make some clarifications. Winnie was going to be spending Thanksgiving week with us at the parsonage, and by now I knew that I was in love with her. Yet I was still not sure whether our love needed to be expressed physically. I knew that if she was willing, I wanted to explore my sexuality with her. Deciding to explore the physical possibilities of my lesbianism was perhaps the most difficult and frightening choice I have made in my life. Nothing in my upbringing, education, or religious training had prepared me for this kind of stark honesty. Once again I held on to St. Augustine's words. If it was true that I was a lesbian, then that truth must be God's truth. There was no turning back. I had come too far. I wanted to know who I was completely, no matter what I discovered.

Winnie had gotten a ride with a friend to Mexico, Maine, a little town across the mountains about an hour's drive from Conway. I spent the week before her arrival cleaning the parsonage, planning wonderful meals, and doing as much advance church work as I could so we would be able to spend more time together. She arrived the evening before Thanksgiving, and I had targeted Sunday night as the time when I would approach her about taking our already close relationship farther. I had decided that I needed as much time as possible between Sunday services for my time of discovering. My style of preaching was to communicate with my congregation from my heart. If I was a basket case when I climbed into the pulpit, everyone would know it. If my exploration with Winnie was going to leave me with any guilt or in a state of turmoil, then at least I would have a week to get myself put back together before I had to give a sermon again.

Sunday evening arrived all to quickly. Winnie had been using the guest room since her arrival, the same room she had used all summer. As we said good-night, I was afraid I would not have the courage to raise the subject. I was lying in bed as she passed the doorway on her way from the bathroom.

"Winnie, are you OK?"

"Yup, why do you ask?"

"Just wondering. Are you tired?"

"Not particularly. Why? Do you want to talk?"

"No, but would you give me a back rub?"

"Sure."

I loved back rubs, and Winnie knew that. It didn't seem at all unusual that I would ask her for one. As her hands rubbed the oil into my skin, I lay there wondering how to broach the subject with her. I hadn't thought to rehearse the moment, and there didn't seem to be a particularly casual way to handle it. What was I supposed to say? "Hey,

Winnie, how would you like to make love to me?" At this point she still thought that I was convinced I was straight.

After a half hour or so the back rub was finished, and Winnie prepared to go back to her room. We said good-night, and she went back into the bathroom to wash the oil off her hands. As she shut off the light and headed down the hall, I called to her. "Winnie, would you like to sleep in here with me tonight? I really don't feel like being alone."

I could sense her surprise, and the few seconds of silence seemed to last an eternity. She didn't answer me in words. Instead, she walked into my room, took off her nightgown, and slid under the covers on the other side of my bed. There were a few awkward moments until I reached over and put my hand on her shoulder.

"Winnie, I'm scared, but I need to know who I am. Will you help me?"

"Are you sure?"

"I'm nervous, but I'm sure that I need at least to try. But let's go slowly, and please, if I get too scared, I need to be able to say we have to stop."

It wasn't physical pain, or the idea that my growing love for Winnie was bizarre, or even the fear that people would think terrible things about me if they knew that frightened me. What had caused me to lie awake for so many nights during the past months and had fired in me a need to read as much as I could on the subject was the fear of losing God's blessing in my life and my own self-respect. Those were the two most important things. I knew that God would never condemn me for doing whatever it took to know and understand myself. It would be what I did with the knowing and understanding for which God would judge me.

Winnie lay on the bed facing me as she gently stroked my arms and neck and face. Her touch was soft and reassuring, and slowly I was able to relax. We were beginning to say with our bodies what we had been feeling with increasing intensity in our hearts and souls. It felt so right for us to be holding and caressing and loving each other, and as our experiencing of each other's bodies continued and grew more bold, I began to weep.

"What's wrong?"

"Nothing's wrong. Everything is right. I feel as though I'm having a birthday. Thirty-seven years old, and I'm being born."

She held me close as I shed tears of joy and relief for having finally discovered such a huge part of the puzzle of who I was, and through the tears we continued to hold each other and to reverence the gift that God had given us in each other. I felt like a giddy child as a whole new and wonderful world unfolded before me, and as it did, I sensed God smiling. "Ah, you've finally figured out who I created you to be."

The next days flew by as Winnie and I shared more deeply in each other's lives. We took delight in exploring the newness of warm curves and sweet scents as our bodies familiarized themselves to our closeness. Our hearts and souls touched in a different, closer way as well, and these new experiences of each other quickened our love. On the following Sunday, the day that Winnie was due to go back to the seminary, I led worship at my two little churches with new understanding of the word "love." It wasn't more difficult to speak about the love of God because of what Winnie and I had experienced together, but easier, for I was experiencing God's love through her, and it seemed that God was spending a lot of time smiling at me lately.

Later that afternoon I drove Winnie back to Mexico, Maine, where she would be meeting her friend from the seminary. We had decided that she would spend every long weekend and holiday in Conway with me and that I would get up to Bangor as often as I could. We had compared schedules, and our longest separation would be four weeks. My heart was heavy as I drove back to the parsonage alone. Now that our love for each other had taken on a whole new dimension, I would miss her even more than before.

For the next two months when we couldn't be together, we were on the telephone. We wrote each other every day, and still, we seemed never to run out of things to say to each other. We were excited about life and our love, and the future stretched before us full of possibilities for our life together.

I had become close friends with the American Baptist minister in Madison, New Hampshire, one town west of Conway. Linda and I had met at one of the monthly ecumenical clergy gatherings, and being the only two women clergy in the area, we had automatically gravitated toward each other. Linda had been the pastor of the Baptist church in Madison for four years. Her husband, David, also clergy, had decided to take time off from parish ministry to be a full-time daddy to their son, Jonathan. I had quickly come to cherish my friendship with Linda and her family and wondered if it could stand the test of her knowing about my relationship with Winnie. Two weeks after Thanksgiving I asked

Linda to join me for lunch at a local restaurant. I had decided to tell her about my discovery. As we talked over lunch, Linda sensed that I was nervous. When I finally blurted it out, she reached across the table, took my hand, and smiled at me. "Oh, Rose Mary, were you afraid that I would be mad at you if you told me about you and Winnie?"

"Yes. I guess I felt that because you're a Baptist, you might not understand or approve, that you might think that you couldn't be friends with me anymore."

"Rose Mary, I love you because of who you are. It doesn't matter to me. I think it's great that you and Winnie love each other. God knows there's certainly a shortage of that around these days. People kill and hurt each other every day. Isn't it nice when you see people loving each other for a change?"

Tears of joy were welling up in my eyes, and Linda gave my hand a little squeeze for emphasis. "Come on, kid, you've worried about this enough. Now knock it off and let's have lunch."

I was so grateful for Linda and her warm and understanding heart. We talked about Winnie and our relationship for a while, and then I asked her if she knew any lesbians in the area. She said she didn't but added that she knew how to locate some. She knew a woman therapist who had several lesbians as clients and would call her later that afternoon. As we left the restaurant, Linda and I hugged, and I knew I had a wonderful friend in this woman. That evening she called to say she had spoken to her friend, who was going to contact a couple of her clients to ask if they would call me. Even with my need to be careful about who knew about Winnie and me, I hoped we could find other lesbians in Conway with whom to be friends. It was important to know other women with whom I could share this part of my life, a part that I could not share with any of my parishioners.

Winnie and I saw each other as much as possible. Between our times together she was busy with classes, writing papers, and making new friends at the seminary. I was busy with my work in the parish, and except for the fact that we didn't have as much time together as we would have liked, we both felt that our lives were good and full. Matthew seemed to be settling into his new school and was even talking about finding a part-time job.

A week after our lunch I received a phone call from a woman who said that she had been asked to contact me. She said that she was a friend of Linda's, the signal we had decided to use. She asked if I would like to meet her and her partner the following weekend. I was thrilled. Winnie was coming for a three-day visit, so we would be able to meet the couple together. Terry asked us to meet them on Saturday at her mother's house, where she and her partner had been building a garage.

Saturday came, and in the afternoon Winnie and I set out in the car with Winnie reading the directions while I drove. We were excited and nervous. We hoped that we would like the two women and that they would like us as well. It wasn't hard to find the house. We pulled up the long gravel driveway and, as we pulled to a stop, noticed three women standing near a half-built carport. They waved to us, and we waved back as we got out of the car. As the five of us walked toward one another, I drew a sharp breath. I knew one of them, the oldest. My heart raced, and I wanted to run back to the car and drive away as fast as I could. Winnie heard my gasp and whispered, "What's the matter?"

"I know that older one."

"Oh, God. What do you want to do now?"

"It's too late. She's already seen me."

We kept walking toward the three women. The older one was smiling at me. The two younger ones were looking back and forth at us, wondering what was going on.

"Hi, Louise."

"Hi, Rose Mary, how are you?"

"OK, I guess. I didn't expect to see anyone I knew today."

"Don't worry, Rose Mary. You're safe here. I want you to meet my daughter and her lover."

I began to breathe again as introductions were made and we headed into the house. We talked and laughed as Louise and I filled everyone in on our exchange in the yard. It was comfortable and good to be sitting in this cozy house with these other women. It was even better to watch a mother and daughter so easy in their exchanges with each other. As I watched them, I wondered if my own mother would be able to take my relationship with Winnie in the kind of easy stride with which Louise accepted her daughter and lover. After dinner, and a game of Trivial Pursuit that Winnie and I lost miserably, we ended our visit with our new friends. As we drove home that evening, we both felt blessed and full of good feelings. Life was wonderful.

Over the next weeks I continued to read books on feminist theology and lesbian issues. I grew increasingly frustrated and angry. More and more I began to realize that the Church had treated me like a little child, had told me only what it felt was safe for me to know. There wasn't only one right way to know God, but many, and they were all right. There were many names for God—Great Spirit, Mother Earth, Ground of Being, the Source, Our Higher Power, the Universe—and they all were good. I began to realize that the Church had lied because the patriarchy was afraid that if I, and others, really knew the truth, we would leave. They were right. The more I read, the more I thought; and the more I prayed, the more I realized that I had been held captive in a benevolent prison that I had helped create out of my own ignorance and willingness to please. It became increasingly difficult for me to plan sermons that felt whole and integrated yet also stayed in line with Christian theology. Slowly I began to see more clearly that the Jesus of the Bible, the Jesus with whom I was in relationship, was nothing like the Jesus the Church had presented to me. My reading was beginning to change my concept of the person of Jesus, and as He became more human to me, as He was stripped of all the mythological hocus-pocus the Church had superimposed upon Him, His life had more to say to my life. His integrity spoke to mine. His humanity challenged the possibilities of my humanness. It was a brand-new love affair but one I didn't think I could readily share with my congregation.

Being a minister in the United Methodist Church became more and more difficult as I tried to integrate my new understanding of the spiritual in my life. What I preached from the pulpit every Sunday was the very stuff that had come out of my life, and now, in order to be able to parrot the Church's interpretation of the person of God and Jesus, I was having to compromise what I was learning and knowing in my reading and experiencing of God. By the end of December I had made my decision. I called my district superintendent and told him that I wanted to take a leave of absence from parish ministry beginning in July of the next year. I wanted to finish out the year with my congregations before I left them. I did not know whether or not my decision to take a leave of absence meant that I would never be a parish minister again. I just knew that I needed time to integrate my new discoveries.

Winnie had already decided that much as she loved her life at the seminary, her first semester would be her last. Being a practical person, she had decided that she didn't want to put enormous time, effort, and money into preparing for a ministry that the Church would not allow her to have if they knew she was a lesbian. Until recently she had lived all her life in denial of her sexual orientation. She had tried to push that consciousness deep down inside herself when she had married Jim, and all it had brought her was fragmentation and a deep sorrow. She knew that she never wanted to live that way again. When I called Winnie to tell her about my decision to take a leave of absence, she became worried and upset. I think at first she thought I was making the decision to leave parish ministry because of our relationship. That may have been a part of it, but more important was the realization that I could not bury my own theological and spiritual discoveries just to be safe in my job with the denomination. It took awhile, but I finally convinced Winnie I would never leave the ministry "just" because of her and our relationship. It was a decision that I was making for me.

Winnie was planning to spend her two-week Christmas break with me in Conway. We spent a lot of time on the telephone discussing what we wanted to do and talk about while she was there. There was only one small problem: The small ecumenical clergy group, of which I was a member, was planning a Christmas party, which included dinner at one of the lovely inns in the area. The other clergy were planning to bring their wives, and I had already been asked if I was going to bring a boyfriend. There were eight of us, and a Roman Catholic sister and I were the only women in the group. I had not spoken of my relationship with Winnie with the group. I was afraid of placing my congregations and myself in a very embarrassing situation. On the other hand, strict confidentiality had been established among the members of the group because we discussed many delicate personal and professional matters with one another. Others in our group had been very vulnerable, sharing both personal and parish struggles. Two weeks before the party the leader of the group, Dick Wilcox, minister of the Congregational church across the street from mine, started to banter with me about who I would be taking to the Christmas party. The other members of the group grinned at us as I blushed and tried avoid answering Dick's question.

"Come on, Rose Mary, are you going to bring a boyfriend to the party?"

Dick was enjoying the fun. It was the Catholic sister who helped out. "Dick, why does Rose Mary have to bring a boyfriend? Maybe she wants to bring a woman with her to the party."

"Hey, I don't care. She can bring anybody she wants. Why do you want to bring a woman with you, Rose Mary?"

I decided to be vulnerable to my colleagues. I told them that I was afraid to hand them such potentially damaging information about myself, but as I continued, each member of the group affirmed me and my relationship with Winnie and also helped me understand that they took our covenant of confidentiality very seriously. I brought Winnie to the Christmas party, and we had a wonderful time together. Over the next months this group was to become a great support to me when I told the congregations that I would be leaving them at the end of the church year. I will always be grateful for the love and support that they offered us during such a difficult time.

Winnie finished the semester at the seminary, and on January 25, 1985, I drove up to the campus to take her back to Conway with me. Our whole lives stretched before us as we drove south on the highway. We held hands, grinned at each other like two lovesick teenagers, and talked about the decisions that we were facing. We knew that we would be moving away from the Conway area the following June but had not, as yet, decided where to live. Being methodical, I had bought a large posterboard and put my name and Winnie's on the top. Along the sides I had made a list of categories important to each of us: social, spiritual, emotional, intellectual, geographical, family, job, and cultural needs. My plan was that each of us would spend some time thinking about what her personal needs were in these areas, place them on the chart, and compare them, and after assessing our needs, we would decide where we would live. Winnie wanted to be close to her son, Adam, who was living with his father in Skowhegan. It was important for me to live near the ocean. We both liked New England, and it was important to us that we each be able to find fulfilling and good-paying work. We wanted some cultural outlets available to us and hoped that we would be able to find a spiritual community open to our growing eclectic taste as well as our lesbian relationship. It was a tall order, and at first, as we looked at our completed chart, we thought that perhaps we were asking for too much. By February we had come up with what we thought was the perfect solution, Portland, Maine.

After she had moved into the parsonage, we spent the first couple of weeks rearranging the house to accommodate Winnie's belongings. It was important to both of us that she feel the parsonage was her home, too, not that she was a guest. Matthew and I had been involved in family therapy for several months, and now Winnie and I wanted to tell Matthew about our relationship. I spoke to our therapist about Winnie and suggested that the following session would be a good time for me to tell Matthew. He agreed.

Matthew was sixteen years old at the time, and I worried that it would be difficult for him to accept the fact that his mother was a lesbian. Yet regardless of the risks, I knew it was important he know. We needed to be a family, and I hoped Matthew would feel that way, too. We met with the therapist, who explained to Matthew that I had something very important to tell him. Matthew stared at me, and tears began to well up in his eyes.

"You're going to tell me that you're dying, aren't you?"

"No, Matthew, it's nothing like that."

"Well, then it's Nanna or Grampa, right? Something's wrong with one of them."

"No, Nanna and Grampa are fine, too."

"Then what is it, me? Am I gonna die or something?"

"No, Matthew, you're fine."

"Are you sure? I mean, everybody is OK? Nobody's going to die or anything?"

"No, everybody is OK, I'm sure. I want you to know about something that I've discovered about myself, Matthew. You know that Winnie and I are close and that we care about each other a lot."

"Yeah, I know that, so what?"

"Well, we've discovered that we love each other very much. I'm a lesbian, Matthew, and I want to spend the rest of my life with Winnie. Do you know what a lesbian is?"

"Yeah, I think so. It's a woman who's a homosexual, who makes love to another woman, right?"

"Yes, that's part of what it means to be a lesbian. How do you feel about that?"

"Well, I don't care. You're still my mother, right?"

"Yes."

"And Winnie's going to live with us all the time now?"

"Yes. How do you feel about that?"

"Is she supposed to be like my father or something?"

"No, Matthew. But she is an adult who will be a part of our family, and I will expect you to respect her."

"Yeah, she's nice enough. I guess that's OK."

"Do you have any questions, Matthew?"

"Just one. Is homosexuality hereditary? I mean, I like girls, and I don't want that to change."

I chuckled. "No, Matthew. I don't think it's hereditary. If you like girls now, you will probably always like girls."

"OK, as long as that doesn't change. It's your life, and you have a right to do what you want. As long as you're happy—does this make you happy, Ma?"

"Yes. It makes me very happy, Matthew."

"So that's what this was all about? Did you think that I would fall apart or something like that?"

The rest of the session was spent with the therapist and me making sure that Matthew understood and really was comfortable with what I had told him. By the end of the hour we were convinced. Matthew was a terrific kid, and I was proud and grateful for the way he had responded. When we got back to the parsonage, Winnie was waiting for us in the kitchen. I could tell she was anxious to know how our session had gone.

"So, Matt, everything OK?"

"Yeah, why? Did you think that I would have a fit or something?"

"No. I just wondered how you were feeling."

"Hey, I'm OK. It's no big deal. Is it supposed to be?"

"No, not to us. It's just that for some people it is a big deal, that's all."

Over the next few months we settled into a routine with a certain degree of ease. Matthew tested both Winnie and me to see how the situation would affect who had the authority in the house. He soon discovered that things really hadn't changed much and that Winnie wouldn't let him get away with any more than I would. He also started asking more questions about what it meant for me to be a lesbian. He was afraid that I had turned to Winnie out of loneliness because his father and I had been divorced for more than fourteen years by then. Once I convinced him that Winnie was not a fill-in until the right man came along, Matthew decided that everything was quite all right. He was happy about moving to Portland; the years we had spend living in small towns were hard on him. He made no bones about the fact that he hated them. He'd always made it clear that when he was old enough, he was planning to move to a big city. Three years later, after having gone to the University of Southern Maine in Portland for one year, Matthew and a friend drove off to Los Angeles and the fulfillment of their dreams. Four months later he moved to Arizona, where he lives with my mother, attends the university there, and has a job working with computers. I think that's great. We all need to search out our dreams.

By March I had told the lay leader of the Conway church I would be leaving at the end of June. George was a sweet, fatherly man who always had a smile on his face and a word of encouragement on his lips. He and his wife, Ruth, are wonderful people, and I had come to love and respect them a great deal. George was visibly upset when I told him the news and wanted to know what the church had done to make me want to leave. I'm not sure that I was ever able to convince him that the church had done nothing wrong. I couldn't tell him, or anyone else, my real reasons for leaving. It wouldn't have been fair for me to tell them about Winnie and me. The denomination had its rules, and a minister was appointed to a church by the bishop. In most cases neither the minister nor the congregation has much more than a cursory say in how appointments are made. For me to have told the congregations about my relationship with Winnie would have placed them in the awkward position of having to choose between me and the denomination. I didn't think that a local congregation was an appropriate battleground for that kind of issue. I also felt it was inappropriate to share my spiritual, theological, or biblical dilemmas with the congregations. They were my own personal concerns, and even though I was in turmoil, I needn't drag them into it. No, I needed to leave parish ministry, and I saw it as my responsibility to make my leaving as easy and graceful for the people in my churches as possible. So, whenever George came to the parsonage "just one more time to try to talk you out of this," I would stick to the same story. I was leaving because I needed time to think about my changing theology, as was partly true, and to think about whether or not parish ministry was right for me, as was also true. George never really bought my reasons for leaving. He lost no opportunity to tell me that I was their minister, that I should stay with them, and right up until a month before I was due to leave, George insisted that it wasn't too late. Even though another minister had already been appointed and was due to move in only days after we left, George insisted we could make it work so I could stay. I need only say the word, and he would make it happen. It saddened me to hear the pain and confusion in George's voice. He and Ruth were convinced that I was making a mistake. When I told my congregations that I would be leaving, many of them joined George and Ruth in trying to convince me to stay. They encouraged me to believe that I did belong in ministry, that I did belong with them. As they told me these things, I wondered: *Would you feel the same way if you knew?*

There were many people in the two congregations whom I would miss.

They had proved to be wonderful people, full of love, compassion, and genuine caring for those in the community who were in need. Any minister fortunate enough to be appointed their pastor would be very lucky indeed. Two other people who had become very dear to me were Michelle and Frank. They were a young couple in their mid-twenties who had been married three or four years when I met them. They started to attend the Conway church shortly after I arrived and by winter had become members. Frank was a native of the area and had met Michelle in Florida. She had a rare heart disease for which there was no cure. When she was born, her parents were told that she would die before she was ten years old. When she reached puberty, the doctors said that she would not live to graduate from high school. Michelle proved them wrong every time, but by the time I came to know her, her heart had grown weak to the point that she could not do even the lightest work. Frank worked two jobs just to keep up with living expenses, Michelle's medical insurance, and her hospital and medication bills not covered by insurance.

Yet they were a happy couple, happier than many couples I have met who have far fewer obstacles in their lives than they. I visited Michelle often and most times left her home with a lighter heart and a smile on my face. She was full of stories, most of which were either extremely funny or deeply touching.

The one I remember most vividly as a demonstration of Michelle's gift of compassion is about an old blind woman she had taken care of before she got too sick to work. Frank would take Michelle to the woman's house in the morning on his way to work. She was responsible for bathing and dressing the woman in the morning, getting her meals, and entertaining her until the woman's daughter got home from work in the evening. Michelle told me how she tried to help the woman recapture experiences from her childhood. They sang old childhood songs together, and Michelle read stories to her. In the summer Michelle picked wild flowers, and the woman tried to identify them by smell and touch. In the fall Michelle brought in a paper bag full of colorful dried leaves and pinecones and described the colors to her charge as they felt the crispness of the leaves and the ridges of the pinecones. In the winter Michelle put newspapers on the kitchen table, covered them with plastic sheeting, and brought in a bucket of snow. She and the old woman sat for an hour making a miniature snowman. And in the spring they made mud pies at the same kitchen table as they mushed the cool, slippery substance through their fingers. I wept as Michelle told me about her year with this blind woman. I thought of the countless old people I had seen over the years in nursing homes, and I wished they could known someone like Michelle.

Michelle was also fond of telling stories about Frank's and her courtship and marriage. On the night he proposed—Valentine's Day—Frank had saved up enough money to splurge. He bought a red velvet dress and shoes for Michelle and left them with a note asking her to put them on and be ready to go out by six o'clock. At six a driver arrived at her door and escorted her to a limousine. The driver took her to the fanciest restaurant in town, where she met Frank, dressed in a tuxedo and holding a corsage. After dinner and dancing, the driver took them up into the mountains, where Frank proposed to Michelle, producing a small diamond engagement ring wrapped in colorful foil and nestled in a box of chocolates. They made a champagne toast and dreamed of their future all the way home. Frank knew that they would never have what some people would call "a normal life." He knew that Michelle would probably die at a very young age. But he loved her, and she loved him, and together they were determined that whatever years they did have would not be wasted. They had too much love for that.

In spite of their situation, perhaps the greatest sadness in their life together was that they could not have children because Michelle's heart was too weak to tolerate a pregnancy. They took every precaution to be sure that she did not conceive. Michelle was seldom depressed, but when she was, it was usually because she wanted a child so badly. One afternoon she called to tell me that a friend was pregnant with her third child. Her friend was not married and had decided to have an abortion unless Frank and Michelle would adopt the baby when it was born. As much as the possibility excited Michelle, she was in tears. Even this arrangement would cost two thousand dollars for the attorney's fees and the investigation required by the state. Being this close to having a child of her own, yet knowing that she and Frank couldn't afford to make it happen, caused more pain than if the possibility had never presented itself. I told her to hang on and give me some time to do some investigating. I asked her to trust me and not to worry.

It took much less work than I would ever have imagined. I called the only woman lawyer in town, whom I had not even met. I explained the situation to her and asked if she would take the case *pro bono* (for free). She immediately agreed to represent Frank and Michelle in the adoption. Then I called the state office and asked what its requirements were and how much the investigation would cost. Once I had the figures, I began calling key people in the congregation to ask them to make a donation toward the amount we needed. Within two hours I had raised all the money, with a little left over. Winnie and I walked over to Frank and Michelle's house to tell them the good news. The four of us sat at their kitchen table and cried tears of joy together. Their church family was making it possible for them to have their baby!

Little Richard was born that next summer, after Winnie and I had left Conway and moved to Portland. Michelle was able to spend the last month of her friend's pregnancy with her and accompanied her to the hospital when it was time for Richard to be born. She was at the foot of the delivery table at the moment of his birth when her longed-for little baby was delivered right into her arms. Her friend went home from the hospital the next day, but the hospital allowed Michelle to stayed until it was time for Richard to leave, too. Three days after Richard's birth Frank, Michelle, and Richard drove home from the hospital to begin their lives together. Several weeks later Winnie and I drove back to Conway so that I could assist at Richard's baptism. It was only later Michelle told us she and Frank had made two requests of their new pastor: that I be allowed to perform the baptism myself and that Winnie and I be named Richard's godparents. They were refused both requests because by then their pastor knew I was a lesbian. In light of the fact, he said he did not think it at all appropriate that he grant either of their requests. Frank and Michelle didn't argue, but they refused to name any other godparents. After the service they told us that as far as they were concerned, Winnie and I were Richard's godparents. We were proud and honored to be chosen.

Leaving the Conway and Center Conway congregations was difficult. A few weeks before our departure we told a few select members of the congregation in Conway about Winnie and me. In each case their response was the same: "You mean that's why you're leaving? That's crazy. What difference does it make?" I would then mention the names of a few other members of the congregation, those known for being particularly conservative, and asked if they thought that these folks would have responded as they had. In each case the person shook his or her head and said, "No, you're right. He [or she] would not have understood, but it's too bad. We're all losing because of it. Being a lesbian doesn't make you any better or worse a minister. It just makes you you."

My last Sunday in the pulpits of my churches was an emotional one for my congregation and for me. My sermon was short. I couldn't keep the lump out of my throat or the tears from my eyes. It really wasn't a sermon anyway. I used the occasion to thank the congregations for all that they had meant to me in my role as their pastor. I encouraged them to look to their future and know that because of the blessings they had given to the lives of others, they, too, would be richly blessed. By the time the services were over, both the congregation and I were spent. My sadness in leaving them took a long time to disappear, and I think that was good. It would have been wrong not to have allowed the sadness to wash over me. It brought cleansing and new life.

CHAPTER 7

During my last two months as pastor in Conway and Center Conway, Winnie and I had been spending my day off driving into Portland to look at apartments. She had been a minister's wife for eighteen years, and I had been living in either seminary housing or parsonages for seven years. Neither of us had had to pay rent in all that time, and we both were shocked by the prices of decent places to live. We looked at one small, dingy apartment after another until we began to think there was nothing available that was both affordable and attractive. Finally, two weeks before we were scheduled to move, we found a lovely five-room apartment just a mile out of town. It was clean, neat, bright, and perfect for our needs. It occupied the second and third floors of a two-family house. The third-floor attic had been made into a loft bedroom with two skylights, and we decided immediately that the loft was going to be our room.

On moving day Winnie and I headed for our new home, experiencing a mixture of excitement and fear. Neither of us had gotten a job yet, and we didn't have much money. We would spend the weekend unpacking and on Monday morning would begin looking for work. We felt we could find good jobs. I had a lot of education and experience behind me and was hoping to find something in the area of personnel. Winnie had done some pretty high-level volunteer work over the years. She had single-handedly established and run a large food cupboard in the town of Skowhegan, which started with loaves of bread and pastries donated by a national baked goods distributor. Two years later her garage was filled with frozen, canned, and baked foods which were distributed to the poor twice a week. We had valuable skills that would command good salaries. We had spent months dreaming about our future together, and now our future was here.

Our first day in Portland was a rude awakening for both of us, the first of many such awakenings. This may sound strange to those who have never experienced parsonage living, but our first shock was in walking into an empty apartment, listening to the silence, and looking at the emptiness. Over the years we had each moved into new parsonages several times. It was always the same. Members of the new congregation were always there to greet us with smiling faces, waiting to help unload the moving van. There were flowers on the kitchen counter and casseroles in the refrigerator. With every move there was a ready-made community of new friends awaiting our arrival. In small towns such as the ones in which Winnie and I had lived, it was not unusual for the whole community to know we were the new parsonage family weeks before we arrived. Our move to Portland was different. Life was going on outside our new apartment door as usual, and no one knew, or cared, that we had arrived. There were no casseroles or flowers, no notes of greeting, and no phone ringing with a friendly voice on the other end to welcome us into the community. It was a cold and isolating experience for both of us, and we felt it keenly. For the first time I began to realize how dependent that life-style can make a person. I had been in the system for only seven years and I wondered how much more difficult it must be for those who retire from the ministry after having spent forty or more years in that kind of dependency. Years of not having to find a house to live in, not having to worry about rent or mortgage payments, not needing to consider heat or electric bills, and not needing to be concerned about where one will find new friends leave a person with few resources.

Monday morning came quickly. Winnie and I had spent much of Sunday scouring the want ads. I had also decided to stop in at one of the professional placement offices to see what it could do for me. We left that first morning full of excitement and anticipation. We returned home that evening feeling depressed and deflated. No one was impressed by all the volunteer work Winnie had done over the years. She had not been offered one job. I, too, had had a dismal experience. Companies want employees with previous experience in the precise area for which they are hiring. The fact that I had graduate-level education in counseling and had pastored several churches, thus proving my personnel skills, did not interest the interviewers. Personnel work requires that the individual be familiar with the red tape involved in insurance forms and workers' compensation. Interpersonal skills did not reach the top of the list of desired qualities. It was depressing to realize that employers place little value upon the person of the employee. The big business of making money is all that counts. Meeting with the representative of the professional placement office was no less disillusioning. It seemed that I had nothing marketable to offer. It's damned near impossible to convince prospective employers that ministers have skills that can be easily translated into the marketplace.

Winnie and I sent out copies of our résumés and went to interviews for two weeks without a nibble. We both were discouraged. We were also broke. As the days wore on, I realized I would need to take the first job I was offered, no matter what it was. After I had been working for a while and we had gotten on our feet financially, I could begin to concentrate on getting a really good position. In the meantime, we needed to worry about the rent!

My first job was as the assistant manager of a women's clothing store. Five days a week, eight hours a day I rang up purchases on a cash register and straightened out racks of clothes. At the end of each day it was my responsibility to close the register, prepare the night deposit, and put the bag of cash and checks into the box at the bank on my way home.

I believe that everything happens to us for a reason, that there is something for us to learn from all the events of our lives. What I learned most from my job at the clothing store was that life requires both humility and a sense of humor. It was a boring job, but I never really hated it until someone I had known when I was a pastor came into the store. Whenever that happened, I felt a sense of failure and always made sure that during the course of the conversation the other person knew I was the assistant manager. Even as I did this, I realized how silly it was. Deep down, I knew that my success or failure as a person had nothing to do with what kind of job I had, yet it was almost as if there was a war going on inside myself. Part of me was happy with Winnie and our new life together, and my work didn't matter. Another part of me felt that unless I had a really important job of which I could be proud, I was a failure. It was as if I could hear the voices of my father, the nuns from St. Margaret's, and all the kids in my class from grade school shouting in unison: "See, you can never really amount to anything. We always knew you were a fake."

The situation grew worse as we realized that my salary would not be enough to pay the bills and meet the rent payment, which was due in two weeks. As my sense of failure and frustration mounted, I took it out on Winnie. She still hadn't found a job, and in my anger I blamed her for our dismal financial situation. The only solution was to go to the city welfare office and ask for help with the rent. I hadn't been in that kind of situation for years, and the sense of being a failure grew as I surveyed our predicament.

The next morning we visited the welfare agency. The outside door led directly into a long, narrow hall where people were already in line, waiting to talk with a woman who sat behind a protective wire mesh. As I stood there, I remembered all the times that I had sent parishioners or needy townspeople to the local welfare office for help. I had never been in such a dirty, smelly hellhole in my life, and as we continued to stand in line, it was as if the very walls were closing in around me. I felt that I would suffocate if I did not get out into the fresh air. I looked up at Winnie through eyes that were clouding over with tears. "I've got to get out of here. I can't stand this anymore." I walked down the long corridor as fast as I could and didn't take a breath until I was out the doors. Racing to the car, I shouted at Winnie like a madwoman: "I can't stand this life. I hate it. I'm not like them. I refuse to stand there talking to a woman who is behind a wire screen in order to be protected from me! How can they treat people that way? It smelled in there. I won't do this, Winnie, I just won't. There has to be another way."

We drove home in silence. The air was thick with my anger and our joint sense of fear and helplessness. Later, after I had calmed down, I began to realize that like it or not, we were going to have to ask for help. I called the central office of social welfare in Portland and asked to speak to the supervisor. I tried to be coherent and businesslike as I explained our situation, but early in the conversation I began to cry as I sought to help her understand what a humiliating experience we had earlier in the morning. She asked if we would come back the next day and assured me that we could have an appointment time, go into an office, sit across a desk from someone, and receive the help we needed with as little embarrassment as possible. She was offering us a life preserver, and I grabbed on to it with as much gratitude as I have ever felt about any gift I have received.

We got help with the rent, plus a one-week food voucher. We were temporarily out of trouble. The next day Winnie signed up with a temporary employment agency in town and was sent on a long-term assignment right away. Our jobs weren't great, but at least they were paying the bills.

Our first year in Portland was difficult for us. There seemed to be so many adjustments to make. Winnie's temporary job landed her a full-time permanent position as a printer in the same company. She had known absolutely nothing about printing, but over the few months there, had hung around the printshop as much as she could and had picked up some tips from the man who had been running the machinery. When he suddenly quit his job, Winnie asked to be given a chance to prove she could handle the position. The first thing she did was call the company which serviced the printer and ask one of its representatives to help her become more familiar with her new responsibilities. It didn't take long before she knew how to make the printer do everything it was ever meant to do, and sometimes more. She had found a new skill and was enjoying it. She works for a different firm now but is doing the same kind of work. Winnie is supervisor of the printing department and receives a respectable salary and good benefits. It has been a long and hard battle, but she is winning!

I stayed at the women's clothing store for six months until I landed a good part-time job doing behavioral education classes for a weight-loss clinic. Getting the job was important to me for two major reasons: First, I had been trying to get into good eating habits and had lost a total of seventy pounds. Being hired for the position was an affirmation of my success in learning to live a healthier life-style. Also, it paid well enough for part-time work nearly to match what I had been making at the clothing store working full time. I had decided that I wanted to be self-employed. Now I would have time and energy to build a small part-time private practice in counseling. I also wanted to begin leading retreat and workshop weekends for women. This was my opportunity. Working for myself was a way out of constant financial stress as well as doing what I love to do most. Since then I have continued to work on this dream.

CHAPTER 8

When Winnie and I first moved to Portland, we were in a state that can only be described as religion burnout. By then I had spent nearly a year reading everything I could about feminist theology. I felt that I had been lied to, robbed, and spiritually raped by the Church. After ten years of college, graduate school, and seminary education, it was as though I had wasted my time, energy, and spirit, not to speak of the thousands of dollars it had cost. I had been conditioned to carry on the legacy of a patriarchal system which held women and other "minorities" docile captives. My anger at the Church was coupled with feelings of depression and defeat. How would I ever be able to sift through all the lies and deceit in order to discover a healthy spirituality? Early in my reading I had tried to change my language about God, calling God "Mother." It didn't work for me. It wasn't real or authentic, more like putting a dress on Father God. It was as though I were trying to put clean clothes on a dirty god, a god who had been smudged and soiled by centuries of patriarchal dirt and grime. Not having the emotional energy to cope with it all, I put religion, and God, on the back burner. I knew I could not attend a United Methodist church. Between the lies of all patriarchal religions and the stance of the United Methodist Church toward gay men and lesbians, there was too much hurt, pain, and disappointment in the system for me to be able to find nurturance and strength there. The answer was in another place, but I had no idea where, and I was not ready to search for it. Meanwhile, we chose not to attend any church.

The United Methodist Church has no official committee or task force which supports or recognizes the validity and ministry of gay men and lesbians. Strangely enough, even though the Church seeks to help its people understand that there is no difference in the expectations placed upon its clergy from those placed upon the laity, there are Church laws which govern its response to gay/lesbian clergy, but there are none directed toward gay/lesbian laypeople. As one black lesbian acquaintance aptly observed, "Women, gays, and lesbians are good enough to raise money for you [the Church] by making pies and serving chicken dinners, teaching your children in Sunday school, and directing your choirs, but we're not good enough to share the Word of God with you." In the United Methodist system you can be a gay or lesbian minister and be appointed to a church for only as long as you are willing to pretend that you are straight. You can be an openly gay or lesbian layperson and, depending upon the tolerance level of your pastor and the congregation, can be active in the life of the Church and can even hold office on the local, conference, or national level without repercussions. With this observation in mind, I'm not sure who should be more angry: the ministers, who, in fact, do have different expectations placed upon them by the Church, or the laity, who are, in reality, being told that their standards don't count as much as do those of the clergy.

At this time, most faith communities, regardless of their formal stance on the gay/lesbian issue, have either an official or unofficial gay/lesbian support system. In the United Methodist Church the unofficial group is called Affirmation. It receives neither emotional nor financial support from the denomination. It must raise its own monies, pay for all its mailings, and be totally independent of all assistance afforded other groups in the denomination. As far as the hierarchy is concerned, Affirmation does not exist. Most of its members are gay men and lesbians. However, there is growing support coming from straight laypeople and clergy in the denomination.

When Winnie and I moved to Portland, one of the key leaders of Affirmation called to ask if I was willing to be a test case in a battle with the United Methodist Church for the recognition of gay men and lesbians in ministry. She emphasized it would, in all probability, mean I would find myself facing an ecclesiastical (church) trial. She warned me it would take a lot of time, emotional energy, and money to see the fight through to the end. She also said if I accepted the challenge, Affirmation would support me in every way possible: with financial help, legal assistance, and emotional support. After a week of thinking it through, I called her to say I was not willing to take the risk she had proposed. I was already feeling very fragile. I didn't see how I could possibly withstand the kind of emotional drain I knew was inevitable if I chose to accept the challenge. "Besides," I told her, "I'm not a fighter. I've always been a company woman, doing what was expected of me. Choosing to leave quietly was enough of a switch in my behavior pattern. I'm sorry, but I don't think I'm the person who should do this." When the conversation was finished, I thought I would never need to talk to anyone from Affirmation again. I knew that for my own sake, I needed to leave the United Methodist Church. I wanted to find a faith community with which I could feel comfortable. I wasn't even in a hurry.

The summer of '85 was a busy one for us. It was hard work settling into a new community, new jobs, and our new relationship. By fall we both felt more settled and began to recognize our hunger for spiritual community. We decided to search out alternatives to Christianity. I was emphatic I would never again allow myself to be a part of any group that made dictates regarding my belief system. I didn't want to be part of a community that told me certain investigations and experiences in the realm of the spiritual were "bad" or "evil." I had already spent too much of my life denying avenues to God and the spiritual other than those approved by the Church. I was scared; but I wanted to try it all, and for the next two years I glutted myself on a spiritual smorgasbord. We researched Baha'i and discovered it, too, was patriarchal and offered its followers a narrow interpretation of faith. We attended a Women's Spiritual Community group meeting several times, and there was much there that appealed to me. But it soon became apparent that in order to be a real part of the group, one needed to volunteer to work at all sorts of fund-raising events, and I realized that not only was I suffering from religion burnout, but I was also burned out on "doing." Struggling just to "be" sometimes seemed more difficult than dealing with the identity of being a lesbian. Faith communities don't seem to know what to do with someone who needs to gather nurturing, strength, and healing by being among them. Attend services too often, and someone is bound to approach you with an offer to be on a committee, teach a class, or work at a potluck supper.

The one saving grace for me in all this searching was that I had begun to see a spiritual guide once a month. Her name is Mary Lou Evans. At first I doubted Mary Lou had anything to offer me in my state of anger with and confusion about the Christian Church. She was a

United Methodist, who even had the stamp of approval of the bishop. I went for our first meeting together with more than a small chip on my shoulder.

Mary Lou is a gentle but firm woman in her sixties. Many of her clients are United Methodist ministers who feel the need for some authentic spirituality in their lives. Mary Lou is not a minister but has received a great deal of training in the way of the spiritual path over the years. One of the things I like most about Mary Lou, and the major reason I chose to continue working with her after our first meeting, was that she doesn't try to impose her own understanding of God and the spiritual on her clients. In fact, it's quite the opposite. Mary Lou encourages searching, questioning, and playful, but serious, romping through all sorts of spiritual alternatives. At the time of our first meeting she offered a safe harbor for my soul. And for two years it was with Mary Lou that I did most of my spiritual searching and testing.

My relationship with the United Methodist Church was over. However, I also knew that my ordination was important to me. God, whoever God was, had called me to ministry. Of that much I was, and still am, sure. I knew I needed to find another spiritual community with which to identify. Some of us, by creation or conditioning, are spiritual community creatures. We need to do at least some of our spiritual living with others. I am one of those people. Yet, thus far, I had not been able to find a group with which I felt comfortable.

There are two Unitarian Universalist churches in Portland, Maine. One is the older, more established church in the center of the city. The other is a newer congregation in the suburbs. Our first encounter with the Unitarian Universalist Church was less than ideal. We attended the service in town. The church building is old, ornate, and probably very beautiful. Yet it is so traditionally "churchlike" that I felt uncomfortable from the first moment I stepped foot inside the doors. In the middle of the sermon one of the members of the congregation had a heart attack. We tried attending a second time, but it didn't feel right to us.

Finally, we attended the Unitarian Universalist church out in the suburbs. I can't say it was an experience that wiped out all doubt about Unitarian Universalism. Quite the contrary. It was pleasant, but nothing that got us all excited about wanting to join. The members of the congregation were friendly; but the minister was in the process of leaving after more than ten years of being with the congregation, and it was obvious there were lots of separating pains going on between him and the people of the church. This was not a time for new beginnings for the congregation, but of endings, and being there felt awkward. We decided not to go back for a while.

Our next attempt with the Allen Avenue congregation was later in the fall of 1985, after the long-term minister had left and the new interim minister had arrived. Many denominations are structured in such a way that when a minister leaves, the congregation spends a year or more going through the process of choosing and negotiating with a new minister. During the time of search the congregation still needs a minister, and many ministers may, for one reason or another at some point in their careers, choose to serve a congregation which is in the search process. The minister becomes an "interim," and it is understood from the very beginning that this relationship with the congregation is for one year. An interim minister plays a very important role in the life of a congregation in that he or she can help the congregation heal from the loss of the previous minister as well as prepare it for the next long-term minister. By the time we decided to visit Allen Avenue Unitarian Universalist Church again, David Phreaner had begun his year as the interim minister.

We liked David immediately. He is a gentle man who walks lightly into the life of a congregation. He insists upon nothing except the right to be David, and I found his was a refreshing approach to pastoral ministry. Here was someone to whom I could relate as my minister as well as someone who could be my friend and colleague. Attending services at Allen Avenue became a joy and something that we looked forward to each Sunday, yet I was still not sure I wanted to become a member.

We had been attending services regularly for several months. Finally one event on a particular Sunday helped me decide that I wanted to be a Unitarian Universalist. It was the occasion of the naming of a new baby.

Unitarian Universalists do not practice the sacrament of baptism but observe a ritual during which a child is recognized as being a part of the life of the church community. This ritual, which takes place during the regular Sunday service, is called a naming. On this particular Sunday a woman-child was being honored. David stood in front of the congregation and explained how during the naming both little Elizabeth's parents and the members of the congregation would pledge to support and nurture Elizabeth as she grew and matured. Following his explanation, David asked Elizabeth's parents and family members to bring the child forward. To our surprise and delight, Elizabeth was presented by two moms! They were clearly two lesbians and a small child, coming before the congregation as a family unit, and as I looked around at the faces of the people in the congregation, I saw them smiling at Elizabeth and her family. As the ritual continued, and I watched Elizabeth with her parents, her grandparents, and her aunts and uncles, I could feel the tears running down my face. My heart began to hurt as for the first time in almost a year, I allowed it to be open and vulnerable. I had found a place where I could be open as a lesbian, a people among whom I could, once again, become vulnerable, and I was grateful. After months of being without a spiritual community, I had found a people with whom I could be myself. It was then I knew I wanted to know more about these people who call themselves Unitarian Universalists.

Three days later I visited David at his office. I told him that I was considering joining the Church but that I had a lot of reservations. David could see I was on the defensive as I began my litany: "I won't allow myself to be told what I must believe ever again. I won't let any church tell me what is good or bad for my spiritual growth. I will never again allow a church to have such complete control over my life." The list went on for some time, and David never tried to interrupt me. He sat back in his chair with his arms folded over his chest, grinning at me.

When I had exhausted my litany, David smiled at me and said: "Welcome home." His words were few, but they were the words I needed to hear. They offered me a safe haven in my spiritual search, while at the same time they afforded me the freedom to take whatever path the search might present. We talked for a while longer, and when I left his office, I left with an armload of books. I might have felt good about becoming a member of the Church, but I was still nowhere close to deciding whether or not Unitarian Universalism was a denomination upon which I wanted to hang my ministerial credentials.

Over the next year David kept me supplied with books whenever I was ready for more reading. We talked about my doubts and questions, and slowly I began to be comfortable with the idea of seeking to have my ministerial credentials transferred into the Unitarian Universalist Association.

During this time of reading and searching with the Unitarian Universalists, I was also needing to deal with the United Methodist Church. I had been granted a one-year leave of absence when I left Conway. If I wanted a second year's leave, I would need to apply for it by late winter of 1986. I had written an article for the Maine lesbian/gay newspaper, *Our Paper*, which had appeared in the August '85 edition. As large as the United Methodist Church is, the underground network is well established and in top form. When I wrote the article, I had already come to terms with the fact that in all probability, it, or other information about my relationship to Winnie, would get into the bishop's hands. I had come to the decision that regardless of the consequences, I needed to be a whole person, and being whole meant not being ashamed of being a lesbian.

I knew I was taking a great risk. In 1984, at the General Conference, the United Methodist Church had made several formal statements regarding lesbian and gay clergy, which in my own classic state of homophobic denial, I had wholeheartedly endorsed. *The Book of Discipline*, the official book of Church "law," states: "No self avowed, practicing homosexual may be accepted as a candidate, ordained, or appointed to a ministry in the United Methodist Church." In late fall, just two months after my article had been published in *Our Paper*, I received a phone call from a friend in a position close to the bishop's office. My friend informed me that one of the district superintendents had a copy of the article I had written and was planning to give it to the bishop at their next meeting. To the best of my knowledge, it was Winnie's previous lover who had made sure the district superintendent got a copy of the article. *Our Paper* can be obtained only by subscription or at local gay/lesbian hangouts. Most straights (nongays) don't have easy access to it or even know of its existence.

I had shared a close relationship with the bishop and his family. I respected George Bashore and considered him an honest and honorable man. Out of respect for our friendship, as well as for his position as my bishop, I chose to write a letter to him in which I shared my identity as a lesbian.

Dear George,

It is with some reluctance that I write this letter to you, yet the information I have to share with you is better coming directly from me rather than from another source.

I am sure you have suspected all along there was more to my decision to take a leave of absence from parish ministry than

I have told you. I want to share some of those reasons with you now in this letter.

My decision to leave parish ministry was not an easy one to make. Conway and Center Conway were filled with warm, gracious, and generous people, and my year with them was a good one. However, there were many struggles of self identity going on within me, and as I saw these struggles and questions taking shape, and especially as the answers to some of these questions began to form, I realized that I needed, at least for a time, to be away from parish ministry in order to give myself the freedom and opportunity to explore the depths on my struggles and identity . . . for they were both theological and personal in nature.

I am remembering particular conversations we shared in your living room regarding the then up-and-coming vote at General Conference on the issue of homosexuality and ordination. We were both adamant about our personal stands, and I even said that if General Conference voted to allow homosexuals to be ordained and to function in the ministry I would probably choose to leave the United Methodist Church. I am also remembering the quote: ". . . Thou dost protest too much." Often we discover that that against which we protest the most is also that which threatens us the most personally. Last fall I made the discovery that I am a lesbian. Living with this knowledge about myself and being in relationship with another woman, while at the same time trying to function as a pastor in a denomination which, by General Conference vote, has chosen to close the door of parish ministry to gays and lesbians was too much of a struggle and conflict for me. I found myself in the position of living a double life—of presenting myself and my lover one way to the church, and living a much deeper relationship with her in reality and in secret. I therefore chose, what for me was, the only real alternative—to leave parish ministry and begin a private practice counseling other lesbians. As I suspected, and now find to be fact, there are many gays and lesbians who find themselves outside of the organized church, not out of their own choice, but because the organized church refuses to accept them as whole, good, and healthy individuals. This is truly a dilemma.

I realize my writing all of this to you places you in a rather awkward position. Yet, as I wrote in the beginning of this letter, I would rather you heard this information directly from me than from any other source. I had hoped I would be able to come to a decision myself about what I needed to do about my relationship to the Conference and the Denomination before I felt the need to write to you with this information. It would make matters so much easier for everyone concerned if I could simply state that I was requesting voluntary location. I am not clear, however, at this point in time that this is indeed what I need to do. I guess I would prefer to remain on leave of absence until I can decide what status I would want to seek with the denomination. I think there is a part of me that has always hoped it would some day be possible to seek special appointment to a ministry in counseling gays and lesbians in the name of the church.

I am certainly open to discussing this matter with you George. I am not seeking to challenge you with this information, but to be forthright with you about what is happening in my life that might very well affect my relationship with the church.

This is certainly a time of challenge for all of us. Let us hope and pray we will be made equal to the task.

Warmly,
Rose Mary Denman

It was midwinter before I finally received a letter from the bishop. In it he indicated that we both were facing some difficult and complicated choies. He asked if I would call his office for an appointment so we could discuss the matter in person.

Rather than any meager attempt to respond to you through a letter, I prefer to arrange for a consultation together. I do believe that it has been important for you to have some time to reflect on the meaning of this for your life and future. It will be very important for us to talk together regarding your future status in ministry.

Much more important, I would love to talk with you per-

sonally about your life and aspirations. Much is happening in this whole arena bringing about alternatives for life-style.

In April 1986 Winnie and I drove to Boston for my meeting with George Bashore. She waited in the lobby while I spent the next two hours talking with the bishop. Our visit was cordial but guarded. I needed to make it clear to the bishop that although I knew I did not want to be affiliated with the United Methodist Church, I was not yet ready to make a decision regarding my ministerial credentials. I was asking him to put everything on hold until I could reach a decision.

There were only two elements of our conversation that made me uncomfortable then and which even now confuse me. George and I were sparring around the issue of my lesbian identity when finally he said: "Rose Mary, it doesn't matter what I read or what someone else says to me. Unless I hear it directly from you, I can consider it hearsay and need not take any action." I realize now, and realized fully even then, that this was his way of trying to protect me, yet to me, it seemed to be contradictory to what both of us had given our lives to: truth. I looked at the man who had laid his hands upon my head and ordained me five years before, and I felt overwhelming sadness. We were drifting apart in two totally different directions, and my sadness came from the awareness that, from my vantage point anyway, it was I who was breathing fresh air and new life into my being. My other concern was that the bishop continued to refer to his belief that with prayer and the right kind of counseling, a gay man or lesbian could be healed—or at the very least, our faith in Christ and our willingness to be obedient to the Church would give us the strength necessary to live a celibate life-style. Never once did George indicate a willingness to examine his understanding of homosexuality. Never once did he express a willingness to consider the fact that he might be homophobic and therefore wrong in his thinking and attitudes. I felt almost physical pain as I watched a man I loved and admired being so stuck in a tradition built out of fear and ignorance.

I looked at George and knew from that moment on I could not bring myself to think of him as my bishop. He was still a very warm and gracious man but no longer my pastor and leader.

"George, can you see what you are asking me to do? As ministers we believe what Jesus said about 'the truth setting us free.' We climb into pulpits every Sunday and tell our people that searching for, knowing, and living out the *truth* in our lives is what will bring us to wholeness. Yet you are telling me that in order to be allowed to preach truth, I must live a lie. You are asking me to live a fragmented life so the Church can be comfortable with me as a person. I can't do that, George. Regardless of the consequences, I must strive for wholeness. I am a lesbian. I am living in relationship with another woman. We love each other. That is my truth, and I must live it freely and openly."

There was a long silence between us, and it was evident George was struggling with my words and how he needed to respond to them. Finally, when he spoke, it was to say he would grant my request for a second year's leave of absence. Later, in a letter to me, he outlined the alternatives from which I would need to choose: leaving Winnie and living a celibate life-style or surrendering my ordination. When I left his office, we parted with a warm and genuine hug. Right to the day of the trial, over a year later, we were always happy to see one another and greeted each other with kind words and an embrace. I think it was confusing for other ministers in the church and the media to witness our relationship and to understand that in spite of the conflict resulting from our opposing positions, we still cared a great deal for each other.

I was glad for the second year's leave of absence granted by the bishop. During those twelve months I was able to begin feeling comfortable about taking the next step in my involvement in the Unitarian Universalist Association (UUA), seeking transfer of my ministerial credentials. I contacted the head of the Department of Ministry at UUA headquarters in Boston. We made an appointment to have lunch and to discuss the steps I would need to take in order to complete the transfer.

The transfer of ministerial credentials from one denomination to another is a lengthy and complicated process. The receiving denomination needs to be assured that the candidate is well versed in matters of denominational history and polity, that the individual is of reasonably sound mind and body, and that he or she would be an asset to the profession. Many books need to be read, interviews held, questions asked, and testing completed before the transfer can be granted. I was in this process for more than a year. I attended a class through Bangor Theological Seminary taught by a Unitarian Universalist minister in the area of denominational polity and read stacks of books on UUA history and development. I took a three-hour battery of psychological examinations and, finally, spent one long, tough hour being examined by the Ministerial Fellowship Committee, first delivering a short sermon to its members and then answering questions in the areas of theology, spirituality, history, and polity. It was a nerve-racking experience, but it was also a fair and necessary one. While I went through this process, it was important for me to maintain my credentials with the United Methodist Church. After all, one can't seek to transfer something that doesn't exist!

By the middle of my second year's leave of absence I was only halfway through the transfer process. It became increasingly obvious that I would need to seek an additional year. I wrote what I thought was a perfunctory letter, explaining to the bishop that I was in the process of seeking transfer of my credentials to the Unitarian Universalist Association but would need an additional six months' leave of absence to complete the necessary steps. Everything I knew about George Bashore indicated he would grant my request. After all, the alternatives were not attractive for either of us. His response to my request shocked me.

CHAPTER 9

Nothing in my background, upbringing, education, or experience with the Church had ever helped me explore the benefits that fighting for what I believe could give my self-esteem or dignity. I thought long and hard about the situation and talked to friends in the ministry, with Winnie and with Mary Lou Evans. All of them seemed to say the same thing. They couldn't make the decision for me, yet every one of them suggested that what I needed most was to ask myself: "Which decision would most nurture my own sense of self-worth?" With that question in mind, it became increasingly clear there was only one real alternative for me: to fight the United Methodist Church for the right to keep my ordination credentials.

I wrote a second letter to the bishop in which I clearly stated my desire was not to stay in the United Methodist Church but to transfer my credentials into the Unitarian Universalist Association. I once again requested an extension of my leave of absence.

It was more than a month before I received a reply to this second request. This time it came from Ann Partner, the chair of the Board of Ordained Ministry for the New Hampshire Conference. She stated that the board, upon recommendation from the bishop, had made a decision not to continue my leave of absence. The next day I received a letter from George Bashore:

Dear Rose Mary,

It is with deep regret that I must write this letter to you. The Executive Committee of the Board of the Ordained Ministry of the New Hampshire Conference is not recommending renewal of your leave of absence. . . .

Therefore, I would suggest that you may wish to submit to me in writing a more formal request to withdraw voluntarily by surrender of your ministerial office. This would include the deposit of your credentials. . . .

. . . If you intend to request involvement within another denomination, I would think that you would prefer a reference of "voluntary termination."

Rose Mary, this letter brings great pain to me. We have shared together in many deep concerns, and you have been helpful to me and our family personally. For that we are indeed grateful. . . . I have been studying this area [homosexuality] very much lately. Dr. Gerard van den Aardweg in the Netherlands specializes in the treatment of homosexuality that offers a new approach in therapy in the context of hope for change. He knows that the homosexual cannot simply be ordered to change; however, there is a growing body of evidence that homosexuality is not a "given," and that there is successful treatment for those who desire it. . . .

I am sending copies of this letter to the district superintendents and the chairperson and registrar of the Board of the Ordained Ministry. Your response will be reported to the executive session of the annual conference in May for final action. . . .

Receiving this letter from the bishop was a shock that somehow catapulted me into clear thinking. The gears of my mind shifted into full throttle, and from that moment on my life would never be the same. Something inside me was giving birth to courage and self-respect, and these newborn attributes were maturing with a speed impossible to attain by pure act of will. It was as though all the spiritual strength and nurturing I had sought over the preceding months had been stored away and incubating just for this purpose. I was being confronted by the giant and, to my utter amazement, was not afraid. A sense of calm and well-being washed over me, then made its home in the center of my being, and I knew I would be all right. I had somehow tapped into the resources of my personal power. I was being introduced to a new kind of inner strength, one which no person can manufacture for him- or herself. It was a gift from the Universe and Mother Earth, and I was humbled by their generosity.

The day after receiving the bishop's letter, I called Unitarian Universalist headquarters in Boston and spoke with the Reverend Joan Kahn-Schneider, director of ministerial education. I brought her up-to-date on the process of my seeking transfer of my ministerial credentials and read the bishop's letter to her. I then outlined the three alternatives from which I had to choose: (1) taking the bishop's suggestion and voluntarily surrendering my orders; (2) doing nothing and waiting until the executive session of the Annual Conference, when my colleagues would be sure to vote involuntary termination; or (3) choosing an ecclesiastical (church) trial, by which I would be allowed to state my case before my colleagues passed judgment on me. As Joan and I spoke, I was clear that I was not asking for her advice. I knew full well the final decision was mine alone. What I wanted from her was an outline of how these alternatives would affect my transfer into the Unitarian Universalist Association. Joan's response helped me reach my decision.

"Rose Mary, because of the reasons for your struggle with the United Methodist Church, the Unitarian Universalist Association's decision about your fitness for ministry will not be determined by how your separation from the United Methodist Church takes place. If, after your study, preparation, and meeting with the Fellowship Committee, the committee determines that you are fit for ministry in the Unitarian Universalist Association, you will be welcomed into the ministerial fellowship. If, at that time, being reordained feels like a healing act to you, then we will reordain you. If, on the other hand, it feels more empowering that we recognize your ordination from the United Methodist Church, then we will recognize it as valid, regardless of what the United Methodist Church does with your ministerial standing."

Joan's words brought tears to my eyes and determination to my heart. I had made my decision. George Bashore had thrown down the gauntlet, and I was accepting the challenge. I was going to fight the United Methodist Church for my ordination and the right to transfer my credentials. I would choose church trial.

My first action was to respond to the bishop's letter on April 18, 1987.

Dear George;

It was with a great deal of sadness and disappointment

that I read your letter to me earlier this week. I had hoped that my transfer out of the United Methodist Church into the Unitarian Universalist Association could be a smooth and uneventful one for the sake of all concerned.

I am writing this letter to you so that I can make my position on this matter as clear as is possible.

In your letter you stated: "If you intend to request involvement with another denomination, I would think that you would prefer a reference of 'voluntary termination.'" After having researched this matter with the U.U.A. office in Boston, I have found that because the issue involved concerns my lesbian orientation, how my severance from the United Methodist Church happens is of no negative consequence to me. However, it is still my desire to make this transition as smooth, and with as little conflict as is possible.

*I will not voluntarily surrender my ministerial office with the United Methodist Church until next fall when I will, hopefully [*sic*], be transferred into the Unitarian Universalist Association. I am continuing to seek for an extension of my leave of absence until the process can be completed. . . .*

In view of all of this, as well as the stance you have taken in your letter to me, I am requesting to exercise my right to appear before the Executive Session of the New Hampshire Annual Conference next month in order to present my case before my peers. I understand that the executive session will be meeting on Wednesday evening, May 20th at 7:30 P.M.

No response was forthcoming until a copy of a letter from the bishop to Ann Partner, chair of the Board of Ordained Ministry, dated May 5, 1987, was sent to me.

Dear Ann:

It is my sad responsibility to file a formal complaint against Rose Mary Denman. I am following the procedures of the Book of Discipline, *Para. 455.b. This complaint is based on the offense listed in Para. 2621.1b—"practices declared by the United Methodist Church to be incompatible with Christian teachings." This complaint is based on her own admission that she is a self-professing, practicing lesbian. . . .*

> *It is my understanding that you will convene the Joint Review Committee in order to consider this matter. Thank you for taking care of this very difficult matter. I regret that this kind of action is necessary: however, in order to maintain integrity with the standards of the United Methodist Church someone needs to file this kind of complaint. I will be glad to cooperate in any way.*

The die was cast. In my last letter to him I had tried to provide the bishop and myself with a quiet and easy way out. He needed only allow for less than a year's extension on my leave of absence and I would have been gone from the United Methodist Church. I think all along George was counting on one of two things taking place: either I would become frightened of the idea of trying to fight the huge patriarchal mechanism of the United Methodist Church, back down, and go away in quiet disgrace, or by some miracle, I would see the light and be healed of the affliction of homosexuality. The old Rose Mary whom George had ordained in 1981 would have disappeared without a whimper. The new and empowered Rose Mary would do no such thing.

Ann Partner called to tell me the Joint Review Committee of the Board of Ordained Ministry would be meeting on May 11. I was told that at this time I would be allowed to respond to the bishop's charges. I was also informed I would be allowed to be accompanied by another ordained minister of my choice. The decision of the Board of Ordained Ministry, upon the recommendation of the Joint Review Committee, would be brought to the Executive Session of the Annual Conference on May 20.

I needed to consider which of my colleagues I would ask to accompany me to the Joint Review Committee meeting. I could think of no one I considered able to stand up under the pressure of the occasion. By some strange mixup of information, I unintentionally called the home of Priscilla and John MacDougall, both ministers in the United Methodist Church, neither of whom I had ever met. The three of us talked together for some time. John, a wiz at *The Book of Discipline*, offered to help me to prepare for my meeting with the Joint Review Committee on May 11 and my statement before the executive session of the Annual Conference on May 20. Priscilla volunteered to accompany me to the Joint Review Committee meeting. Both joked about how they had always wanted to be downwardly mobile in their ministerial careers. "Besides," John told me, "if you're headed in any other direction in this business, you must be doing something wrong!" Winnie arranged to take the day off from work, and I told Priscilla we would meet her at the Howard Johnson's in Manchester, New Hampshire, an hour before the meeting was due to convene.

There was little to do in the way of preparation for my meeting with the Joint Review Committee. Winnie and I were up early that morning, and our drive to Manchester was filled with conversation about how we thought the meeting might proceed. Priscilla was waiting for us when we arrived at the restaurant. Neither Winnie nor I was prepared to meet the person who waved to us from a corner booth. I waved back and made my comment to Winnie through clenched teeth and a forced smile on my lips. "We've been duped, hon. She's a right-wing fundamentalist if I ever saw one."

"Oh, God. Now what do we do?"

"It's too late. We've got to meet with her."

Winnie and I made our way to the table. There sat Priscilla, dressed in a conservative pale blue linen suit and high-collared white cotton blouse complete with ruffles both at the neck and sneaking out beyond the sleeves of her suit jacket. She wore conservative pumps and a cross around her neck that must have been three or four inches long. Her light brown and gray hair was done up in a short, wavy no-nonsense bob. There wasn't a stitch of makeup on her face. This vision of conservatism greeted us with a great big smile as she peered out over her wire-rimmed reading glasses. "Hi, you must be Rose Mary and Winnie. I'm Priscilla MacDougall."

And so began our introduction to a woman who was to become a good friend and staunch ally. For perhaps the first time in my life I began to understand the adage my father loved to toss around "You can't tell a book by its cover." Priscilla is anything but stuffy and conservative. The three of us passed the next half hour with small talk mostly. Priscilla encouraged me to stay calm and suggested that we had better not add fuel to the fire by having Winnie wait for us at the church. We decided she would wait for us at the restaurant.

The meeting with the Joint Review Committee lasted for one very long and draining hour of forced civility. There were coffee, tea, and doughnuts for everyone. I felt like Alice in Wonderland conversing with the Mad Hatter as Priscilla and I sat in the circle with the six or eight committee members. We all were behaving as though we had no loftier decision to make than what to wear to the next tea party. I didn't realize then that the meeting was simply a way to go through the proper procedure. As I reflect upon the time we spent with the committee, it would seem that the decisions had already been made.

The committee members took turns asking very perfunctory questions. They wanted to know what kind of work I was doing, where I lived, how things were going for me in my life, why I was requesting an extension on my leave of absence, and what relationship, if any, I was maintaining with the United Methodist Church. Finally one of the members blushed a bit as he leaned forward in his chair and began to verbalize what had been on everyone's mind from the beginning. "Rose Mary, is it true that you are a lesbian?"

I tried not to appear as amused as I felt. *What kind of question is that?* I thought. *I've written an article for the Maine gay/lesbian paper, and every person in this room has a copy. They also have copies of the letters I've written to George. For heaven's sake, do they think that at this point I'm going to sit here and try to deny it?*

I looked my colleague in the eye and responded in as straightforward a manner possible: "Yes, I am a lesbian."

The room was silent as they all held their breaths. My colleague was getting ready for his next and most obvious question.

"Well, Rose Mary, what I mean is"—he cleared his throat as his eyes flashed from one to another committee member, looking for support or perhaps for one of them to bail him out—"well, are you a self-avowed—"

I cut him off before he could complete his question. "Henry, don't ask that question unless everyone in this room is prepared to discuss his or her sexual practices."

Others of my gay colleagues, finding themselves in this kind of bind, had refused to answer any questions regarding their sexual practices. As long as they only admitted to being of gay or lesbian orientation, they were safe. There is no church law which states that one cannot be a gay or lesbian and be a minister, but one cannot be a minister if one is a sexually active gay man or lesbian. The Church's stronghold on us is if you're a gay man or lesbian who is willing to live a celibate life, you will be allowed to continue in the work of ordained ministry. The alternative is to lie. I was not willing to lie, but I was still willing to play the game of refusing to answer any questions about my sexual practices if it would buy me the time needed to complete the transfer process into the Unitarian Universalist Association. I would choose trial only if all other attempts at resolution failed.

Henry sat back in his chair. No one dared pursue his line of questioning. The meeting ended shortly after. As Priscilla and I were driving back to meet Winnie, we both were sure the Joint Review Committee would advise the Board of Ordained Ministry to continue my leave of absence. We were confident it would realize that to do anything else would be to open up a can of worms for absolutely no reason. Winnie and I drove home congratulating ourselves for standing up to the board and the bishop. We were sure that the whole mess was over.

Shock set in when later that evening, I received a telephone call from Ann Partner, the board chair, informing me the board had voted to deny my request for an extension on my leave of absence. We briefly discussed the alternatives from which I now had to choose, and Ann told me I would be receiving a letter confirming the board's decision and our telephone conversation. The letter arrived two days later, May 11, 1987.

> *Dear Rose Mary,*
>
> *It is my responsibility to convey to you in writing the recommendation of the Board of the Ordained Ministry as we discussed this evening by phone.*
>
> *The Board of Ordained Ministry of the New Hampshire Annual Conference voted on May 11, 1987 to recommend to the Ministerial Executive Session of the Conference the termination of your membership in accordance with Paragraph 455.1f (page 245) of the 1984* Book of Discipline. *As a result of this action you have a right to elect trial (Para. 455.3) or withdraw under complaints (Para. 454.5). The recommendation of the Board will be acted upon by the executive session unless you choose withdrawal or trial. You have ten days in which to make this choice and send notification to the Bishop and to me. (Para. 455.1f). . . .*

Later I received a copy of the minutes of the Board of Ordained Ministry meeting of May 11. In reference to the committee's interview with me, the minutes read: "By a vote of 10 'yes' and zero 'no' the motion was passed unanimously to terminate the membership of Rose Mary."

As soon as I finished my telephone conversation with Ann Partner,

I called John and Priscilla MacDougall to tell them about the board's decision. They were as shocked by the news as Winnie and I had been. We talked for some time, and once John was sure I had made my decision to choose church trial, we spent the rest of our conversation outlining my course of action. I had been given ten days during which to make a decision. The Executive Session of the Annual Conference was scheduled for May 20, the ninth day. I was still determined to take advantage of my right to address my colleagues at the Executive Session. The timing was perfect. There was no reason to let either the bishop or Ann Partner know what I had decided until then. That phone call to John and Priscilla was the first of what would be nearly one hundred over the course of the next five months. They would serve as my advisers and my shield. Over the weeks ahead they helped me stay in touch with my sense of humor, and together with Winnie, they were an important source of strength in my life.

CHAPTER 10

John MacDougall and I discussed how I would approach the Executive Session and eventual trial. The Church has a history of doing its dirty work behind closed doors, and we knew this would be no exception. It would to be up to us to make sure the doors were opened as wide as possible. Gays, lesbians, straights, United Methodists, other Christians, and non-Christians needed to know how the blindness of narrow patriarchal rule can hurt real live flesh-and-blood people. We decided that I needed to get as much media coverage as possible.

I quit my job. Winnie's paycheck would have to carry us through the next several months although it would be tight. We knew I would need to concentrate so heavily upon the events ahead of us there would be neither time nor energy left for me to work. My first phone call was to a woman from Affirmation. On the basis of my conversation with her the year before we were confident we would receive the help we needed. However, we discovered that there would be no financial or legal support from Affirmation. It was discouraging to have firsthand experience of the gay/lesbian community's impotence in the Church. Its strength is mostly used up keeping itself as spiritually and emotionally healthy as possible while trying to function within a community which denies it the basic rights of human dignity.

For one full day I located and called every small newspaper in Maine. I also called the Portland *Press Herald* and the Bangor *News*. In each case I asked to speak to the human interest or religion reporters. I received the same response from them all: The reporters didn't think their papers would be interested in carrying the story. I was beginning to get discouraged and the fight had hardly begun.

On the night of May 13 I decided to call Dale McCormick, the president of MLGPA (Maine Lesbian and Gay Peoples Alliance). I had met Dale only once; but she was a strong voice for the gay/lesbian community in the state's political arena, and I hoped she would be able to give me some advice about getting media coverage of my struggle with the United Methodist Church. At the time Dale and many others were working hard lobbying for the equal rights bill in Maine. We had a good discussion during our phone conversation that evening. Dale was excited about what I was trying to do. She wanted very much to help me and told me that her partner was the person who handled all her media coverage. Dale said she would talk with her and get back to me the next day. She promised they would put together an idea sure to get me all the coverage I needed. I went to bed feeling confident.

By the next evening Dale had not called, so I called her again. This time she was not as effervescent as she had been the previous evening. She told me she and her partner had discussed the situation and thought it was not a good idea to help me get media coverage. They were afraid that any publicity on my struggle with the United Methodist Church would hurt the gay/lesbian community's chance of getting the equal rights bill passed in the State of Maine. Once again I was being rejected by the very community I was counting on for help and support. Winnie and I were frustrated and angry. Was the gay/lesbian community its own worst enemy?

The next morning, in desperation, I called the Boston *Globe*. My hope was that because the bishop resided in Boston, the *Globe* would be interested in any controversial story in which he played a major role. I was right. Jim Franklin, a staff writer, was very interested in the story. We did an hourlong interview over the phone, and he promised to have it in the May 19 edition. After hanging up with Mr. Franklin, I decided to go all the way and call the biggest guns I could think of: the Associated Press. Its reporter, Jerry Harkavy, was also interested in the story and asked if he could come to our home to do an interview. His story hit the front page of the Portland *Press Herald* and the Bangor *News* on both the nineteenth and twentieth. From then on I never had to contact the media again. Reporters from all over the country were calling for interviews; so were radio and television stations. I was careful to tell the reporters only what had happened to date. When they asked what my decision would be regarding trial, I told them I would announce my decision on the evening of the twentieth, when I would be addressing my peers at the Executive Session of the Annual Conference in Groveton, New Hampshire.

I made one exception. Scot French, a young reporter for the Concord, New Hampshire, *Monitor*, had been the only small-newspaper reporter interested in the story before the Associated Press got hold of it. Winnie and I had driven to Portsmouth, New Hampshire, to meet Scot on the Saturday afternoon before the trial, and we had done a two-hour interview with him. Because he had been so good to us before my story became "touchable," we decided to give him a lead on the other reporters. On the afternoon of the nineteenth I called Scot and told him I was planning to announce that I was seeking church trial at the Executive Session the following evening. The *Monitor* carried the story in the evening edition on the twentieth—a bit earlier than I had hoped, but with no real harm done.

On the afternoon of May 20 Winnie and I started out for the three-hour drive to Groveton. We had made arrangements to meet with John and Priscilla at a nearby restaurant for dinner before the 7:00 P.M. session. Another clergy couple joined us on that evening: Tony and Susan Jarek-Glidden. Tony and Susan had not received final ordination (Elder's Orders) and were ordained deacons. As deacons they needed to be cautious about publicizing their feelings about my situation. Supporting me as an openly "self-avowed, practicing" lesbian wasn't then, and still isn't, a popular position for a United Methodist minister to take. Because they feared reprisal from the Board of Ordained Ministry, Tony and Susan asked me to understand that although they were supportive of Winnie and me and would do everything they could for us, they also needed to keep a low profile. We understood and were grateful for their love and support, even if it did need to be private. Before I went into the Executive Session, they gave me a pin inscribed "Patriarchal Religions are Evil." That seemed to say it all quite nicely.

We arrived at the church in Groveton about an hour before the Executive Session was due to convene, and as we suspected, several reporters were waiting for us in front of the church building. We spoke briefly with them, made several appointments for later, and went inside.

The Executive Session of the Annual Conference is a closed session. Only ordained ministers may attend. Winnie was, once again, left waiting in the wings. Because only elders may attend the whole of the Executive Session, Tony and Susan could not be there either. The three of them waited in the basement of the church.

John, Priscilla, and I went into the sanctuary about fifteen minutes before the session was scheduled to begin. It was easy to see that my presence disturbed and surprised many of the clergy who were there. I think they were hoping to be able to vote me away without the unpleasantness of having me present for the process. My address was prepared, and Winnie had run off five hundred copies, which were sitting in John and Priscilla's car trunk ready to be distributed to anyone who would take a copy during the three days of the Annual Conference. The Executive Session might be a closed meeting, but I was determined that what I had to say would be known far beyond that small room.

About a third of the clergy who would participate in the Executive Session were already seated in the pews. John, Priscilla, and I sat about three quarters of the way back on the right-hand side. From the time we took our seats until the meeting began, not one other clergyperson took his or her seat on the right-hand side of the sanctuary. It was as if they thought that by even sitting near us they might be viewed as being supportive of our position. Fear is such a peculiar beast.

As the convener of the Annual Conference and the president of the Executive Session, the bishop was at the front of the sanctuary, making last-minute preparations to call the meeting to order. He saw me enter the room with John and Priscilla and watched as we took our seats without speaking to him. Finally he came up the aisle to me. John asked if he would like to speak with me privately, and when the bishop indicated that he would, they moved to the back wall of the sanctuary, far enough away to afford the bishop and me privacy yet close enough to jump in with support if needed. This would be the first, and last, time they allowed me to be alone with church officials. I wasn't to find out until the next morning that John was genuinely concerned for my safety that night.

George and I greeted each other with a hug, and then he asked my intention for the meeting. I told him I intended to exercise my right to address my peers. He nodded his consent and asked what else I intended. It was then I gave him the answer I had known since my telephone conversation with Ann Partner on the night of the eleventh. "George, I will be requesting ecclesiastical trial."

The bishop was visibly shaken. I don't think he ever expected me to go that far. It was out of his hands now, and he knew it. I could sense his sadness and fear, and I hurt for him. But it was too late now. We each had to do what we felt we must. Isn't that all any of us can expect from ourselves or each other?

George walked toward the front of the sanctuary. It was time for the Executive Session to be called to order. For about an hour the ministers busied themselves with the usual points of order. It was difficult for me to concentrate. I didn't feel a part of this group anymore. My only reason for being at this meeting was to continue to seek the right to transfer my ministerial credentials intact.

Finally I heard the bishop tell the clergy assembled that I had asked to exercise my right to address them. He invited me to come forward. John and Priscilla had seated themselves on either side of me, and throughout the past hour they had been holding my hands. Now I received a gentle squeeze of encouragement from each as I rose from my seat. My mouth was dry, my hands were clammy, and my knees felt as though they were made of flimsy cardboard. Yet somehow I made it to the podium. I used the time it took to get the pages of my address in order as an opportunity to calm and center myself. I took a long, deep breath, slowly surveyed the congregation in front of me, and began to speak.

"I have come before you tonight in order to share with you my reasons for my request for the extension of my leave of absence.

"I am a lesbian—four rather simple words, yet strung together in this way, they become a confession, an admission—no—an AFFIRMATION!—and yet an affirmation which evokes a myriad of responses: anger, fear, pain, confusion . . . or . . . acceptance, understanding and support.

"Four short years ago I stood in the very same place that some of you may be standing in now in my response to this issue of homosexuality. I truly believed that anyone who made such an affirmation about themselves . . . who they were, who they loved, and how they chose to live out this love relationship . . . that this person was living outside of the will of God and the Church. My response to this issue was so strong that I once told Bishop Bashore . . . it was just before the last General Conference . . . if those who were self-avowed, practicing homosexuals were ever allowed Elder's Orders and to pastor a charge, I might very well choose to leave the denomination. This, my friends, was blatant, raw, fear-filled homophobia!

"Three years ago I was appointed to the Conway/Center Conway charge. I was pastor of those congregations for only a year, but it was a good year for me as their pastor, and I hope for them as well. We shared together in many of the typical ways pastors and congregations share. We had our struggles. We also had our triumphs and joys, and I believe we grew because of our ministry to one another. Yet, just as I suspect there are some secrets of the heart a parishioner never shares with a pastor, regardless of how close their relationship, there were struggles and secrets of my heart that I did not share with these warm and accepting people because, like all of us, I too wondered about the limit of their warmth and acceptance. I wondered if their love for me as their pastor had a boundary, and I was afraid to discover there might indeed be a limit to their acceptance and love. I became afraid I might push that limit and cross over the boundary; cross over to a place where respect and acceptance would be turned into disdain and disillusionment. You see, it was during that year in Conway I discovered this truth about myself . . . that I am a lesbian.

"God knows what She is doing, though, because before She allowed me to make this discovery about myself, She first began to chip away at my thick-walled, self-serving . . . no . . . self-destructive way of thinking about Her, my relationship to Her, my relationship to myself, and my way of relating to others. In other words, God began to do a real number on my theology! God did this strange and powerful work by putting a woman in my path, a woman who made herself known to me in a slow and initially very subtle way. First she became my friend. Later she told me she wanted to be a minister. Much later she told me she was a lesbian. It was while I was in Conway she told me she loved me.

"I was filled with fear when this woman made this last statement to me. Yes, I loved her as my friend, my very dear and wonderful friend, but didn't she know that I was a heterosexual, that I was straight? This woman, this friend, never pushed me. She quite simply and strongly loved me, and in that love she also made herself vulnerable to me.

"She was vulnerable to me in that she trusted me. She trusted me even when I told her I was her friend, but could not accept her declaration of being a lesbian. She trusted me when I presumed to tell her that she could change her orientation, that there was help from psychologists and healing from God. She trusted me even when I told her I would stand in her way of ordination by exposing her as a lesbian if she ever went to seminary and sought orders. In all of this she was vulnerable to me, and she trusted me.

"My journey toward the discovery that I am a lesbian was a slow, painful, and confusing journey, yet God was patient with me. I always knew She was my companion and strength and that we journeyed together. My friend, too, was my companion in this journey. Her companionship continued to grace me with love, while still affording me the distance and security I needed in order to feel the most safe during this time of exploring my theological, cultural, and ethical values, of exploring the very core and essence of my personhood. Until God began to help me to expand the perimeters of my personal theology, as well as my cultural and ethical values, I stood firmly within the boundaries that declared I was not even free to explore my sexual identity. I blindly accepted the supposition that I was a heterosexual, because to stand in relationship to God and to the Church was seen as synonymous with being a heterosexual.

"Augustine once said: 'All truth is God's truth.' This one simple statement has served as a support and beacon for me during my time of searching and struggling to know the truth about myself. If, in fact, all truth is God's truth, then I did not need to be afraid to discover the truth about myself, about my sexual orientation. If to discover that part of the truth of who I am is to discover that I am a lesbian, then this truth, too, must be God's truth. If all truth is God's truth, then all truth must be celebrated. I am a lesbian. Could I honor God more than by rejoicing in and celebrating this truth?

"When I first began my journey toward ordination as a candidate, I was taught that the test of truth is fourfold: that 'truth stands revealed in scripture, illuminated by tradition, vivified in personal experience, and confirmed by reason' (*Book of Discipline*). Let us test the truth together.

"I am a lesbian. I am also an ordained elder in the United Methodist Church. As of the 1984 General Conference, *The Book of Discipline*, which is the book of law of the United Methodist Church, states: 'Since the practice of homosexuality is incompatible with Christian teaching, self-avowed, practicing homosexuals are not to be accepted as candidates, ordained as ministers, or appointed to serve in the United Methodist Church.'

"In spite of the fact that there are many theologians and New Testament scholars who would argue the fact that the practice of homosexuality is not incompatible with Christian teaching, the United Methodist

Church has seen fit to rule otherwise. The truth, as revealed in Scripture with regard to homosexuality, is, however, the truth of the law of love, the truth of grace, stands above all other truths . . . for when the religious leaders of the day attempted to undermine his ministry by pointing to the 'law,' Jesus' response was to remind them of the greater law, the law of love and grace!

"On May 11 of this year, a Joint Review Committee of the Board of Ordained Ministry for the New Hampshire Conference of the United Methodist Church met with me to discuss my request for the continuance of my leave of absence. I made it clear to the committee that I was in the process of transferring my ministerial credentials and membership into the Unitarian Universalist Association. I also made it clear to them that my request for the continuation of my leave of absence was made out of a desire to make this transition a smooth one, one that would leave my ministerial office intact during the process. My hope is that I will be received into the Unitarian Universalist Association this fall following my meeting with the Fellowship Committee. The Joint Review Committee recommended my leave of absence not be renewed and my orders be involuntarily terminated unless I voluntarily withdraw or choose ecclesiastical trial. The Board of Ordained Ministry supported that recommendation, and this is the motion before you now. The Joint Review Committee and the Board of Ordained Ministry have chosen the law of the Church over the greater law of love and grace. This action, to me, undermines the first test of truth.

"The second test of truth is to examine the hypothesis against the tradition of the Church. On the one hand, we could examine that part of the tradition of the Church which has sought to uphold the law of the Church rather than the law of love and grace: Constantine's persecution of all those who would not embrace the Christian faith; the Church of the Crusades that would plunder, destroy, and kill all in its path; the Church which sold indulgences to the poor, a piece of paradise in exchange for the building of cathedrals; the Church that burned over seven million people, mostly women, as witches because they healed and sometimes called God by other names; the Church which supported slavery, as long as those slaves were treated well; the Church that closed its eyes while six million perished in the ovens of Nazi Germany; the Church which sought to keep women silent and protected from the pressures of power, position, and decision making.

"On the other hand, we could examine that part of the tradition of the Church which has sought to uphold the greater law of love and grace above its own law: Francis of Assisi, who chose to identify himself with the poor; Martin Luther, who chose to challenge the Church as it took advantage of people's fears of the loss of heaven; John Wesley, who chose religious fervor and experience over form; Matthew Fox, who chose to campaign for the equality of all people above the practice of slavery; Carter Hayworth, among those who chose to defy the Church's stand on the ordination of women; Julian of Norwich, who first dared to call Jesus 'Mother.'

"The Church has two traditions, one of which is a record of its blindness and mistakes, mistakes made at the expense of people's lives, a tradition that has twenty-twenty hindsight in its generous apologies to those it persecuted centuries past. The other tradition of the Church is one of integrity, self-examination, and self-correction, a Church which stands for the belief that self-knowledge and truth offer nothing less than a theological justification for refusing to obey the laws of the Church above the laws of love and grace. One tradition supports the status quo, while the other seeks to grow beyond itself. Which of these two traditions will you choose to uphold tonight? This is the second test of truth.

"The third test of truth is experience . . . personal experience. My personal experience is that I am a lesbian. I believe sexuality is a precious gift from God. I will not diminish this gift by choosing to renounce it in the name of Church law!

"The Church has consistently shouted from the steeple tops that its ministry is a ministry toward wholeness, yet by its ruling on homosexuality, it encourages, no, it mandates, that those who are gay and lesbian live fragmented lives, lives that negate the living out of God's gifts of love for one another in a way that includes commitment to and sexual experience with that precious other. I do not stand alone in this experience. There are many gays and lesbians in the United Methodist Church, among both the laity and clergy. As I stand before you now, I stand alone, and yet in a very real sense, I also stand before you joined together with my gay brothers and lesbian sisters. We seek God's truth for us in our lives and in our experience. This is the third test of truth.

"The fourth test of truth is reason. It is not reasonable for me to turn my back upon the truth God has revealed to me about myself. The only reasonable thing for me to do is face God, myself, and you and to declare that as I have searched my heart and the voice of my Creator speaking within the depths of my soul, I can do nothing but reflect the truth I have discovered . . . I am a lesbian. Is it reasonable for me to deny my love for my partner, both in word and in action in order to be accepted by the lawgivers and enforcers of the Church? My answer is *no*! Is is reasonable for you to terminate my membership in the New Hampshire Annual Conference and to declare my orders rescinded in view of all of this? I don't believe so, but you must choose where you will stand, with the law of the Church or with the greater law of love and grace.

"On June 14, 1981, I was ordained on the last day of the Maine Annual Conference. That act of ordination was a symbol of what I and the Church had already recognized as being valid. . . . God had called me forth for ministry. My ordination was a confirmation of this call. By terminating my orders rather than allowing transfer into another, more tolerant denomination, you will be negating the validity of my call on the basis of my sexual orientation and life-style rather than upon the proof of my gifts and graces for ministry, a ministry that has borne fruit in this and the Maine Annual Conference, a ministry which continues to bear good fruit . . . in spite of . . . or perhaps even because of the fact that I have become a more whole person in my discovery.

"I have shared my soul with you tonight. I have refused to play the political verbal gymnastics of demanding that you prove I am not only a self-avowed but also a practicing homosexual. That, my friends, would be hairsplitting, pharisaical jot and tittling, an exercise for which I am neither qualified nor in which I intend to become proficient. I have been honest with you and vulnerable to you. I have searched for truth in my life, in my relationships with others, in my relationship with the Church, and in my relationship with God. I have shared that truth with you this evening, now you must search for your own truth."

I had delivered my address. Now all that was left to do that evening was to read aloud a copy of the letter I had handed to the bishop just before the meeting. I once again allowed my eyes to meet those of my colleagues as I scanned the rows of faces before me.

"In view of the recommendation of the Joint Review Committee and the Board of Ordained Ministry that my membership in the New Hampshire Conference of the United Methodist Church be terminated under the complaint that I am a self-avowed, practicing homosexual, I choose to exercise my right to trial. . . ."

My task completed, I left the podium and made my way down the aisle back to my seat between John and Priscilla. On the outside I had presented a calm and confident exterior, and I am told that I succeeded in conveying this stance to my audience. On the inside, however, I was quivering, and as I sat with my hands being held by John and Priscilla, I had to fight to keep away the tears. It would be many months before I would allow myself the luxury to mourn what was taking place. During the spring, summer, and early fall of 1987 there was no room in my life to process what I was living.

One learns early in his or her career as a preacher to know where the congregation is during a sermon, when it is woolgathering and when it's with you. Public speaking has always been a delight and a challenge for me, and it's still very much a part of how I make my living. It's hardly inappropriate to say that a good speaker knows how to manipulate his or her audience. I would like to be able to say that upon the completion of my address there was thunderous applause as my colleagues rose to their feet in solidarity and support and that they demanded justice be carried out in granting my request. However, such was not the case.

I had all but memorized my address, and as I was delivering it to my peers and watching their faces for reaction, I was painfully aware of all that was taking place in the sanctuary: My former district superintendent left the room entirely, probably on some imaginary, last-minute errand; most of those who remained in their seats vacillated between shuffling their feet, looking at the floor or the ceiling, or sitting with their arms folded over their chests, staring down at some invisible image on the back of the pew in front of them. It was only those whom I knew to be supportive who actually listened to what I had to say. The others' minds were set, and nothing I could say would change them. Yet even in the midst of all that was happening, I realized one thing: I was not responsible for what my colleagues heard or didn't hear. I was not responsible for their decisions about how they felt or what they thought about the issue of homosexuality. I wasn't even responsible for their anger, confusion, or fear. My only responsibility was, and still is, to be living in my own truth to the very best of my ability each moment of each day of my life. I can do no more, and I am mandated by my conscience to do no less.

As soon as I was back in my seat and the bishop was standing in front of the assembly, the mood in the room was charged with electricity. Undercurrents of voices, some soft and some not so soft, began to rumble from every corner. Hands shot up as people sought to have the bishop recognize their desire to speak. He lifted his head as he approached the microphone. Slowly the many conversations began to subside until, after a moment or two more, the bishop felt it was quiet enough to speak. He informed the assembly that although he realized there might be many who would like the opportunity to be heard, he could not permit anyone to voice his or her opinion. Because I had chosen trial, church law mandated that no discussion could take place. Therefore, all the bishop could allow was questions pertaining to points of clarification.

If there were those who had been angry before, they were enraged when the bishop finished. Again hands shot in the air, and one by one the bishop allowed the ministers to ask their questions. A few of the ministers had legitimate questions concerning points of procedure when a colleague requests trial. Most, however, preceded some minor question with a lengthy discourse on their indignation. One elderly colleague seated only two or three pews in front of us made what was probably the most profound statement of the evening, although it was not his intention. "But, Bishop," he said, "if we allow a church trial, it will not be she who is on trial but the Church."

I leaned over to John. "Bingo!"

"He's got it exactly," John whispered through a wide grin.

After several long and crude attempts by my colleagues to continue to give voice to their rage, the bishop announced that he would take no more questions, and the session ended after another hour of assorted executive business. The level of anger and perhaps even hatred in the church sanctuary was staggering. I knew then that I had certainly made the right decision in choosing trial. My "brothers and sisters in Christ" would just as soon have burned me at the stake as consider they might need to search their own hearts. It was horrifying to witness just how violent human feelings can become, even and perhaps especially in the leaders of the church.

There were the few exceptions, however. A handful of ministers let me know that they supported me and what I was doing. On the night of May 20 six clergy made their support known to me: two elders in full connection, John and Priscilla; and four deacons—Tony and Susan Jarek-Glidden, Mark Henderson, and another who must go unnamed in order to be protected. Mark Henderson, who was due to be ordained an elder at the end of the Annual Conference and was therefore allowed to remain in the sanctuary passed a note to me during the Executive Session after I had given my address:

Rose Mary, I first heard of this case twenty four hours ago when I read the article in the Boston Globe. I was supportive of your general position upon arriving at Conference, and after hearing your eloquent and personal statement, my support has tremendously increased. In the days to come I hope that I am able to express my support in whatever manner you deem appropriate. If there is no opportunity, please know that I remain personally supportive of what you have taken upon yourself due to your faith in our Sister—God. My hopes and prayers are with you.

As much as I had been fighting to maintain my composure during the three-hour session, Mark's note brought tears to my eyes. I'm not sure this young colleague will ever fully realize just how much his support and encouragement meant to me at that moment. There are many of us who believe that the Church's greatest hope lies in leaders such as him.

By the time the Executive Session ended I was suffering from a mixture of exhaustion and an emotional high. John, Priscilla, and I left the sanctuary and made our way out to the front lawn just outside the church to meet Winnie, Tony, and Susan. The three of us who had been inside spent the next hour trying to explain the intensity of the last hours. As other ministers began passing us on the sidewalk in front of the church, not one of them approached us. My predecessor in Conway, who just two years before had been overwhelmed with joy when he found out that I would be the new pastor, walked by within three feet of us, saw I was looking at him, and quickly turned his eyes away, pretending he had not seen me. It is strange to be five feet four inches tall, weigh a solid 135 pounds, and realize that to many you have become invisible. I was to experience that feeling many times over the next six months.

Winnie and I had made reservations at the same inn at which John and Priscilla were staying. Groveton is a small town, the kind of New England town which closes down by nine o'clock at night. It was nearly eleven by the time we left the church, and we needed something to help calm us as we debriefed together. The best we could come up with was a pot of hot water and little foil packets of hot chocolate in the cozy great room at the inn. By twelve-thirty we were all exhausted and ready for sleep.

When we arrived at the inn earlier that afternoon and signed in at the front desk, the innkeeper had automatically assigned Winnie and me to a room with twin beds. At the time we were too flustered and timid to ask for another room more suitable to our usual sleeping arrangement. Our pictures had been all over the front pages of most papers in the Northeast, and we had no idea of the repercussions the publicity might bring to our lives. That very morning I had asked Winnie to go into the supermarket with me to pick up the papers because I was afraid of facing unpleasant confrontation alone. None ever came. In fact, at the checkout counter, the young woman at the cash register turned the paper over, looked at the picture, looked at me, smiled, and said: "That's you, isn't it?"

"Yes, it is," I said, and waited for her to say something hurtful.

Instead, her smile broadened. "My brother's gay." That was our full exchange, but it was an important one.

The next morning we got up at six-thirty. I had a seven-thirty appointment with a local reporter. Winnie and I were exhausted, but there was too much to do before we could go home. From seven-thirty until almost noon John, Priscilla, Winnie, and I sat in the great room at the inn, talking with reporters. To save time and energy, we doubled and even tripled up on some of them. One of the reporters present that morning, who also followed the story to its conclusion, was Ann Whiting, editor of *Zion's Herald,* a United Methodist paper for the Northeast. When Ann had first called the day before the Executive Session asking if we would meet with her for an interview, I was hesitant. I had found my center of truth, and I believed that exposing myself to negative energy, much of which I knew would come from those in the Church, would be the most destructive thing that I could do to myself. I was afraid Ann would come at me with a lot of negativity, yet if she was willing to talk with me and to hear my side, I determined that she deserved the chance to do so.

All the interviews went well, yet we were most grateful for our time with Ann. Not only was she warm and gracious throughout the interview, but her reporting was honest and fair. In a recent conversation during which Ann and I discussed the possibility of my writing about our talks together in this book, Ann came through once again. Although I knew I had the right to talk about anything she said, it was also important to me that no one feel his or her confidentiality had been abused. Ann said she was willing to stand on record about her thoughts on the Church's response to gay men and lesbians. She is a loyal member of the United Methodist Church, yet she, like so many others, believes that the

Church is wrong in its stand toward gay men and lesbians. I think I honor most those straight men and women of the Church who feel compelled to voice their disapproval of the Church's treatment of homosexuals. They see the pain of others and are moved to speak out. They hear the cry for justice, and they add their voices to that cry. The pain of gay men and lesbians becomes their pain, and the tears of our people are mixed with their tears.

Before we left Groveton on the afternoon of the twenty-first, I had a talk with John. In the short time I had known him, it had become evident that he possesses one of the most brilliant minds in the Church. I was going to need good representation at the trial, and Church law dictates that persons representing both parties must be ordained clergy. I needed John on my side and told him so. He had guessed I would ask him to represent me at the trial and had already given it a great deal of thought. John knew that by accepting the role as my counsel, he would in all probability be destroying any chances he might have of being promoted within the ranks. Yet justice is much more important to John than being appointed to a larger church or made a district superintendent. He agreed to represent me at the trial and also suggested I find a good lawyer to act as cocounsel. By Church law, this attorney would be able to help us prepare for trial, would be able to be seated at the table with us at trial, and would be allowed to speak to John or me during the trial but could not have voice during the proceedings. John would be expected to call witnesses and to question any who took the stand. By accepting this position, John had taken upon himself a task which would require him to step outside his area of expertise. It would be my lawyer's responsibility to see to it that he was as well prepared as possible. For John's sake, as well as my own, I needed to find the best lawyer available, and we had no money to pay for one.

The Executive Session of May 20 marked the beginning, not the end, of my battle with the United Methodist Church to maintain my ministerial credentials, and the media were to become one of my greatest allies in that battle. Winnie and I knew that if our efforts were to count at all, they would have to be broadly publicized. When we got home from Groveton, there were more than twenty messages on our answering machine. Some were from friends who had called to lend support. Many were from television and radio stations as well as from newspaper and magazine reporters wanting to schedule interviews. For the next four months Winnie and I spent a great deal of our time with these reporters.

Most often they were gracious and agreed to come to our home for the interviews. Before all this attention, I had viewed those in the media as callous vultures willing to destroy anyone's life and reputation for a story. And while this may be true of some reporters, my experience was not like that. There were days when I spent up to eight hours talking with them, and with only one exception, they were always warm, polite, and thoughtful. After an interview I was often not sure of where most of the reporters stood personally on the issue of homosexuality. Some, however, would offer a word of encouragement as they were leaving. Their statements of support did not go unnoticed or unappreciated.

CHAPTER 11

Early in June I received a letter from John Blackadar, pastor of St. John's United Methodist Church in Dover, New Hampshire, and the person appointed to be secretary for the Committee on investigation. It was this committee's task to decide whether or not there was just cause to hold an ecclesiastical trial. The letter confirmed that the first of two meetings of the committee would be held on Tuesday, June 9, at 10:00 A.M. I was advised to be present in the company of my counsel.

John MacDougall and I had already spent many hours on the telephone in preparation for this meeting. We had also discussed hiring a trained attorney, preferably someone with heart and experience in the area of human rights. After several telephone calls to lesbians with a great deal of political savvy, I was given the name of a lawyer in Manchester, New Hampshire, Elizabeth Cazden. I called Elizabeth and described my situation. I told her that I had no money to pay her. Elizabeth was equally straightforward and said she wanted to take this case because she had strong feelings about the lack of justice within the Church. As a Quaker she took the fight for justice seriously and was willing to work for out-of-pocket expenses and whatever else I could scratch up to pay her. The rest, she said, would be forgiven. We scheduled a time when John and I would drive to her office in Manchester, New Hampshire, for our first meeting together.

John seemed pleased with my choice of attorneys. He liked the idea that Elizabeth was a straight married woman with children. He was also impressed with the fact that she was a Quaker. Since slavery was first challenged, Quakers have been the champions of those who have been trodden over by the "system." More than any other faith community, Quakers have stood for justice and equality for all people. Both John and I were to come to realize just how invaluable Elizabeth was to our struggle for justice with the United Methodist Church.

The first meeting with the seven-member Investigation Committee was tense but uneventful. John and I attended together, as did the bishop and the conference chancellor. Most of this first meeting was taken up with procedural questions. The conference chancellor was both an attorney and an ordained minister. The committee did not want to grant us the right to have Elizabeth present, and John pointed out that if the committee continued in this stance, we would be placed in an unbalanced situation, with the bishop (Church) having the advantage of both ministerial and legal counsel, while I would have only ministerial representation. The committee, not wanting to have an even bigger problem on its hands, conceded, and Elizabeth was allowed to be present for all future meetings.

John also wanted the issue of attendance at the trial to be clarified. *The Book of Discipline* states that a church trial may be an open trial (with observers in attendance) only if the accused requests that the trial be opened. We were clear from the very beginning that this was our request. We wanted none of the proceedings held behind closed doors. This would be our way of forcing the Church into a stance of accountability. It also assured us of as fair a trial as circumstances would allow.

It was also established during this meeting that all mailings sent to me would also be sent to John as my counsel. John requested that any written documents referred to in the charges be made available. The minutes contained the following statement in response to John's request: "In so far as it is possible to produce such documents it was agreed to by the committee."

The meeting was called to order at 10:00 A.M. and adjourned at 10:43. A second meeting was scheduled for June 16 at 12:30 P.M. Its purpose was to establish the validity of the charges and to make a decision on whether a trial would actually take place. In the interim, John and I had a great deal of work to do with Elizabeth.

Both meetings of the Investigation Committee were dry and, to be honest, rather boring. There were, however, several instances worth noting. The occasion of the first meeting was, for some of the members, the first time we had met one another. I had spent most of my ministerial career in the Maine Conference, and had only served in the New Hampshire Conference for the one year I was pastor in Conway and Center Conway. Sherwood Treadwell was one of those present at the Investigation Committee meeting. He was my district superintendent during the time I was ministering in the New Hampshire Conference. We didn't know each other well, but as my DS he had introduced me to my new congregations and chaired the annual meetings at both churches. We had also attended many clergy meetings together. Yet, from the morning of the first meeting of the Investigation Committee, Sherwood consistently referred to me in the third person as the defendant, even though I was present the whole time. I'm sure one reason for his doing so was to put distance between the Rose Mary who was his colleague and the Rose Mary being brought to trial by the Church. In fact, the bishop was the only person who consistently referred to me as Rose Mary. At one point it was he who suggested I not be called the defendant and emphasized that the purpose of these meetings was to determine if indeed, I would be placed in that position. Sherwood and the others stopped referring to me as the defendant and began calling me the accused. They had satisfied the bishop's sensitivities while at the same time preserving their need to maintain distance.

Another interesting note had to do with our reimbursement for travel. At the first meeting a sheet of paper was passed on which we were asked to write our names, the towns from which we had traveled, and the number of round-trip miles involved. John and I received reimbursement for our travel expenses. At the second meeting on June 16 the sheet was not distributed. Later, when I called John Blackadar about this, I was informed that John and I would not be reimbursed. In a letter to the bishop I wrote:

> He [John Blackadar] told me these meetings were being held at my "insistence," and that although the committee members were all receiving travel reimbursement, neither John MacDougall nor I would be. He then stated that the pad had been distributed among the committee members at the last meeting only after John and I had left. I reminded John that I am still an Elder in full Conference connection. It would seem that if some present at these meetings are being reimbursed for travel expenses, all should be. A decision to do otherwise would seem to be an indication that in the eyes of some, at least, I

have already been judged guilty and am, therefore, no longer due the rights and privileges of those in full connection.

We were later sent the amount of reimbursement and were informed, in writing, that we would receive no further reimbursement for expenses incurred in travel to and from future meetings or the trial. All other jury and trial participants continued to be reimbursed.

The result of the two meetings of the Investigation Committee was that it was determined the bishop's charges were valid and an ecclesiastical trial was in order. The date of the trial would be set at a future time, after a bishop who was both able and willing to place him- or herself in the position of judge had been found.

The goal in finding a bishop to serve as judge in an ecclesiastical trial is primarily to engage one who has had former experience. Ecclesiastical trials are infrequent, so there were not a great number of bishops in the available pool. The second criterion, one would assume, would be to find a bishop who can be impartial. In view of the fact that bishops are sworn to uphold the laws of the Church, we had our doubts about finding one who could meet that criterion.

The other interesting item to note is that the bishop of the conference in which the trial is taking place is responsible for interviewing and choosing the bishop who will serve as judge in the trial proceedings. In this particular situation the bishop of the conference was also the person who had issued the charges against me—George Bashore.

I was concerned enough about these circumstances to approach George about the process he would use in choosing a bishop to serve as judge. I suggested that he ask Bishop Dale White, a man known for his support of the gay/lesbian community as well as for his commitment to the Church. George agreed and indicated he would contact Bishop White to see if he was available. After my conversation with George I was convinced it was possible to have a fair trial and even allowed myself to become optimistic. In July I received word that Bishop Neil Irons of Pennington, New Jersey, had been chosen as judge. This was not good news. In 1968 two denominations merged to form the United Methodist Church: the Evangelical United Brethren and the Methodist Church. Both George Bashore and Neil Irons had been ministers in the Evangelical United Brethren before the merger. When I asked him about his choice, George told me that Bishop White had not been available because of other commitments. I believed this until much later, after the trial, when I heard that Dale White had never been asked to serve and that in fact, he had assumed matters had been settled administratively, making a trial unnecessary.

Another frustrating point was the dates for which both the jury selection and the trial were scheduled. Once the Investigation Committee had determined that an ecclesiastical trial was in order, I wrote a letter to George Bashore indicating the dates when my attorney, Elizabeth Cazden, would not be available. Two weeks were listed: one during which Elizabeth was scheduled to be at an annual Quaker meeting and the other, in August, when she and her family were scheduled for vacation. Six weeks later we received the schedule. Jury selection was to take place while Elizabeth was away at the Quaker Annual Meeting. The trial date was set for August 24, during the week of her vacation. When I confronted George Bashore with the fact that I had provided him with the dates when Elizabeth would be unavailable before he had even chosen a judge, he said that these dates were the only times Bishop Irons was available.

By midsummer I was far enough along in the process of transfer with the Unitarian Universalist Association to seek a letter of recommendation from my bishop. The president of the Unitarian Universalist Association understood that under the circumstances, I might not be able to secure such a recommendation from George Bashore. A copy of the bishop's response was sent to me by his office. It was dated July 7, 1987.

Dear Bill:

Rose Mary Denman has requested that I write to you concerning her status with the United Methodist Church. Currently this is a very tenuous relationship. In 1985 she requested a leave of absence and was granted that request. Such status remains in effect. Prior to that time she served as an active elder in full connection in the New Hampshire Conference of The United Methodist Church.

As you know, she has declared herself as a self-avowed, practicing lesbian. This places her in conflict with the official position of the United Methodist Church. She is in process of undergoing a trial procedure to determine her offense against the standards of The United Methodist Church. She was requested to withdraw under charges and, if she chose not to do so, told she would be terminated involuntarily. I assume that, unless she renounces her current life-style, she needs to withdraw voluntarily under charges or that she will indeed be involuntarily terminated.

Anyone who is guilty of an offense against The United Methodist Church cannot be in good standing with The United Methodist Church. This means that no letter of transfer can be issued unless a person is in good standing. I hope the above will clarify Rose Mary's present position.

Sincerely
George W. Bashore

This letter did not affect the potential of my transfer into the Unitarian Universalist Association. In effect, all that was needed was validation I had been ordained. This letter, along with copies of my ordination credentials, provided the UUA with the information necessary for me to continue in my application process. If the charges brought against me had been for laundering church monies, a sex scandal with a member of my congregation, or any other such breach of ministerial ethics, the UUA would have taken a dim view of my request for transfer. But because the "offense" had to do with the issue of my lesbian orientation and life-style, the UUA would not consider it, in and of itself, cause to decline my application.

The next step was jury selection. Ministers from Maine, New Hampshire, and Massachusetts were chosen as candidates for duty and asked to be present at St. John's United Methodist Church in Dover, New Hampshire, for the final selection of the thirteen jury members and their alternates. John, Elizabeth Cazden, Winnie, and I met in Manchester the week before so that Elizabeth could familiarize John and me with the process. We had discussed the possibility of Elizabeth's not attending the Quaker Annual Meeting but decided that with her coaching, John would be able to handle the responsibility. We had been sent the names of those ministers who had been chosen as possible jury members. Elizabeth helped us categorize those who might be sympathetic, those who might not, and those who, because we didn't know them at all, would be a gamble. Both the prosecution and the defense have the right to automatically eliminate a certain number of possible jurors without giving reason or argument. After this first elimination has been completed, each candidate is brought forward and asked, in essence, if he or she can be fair and impartial in his or her deliberations. The assumption is the individual will be honest in answering the questions. As I observed the proceedings, I was convinced that most, if not all, of those chosen to serve on the jury had been honest and would approach the trial with a great deal of integrity.

There were several media people covering the jury selection proceedings. Unfortunately the process is closed to all except those who have reason to be present, so Winnie had to leave the room when the selection was about to begin. The drapes had been drawn to foil the photographers, but several stuck their lenses between spaces in the drapery panels.

After the jury selection had taken place, Neil Irons admonished the jurors not to talk with reporters before the trial. He made a point of singling out John and me when he instructed everyone not to leak the names of the jurors to the press. We said we would not, and we kept our word. Several days later I received a telephone call from one of the reporters asking me to comment upon the individuals chosen for the jury. I informed him of Bishop Irons's instructions. My caller then read off a list of the jurors' names and said he had gotten it from Bishop Irons's office.

Once the jury selection had taken place, John, Elizabeth, and I were on the phone almost daily. The three of us met two times during the three weeks before the trial to be sure we were as prepared as possible. One of the first things I did was to write a letter to Bishop Neil Irons. It was short and to the point.

July 15, 1987
Dear Bishop Irons,

Paragraph 2624.12 of The Book of Discipline *of The United Methodist Church states: "All sessions of the trial shall be closed. However, upon written request of the accused to the presiding officer, the trial shall be open to any member of the United Methodist Church.*

This letter is my written request that the trial be open to any United Methodist persons.

I never received a response. John, Elizabeth, and I proceeded under the assumption that my request would be honored.

John and I had asked that the trial be held in the sanctuary. Our purpose for this request was twofold. The sanctuary was larger than the dining hall and therefore would accommodate more people. We wanted to be sure that those who chose to attend would be allowed entrance. The second reason was to make a statement. Even though Christians argue that God is everywhere present, there is a sense of awe and special holiness held for those places of gathering, ritual, and worship. John and I wanted to force the Church into the position of accountability for its actions. Those who had made the rules that banned gay men and lesbians living in committed relationships from serving as ministers needed to be as willing to terminate these ministers' credentials in the same setting as that in which they ordained them. It is interesting to note that it was decided, by Neil Irons, presumably in consultation with George Bashore, that the trial would be held in the all-purpose dining hall/meeting room of St. John's United Methodist Church in Dover, New Hampshire. When John and I questioned the decision, we were told it didn't seem appropriate to hold a church trial in the sanctuary. Neither John nor I had any arguments with that kind of reasoning. A church trial shouldn't be held in the sanctuary of a church. A church trial shouldn't be held at all!

CHAPTER 12

From the end of May, when my story was first published in newspapers, until long after the trial was over, I received hundreds of letters from people around the country. The overwhelming majority of them were letters of strong support and encouragement. They were from straight men and women, many of them United Methodist clergy; from gay men and lesbians who were active in their local churches, yet who felt the judgment of the church upon their life-styles; from those who had left the church years before, who were writing to share their own experience of betrayal by organized religion; from closeted gays and lesbians who wanted to see me as their heroine and mentor, as the quasi savior who would open the eyes of those in Church and society who judge the gay/lesbian community; and from those who were open about their homosexuality and were writing to welcome me aboard the team of those who seek justice. At first I tried to respond to all the letters I received; but all too quickly the task became overwhelming, and I needed to settle for sending out mental messages of gratitude.

Perhaps if this book is read by some of those who wrote to us, they can begin to know just how much their letters meant to Winnie and me. Every card and letter was a cupful of nurturance for the journey. Every word of encouragement felt like a warm hand placed in mine so that I would not feel isolated and alone. At times the letters caused me to feel the weight of the responsibility I had assumed, both for myself and, in the larger sense, for the gay/lesbian community. Most often, however, they were the most pure and simple form of love, and that love sustained me.

There were, amazingly enough, a very small number of letters written by those who sought either to condemn me or to offer me messages of potential healing from my "affliction or sin of homosexuality." These letters attempted to tell me it was not me as a person they hated, but my sin of lesbianism. I came to coin a phrase that has since become my favorite response to those who would approach me with this argument for healing in the name of Jesus Christ. "You can't love me and hate my lesbianism. I don't do lesbian. I am lesbian." Somehow, these folks can't seem to get around the fact that *homosexuality isn't something one does; homosexual is something one is!* Homosexuality isn't a bedroom pastime; it is an identity. Just as naming ourselves men and women is indicative of more than what we do in our bedrooms, so is naming ourselves gay, lesbian, bisexual, and straight. This naming infiltrates the whole of our beings: how we think; how we feel; how we live our lives. One can be celibate or sexually active, but in either case our sexual identity remains the same.

I also received a great deal of support from the Unitarian Universalist Association. From headquarters in Boston, I was encouraged to respond to the United Methodist Church in whatever way would bring me the most inner peace and wholeness and to know that my response would have no bearing on the outcome of my work toward being admitted into the Ministerial Fellowship.

As I've mentioned before, the church we attended in Portland was Allen Avenue Unitarian Universalist Church. One particular occasion of support there will always be a special memory for me. In early April, after I had decided that I would choose church trial, I shared my plan with the congregation during Sunday morning service. My heart pounded as I read my prepared statement before the members of the congregation. Winnie and I were open about our relationship at Allen Avenue, but we had certainly never stood in front of the congregation and asked it to support us in our fight for the right to maintain it.

During the "Joys and Concerns" time of the service, members of the congregation are invited to come forward and share particularly happy or sad situations with those present. It is our way of being in community with one another, of seeking support. People talk about such events as the deaths of loved ones, the births of new children into their lives, recent promotions, engagements, or divorces. Following his or her announcement, the speaker lights one of four candles on the table in the front of the room. After I had read my statement, I lit a candle and returned to my seat beside Winnie. The room was silent, and as I sat there shaking, I wondered if I had just spoken my way out of this new-found community that had begun to mean so much to Winnie and me.

After what felt like a very long time, Sue Butler, another member of the congregation, rose from her seat and went forward. She lit a candle, and still holding it, she turned around and held it out toward Winnie and me. "This is for you," she said. The congregation began to applaud as they offered me this symbol of support. Tears of love and gratitude for the congregation ran down my cheeks as I squeezed Winnie's hand. This was a church that accepted us, all of who we were, and their acceptance warmed and strengthened us.

The interim minister, David Phreaner, and several other members of the congregation offered to form a committee to help raise the funds necessary to cover my expenses during the trial. The first person to approach me with an offer of help was one of the teenagers at the church named Paul. Because some straight people accuse the gay/lesbian community of "converting" young people, I was afraid of the possible repercussions from Paul's parents. I called his mother, told her how David had volunteered to be on the committee, and asked how she felt about it. Terrill told me that Paul was excited about helping, and that she and her husband thought it would be good for him to be a part of the effort. And so Paul became the teen representative on the committee. We sent more than five hundred letters, along with packets of information about the trial, to Unitarian Universalists and others. We also scheduled a benefit concert to be held the Saturday evening after the trial. Kay Gardner, along with Carol Etzler and her partner, Brenda Chambers, all very popular composers and performers, were generous with their time and talents and volunteered to give the concert in exchange for their expenses. Ellen Lukingbeal, a talented member of the church, made her singing debut that night and delighted everyone present with her sweet voice and the depth of meaning in the lyrics to her original music. Small businesses in Portland served as major contributors to the concert effort, and Winnie designed and printed the handsome posters which were distributed through town as well as the booklets distributed that night. With the help of the committee, the business supporters in Portland, these wonderful performers, and the solicited and unsolicited gifts from those who wrote letters of support, we were able to cover most of the trial expenses.

We received no support from the lesbian and gay United Methodist clergy or laity in Maine. Because I had not come out, either to myself or to the Church, until I had left ministry, I did not know who the other lesbian clergy in the Church were. Understandably, they form a very closed society and are known only among themselves. Winnie, however, had known that she was a lesbian from the time she was in her teens and had come out during the months she and her husband were in the process of divorce. She had come to know some of the other lesbians in the conference and had become a part of their group. Once Winnie and I became a couple, this community shut off communication with her, saying that I was a risk to their secret identity. Some even suggested I was really straight and posing as a lesbian in order to provide the bishop with information that would be used against them. They told Winnie I was not to be trusted.

At one point during the summer Winnie was feeling the pressure of the publicity surrounding the trial, so she called one of the women with whom she had been close during the time of her divorce. When I came home later that evening, I found her depressed and angry. She was angry because this "friend" told Winnie that I had no right to be calling attention to my lesbian identity and forcing the United Methodist Church into an ecclesiastical trial. She said I was, in all probability, starting a "witch-hunt," that now none of them was safe, and all single clergywomen in the conference would be suspected of being lesbians. She went on to tell Winnie that being a closeted lesbian minister was not bad or wrong. After all, one could be a lesbian and still be a minister in the United Methodist Church as long as she kept her mouth shut about what went on in her private life.

Winnie had expected her friend to understand why we had chosen to fight the United Methodist Church. This woman has long history of fighting for causes and in the late sixties was very active in the civil rights movement. It baffled Winnie to see her be so much a visionary when it came to defending the rights of others, while at the same time being so blind to the need to fight for her own rights. She was behaving like someone who understands the gay/lesbian life as solely a bedroom issue.

I think I understand this woman's stance of being able to fight for someone else's freedom before her own. As a parish minister I often observed this behavior in myself. I found it to be a happy challenge to ask others for money in support of someone in need. Yet I would rather go without before asking for help for myself. Also, there seems to be a

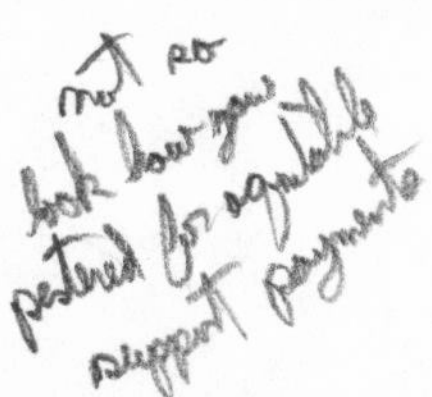

common stance among many who belong to groups suffering from discrimination. The absence of the negative, in spite of the fact that there is no positive, leaves the individual actually feeling grateful. I compare this posture, often taken by gay men and lesbians, with that of the battered wife who reaches the point where she believes that as long as her husband isn't beating her, the marriage is doing just fine.

Before, during, and after the trial there were a number of times when I was approached by gay United Methodist Ministers who were asking me to tell them it was all right not to confront the church as I had done. It was as though my actions were a condemnation of their lack of action, and they needed me to exonerate them. These were difficult moments for me. I always tried to help the individual understand that I was doing what I felt I needed to do for myself, and I could in no way presume to know what is best for anyone else. I believe that a closeted life is an unhealthy and fragmented life, but I must remind myself that it is unhealthy and fragmented for me, not necessarily for someone else who may be in a completely different set of circumstances. We all do what we can and must do. But this in no way gives us license to tell others what they can and must do. We seem to live in a world in which we believe that if one action is right, then the opposing action must be wrong. Maybe we all need a refresher in the sixties slogan coined by Thomas Harris "I'm OK, you're OK" or perhaps even turn to my father's old "Live and let live."

Unfortunately, those who say, "Live and let live," don't always act on it. The second big disappointment Winnie and I had was the reactions of our families. In 1984, while I was still in Conway, my parents were living in Rhode Island. I am part of a large extended family, and we pride ourselves on being able to trace relations all the way to sixth and seventh cousins. Throughout my childhood it was not uncommon for twenty or more relatives to get together for summer barbecues in the backyard. One year, when I was still in my early teens, my father hosted a family reunion, and more than one hundred family members attended. Moving away from home to Maine was exciting, but the hard part was not being able to see my parents or my extended family members as often as I would have liked.

While I was in parish ministry, my father retired, and he and my mother frequently drove to Maine to spend a weekend, often without warning. I joked with them about this and asked what they would have done if they'd driven all that distance only to find Matthew and I were not at home. My father always had the same reply: "We would have had a nice ride."

When Winnie came to live with me in Conway for the summer, we were indeed "just friends," and my parents liked her immediately. They good-naturedly kidded her about being six feet tall and working with an all-women house-building team, but it was easy to see that they, especially my father, admired Winnie for her physical strength and gentle spirit. They thought it was good for me to have the adult company of such a good friend for the summer.

The following January Winnie moved into the parsonage as my lover. We didn't tell our parents about our relationship at first because we suspected they would be far from pleased. For the sake of the congregations we made the guest room look as though it were Winnie's room, and we kept our growing library of lesbian literature out of sight. Therefore, my parents' surprise visits did not threaten the situation. However, as the time drew closer for us to move to Portland, Winnie and I grew more and more concerned about the need to tell our families about our relationship and commitment. We knew that once we were in our own apartment, we wanted to be completely open. We didn't want to have to maintain separated bedrooms for appearances' sake. We wanted to be able to keep our lesbian books with all our other books. We wanted to be able to hang the painting I had done for Winnie the previous Christmas. It was of two women embracing. Most of all, we wanted not to be afraid of slipping in front of our families by calling each other "hon."

Because Winnie's mom lives in New York, and we knew there was no threat of her surprising us with an unannounced visit, I was the first to tell my parents. I chose to do it through a letter, hoping this form of communication would provide them with the time they would need to explode, think it through, calm down, and respond with some level of support. I wrote the letter in May 1985 and waited a month for their response before I called them. Their reaction was, from what I have been able to learn since then, quite normal. They were stunned, angry, and confused and didn't want to have anything to do with Winnie. My father wouldn't come to the phone to talk with me. All my mother would say was that they were very disappointed in me, that they thought I knew better than to hurt them this way, and how could I think I had anything to teach anyone if I was going to be "this way"? I tried to help her understand that Winnie and I were still the same people we had always been; the only thing that had changed was they knew more about us and what we meant to each other. There was just no getting through to either of my parents, and we didn't see each other for more than a year. I continued to send Christmas, birthday, Easter, and anniversary cards and to write to them on a regular basis. I always emphasized the same thing: No matter how they responded, I wasn't going to make it easier for them by hating them; they were going to have to deal with my love. My parents made it clear that I was always welcome in their home but that Winnie was not. I was just as stubborn as they and refused to visit them unless Winnie could be there with me. I insisted she was my life partner and used the same argument for not visiting them without Winnie as they had used, when they were first married, with my grandmother, who didn't want my father in her house. "We're a package deal."

Not seeing my family for more than a year was very painful for me, and I imagine for them as well. Finally, in the early spring of 1985, Winnie and I planned a trip to New Jersey, and Matthew asked if we would drop him off in Rhode Island so he could visit his grandparents. At the end of the weekend I called my mother to tell her when we would be arriving to pick up Matthew. I purposely planned it to be at the time when I knew they would be sitting down to Sunday dinner. As I had hoped, my mother said: "Well, you might as well stay and have dinner with us."

"Does that mean Winnie, too, Mom?"

"Of course. You didn't think I was expecting her to sit in the car while we ate, did you?"

"Is Dad OK with us coming for dinner, too?"

"He's not thrilled, but it's all right."

So Winnie and I visited my parents for the first time as a couple. Our time together was awkward, but I suppose that's pretty much to be expected. Actually my father had an easier time talking to Winnie than he did to me. We breathed a sigh of relief when we left, and I suspect my parents did as well. It hadn't been the easiest time for any of us, but I was hopeful. After all, it was a beginning.

Three months later my mother called to say that while on vacation in Arizona to look at the house my sister and her husband had recently purchased, my parents had bought a new house and were moving there in September. I was stunned. We were just beginning to rebuild our relationship. It was difficult enough with two hundred miles between us. How would it be with thousands of miles to keep us apart? They had never been to visit us since I had told them about Winnie and me. I had hoped they would feel comfortable enough to do so by the next holiday season. Now there was no hope of its happening at all.

Winnie, Matthew, and I attended a family get-together for my parents in August. It was a bit less strained than our previous visit had been, and we could see that my parents were trying to accept us as a couple. Mom and Dad were selling a lot of their belongings in preparation for the move. Before we left, my father gave Winnie all his electric tools. My mother gave me some of her kitchen and cooking supplies. They needed to interpret our relationship by heterosexual standards and obviously had come to the conclusion that because I was so "domestic," Winnie must be the "man of the house." Yet we also recognized the love in their gesture and were deeply moved by it. Winnie and I chuckled about it all the way home, after I finished crying. I knew it would be a long time before I would see my parents again.

Winnie didn't tell her mother about us until the following November. We were planning to go to New York for the Christmas holiday and decided her mom needed to know about us. Again, we were afraid of slipping and didn't want to catch her mother unaware. We also knew we didn't want to spend such an important holiday as Christmas pretending that I was Winnie's housemate. Winnie called her mother about a month before we were due to visit, and her response hurt us both, although it was less harsh than that of my parents. Her mom told Winnie it would take time to adjust to the news, and she thought it was best we not visit at Christmas as we had planned. She did, however, send us Christmas gifts: some for Winnie, some for me, and a couple for us. It felt good that Winnie's mom could recognize us as a couple, even if she didn't like or understand it.

The decision of whether or not to tell parents and other family members that one is gay or lesbian is very difficult. Some gay men and lesbians feel it's an unnecessary burden on their parents. Others believe that what they do in their private lives has no bearing upon their relationships with their parents. Still others are afraid of losing parental love and support. Winnie and I were surprised by the number of straight friends and relatives who judged us harshly not only because of our lifestyle but because we chose to tell our parents. These well-meaning people came at us unmercifully: "Your parents have been through enough already. Why did you have to add to their heartache?"; "They were so proud of you. Why did you have to spoil it for them?"; or, "You could have lived any way you liked, but why did you have to tell your parents?"

These and a host of other responses baffled me. My parents had always brought me up to tell the truth. Also, my father had been fond of telling all his children: "Don't do anything that you wouldn't want the whole world to know about." I had worked through the process of my identity as a lesbian. I felt more whole as a person than I ever had. If I couldn't be honest with my parents about who I was, how could I hope to continue to have a close relationship with them?

There is another reason why it is so important for me to be open about my relationship with Winnie. Not only is it a matter of personal integrity, but it is healthy for us. No relationship, gay or straight, can flourish in the midst of secrecy and shame superimposed upon it by a society which would prefer that we remain invisible. To pass ourselves off as friends would be to deny the depth and commitment of our life together. It would maim, if not kill, our relationship and perhaps even the spirit that makes us who we are.

My accord with my parents suffered a second blow when the news of my choice for church trial first appeared in the newspapers. I talked to my mother about what was happening before the first article hit the headlines. I wanted her and my father to hear it from me first. By that time my father's hearing had deteriorated badly. He was only sixty-three years old, but his hearing had begun to fail years before. I tried my best, over the telephone, to help my mother understand why I was choosing to push the situation to its logical conclusion. Neither of my parents really understood what it was I was trying to do, and any ground we had recovered over the previous two years was lost. As far as they were concerned, anyone who stood in opposition to the Church, Protestant or Catholic, must be wrong. For them, as for many, the Church is never wrong, and when we find ourselves in opposition, it is we who have failed. For so many years, especially since I had begun to prepare for ordination, my parents had been so proud of me and had wasted no opportunity to show me off as their personal success. I had climbed out of a bad marriage, raised my son alone, and still managed to work full time as well as go to school. They were so proud of me on the day of my ordination that my father could not keep the tears from streaming down his face. From then on they wanted me to wear my clerical collar whenever I visited them, especially if we were going to see any of our relatives. Now they let me know just how ashamed of me they were. Not only had I disappointed them, but I had robbed them of their one pride and joy, their badge of honor before their family and friends. The gulf between us widened, yet I couldn't allow myself the luxury of wallowing in self-pity over it. I needed to remain centered and strong for what was ahead.

Winnie's family didn't lend us very much support either. Although her mother continued to call Winnie on the telephone and tried to hear what we were attempting to communicate to her, she, too, as a lifelong member of the United Methodist Church, found it difficult to understand how we could stand in the face of such an institution. She was always clear that no matter what, she loved Winnie and always would, but our choices were confusing to her. She also let Winnie know, in no uncertain terms, that the constant publicity about us in the newspapers and magazines was causing her no end of embarrassment. Yet even though our choices may have stretched her understanding and acceptance of us to the limit, she seemed to be able to find a reserve deep inside herself that allowed her to reach out to us.

And so Winnie and I continued to prepare ourselves for the church trial. We spent a lot of time talking with and caring for each other. We were sure of one thing: We didn't want the struggle to be such a strain on us that we would end up hating each other. That would have been a greater victory for the Church than anything. We became life rafts for each other, and together we reached out for any other signs of love and acceptance that were offered: the letters; the phone calls; the hugs. Whether they came from friend or stranger, they were, each and every one of them, cherished. They were what kept us going.

The greatest gift came from a thousand United Methodist clergywomen gathered in New Jersey for a quadrennial meeting the week before the trial. On Wednesday, August 19, I received a phone call from Priscilla MacDougall, who was attending the weeklong meeting. She called to tell me that many of the women gathered there had discussed the situation and wanted to be sure that I knew I had their love and support. She asked if I would come to the meeting at their expense. It was frightening to consider what their invitation might mean. I was heartened to hear there were a number of women there who wanted me to be with them. But in a group of one thousand there must have been some who strongly opposed my stand. Would I be placing myself in a negative and strained situation by accepting this invitation? After talking with Priscilla and one of the other women at the conference, I decided to join them. Winnie and I were shocked by the invitation. Support sometimes comes from the least expected people and places.

I caught my morning flight on Thursday, and Priscilla was at the gate to meet me when I got off the plane. She talked for the whole hour's drive to the hotel about how much support I was getting from the women gathered at the meeting. She also made it clear that very little was expected of me. There had been an announcement that I would talk with any women who wanted to just before lunch. I was also asked if I would attend one of the discussion groups. Other than those two gatherings, I was free to relax by the pool, soak up some sun, and be with friends.

Priscilla and I had arrived at the hotel by 10:30 A.M., took my bags to her room, and headed straight for a room where I was to meet "a few people." When we walked in, five hundred women rose to their feet in applause, and I was guided to a podium so I could talk to them. Neither of us had been prepared for this reception, and Priscilla gave me a hug as she whispered: "I didn't know it would be like this." I walked up to the podium, looked slowly over the sea of smiling faces before me, took a long, deep breath, and began to speak.

"Well, I certainly didn't expect for this to happen. When I was called yesterday afternoon and invited to be with you, I was told that there might be a few people who would want to talk with me. I didn't anticipate having to give a speech!"

There was a flutter of laughter from the women, and someone called out: "We don't want a speech. Just talk to us."

"OK, I'll just talk to you. I'll tell you what is happening in my heart. I'll tell you why I am doing what I am doing. I'll tell you how brave people say that I am and how scared I really feel. And I'll tell you just how much I need you and the support you are offering to me right now."

For the next hour I told my story. I told it simply and clearly, and I told it from the depth of my heart and soul. In closing I said: "I have a fantasy. There are those who say that what I am doing will only hurt those gay men and lesbians who are in United Methodist ministry. They say that what I am doing will start a witch-hunt, that none of us will be safe. Suppose, just suppose, that every ordained minister in the United Methodist Church was to write a letter to his or her bishop and say: 'I am a lesbian. I am a gay man.' What would happen then? Would they hold a church trial for every one of us? Would they seek to take ministerial credentials away from every minister in the denomination?"

When I had finished saying what I had come to say, every woman in the room again rose to her feet in applause. The minister who had talked with me on the telephone the previous morning stood beside me and hugged me in the name of everyone present. Then she announced that my trial was costing a great deal of money and a collection would be taken to help defray the expenses. Baskets were passed, and more than a thousand dollars were collected. As I looked over the roomful of women, I knew in my heart that no matter what happened, I could be sure there were pockets of support from my United Methodist colleagues, for me and for all gay men and lesbians. This was the greatest gift of all.

The rest of the afternoon was spent by the pool talking quietly with my good friend Pat. Occasionally one of the women from the conference would stop to offer a word of support and a hug. Those short hours seemed to breathe new life and vitality into me.

Just before lunch I was approached by another of the women, who asked if I would take part in the closing worship service that evening. Several of us were asked to meet in the ballroom before dinner. When I arrived there, I walked into a flurry of activity as ten or more women were trying to come to agreement about the order of service.

Susan Savell, a minister in the United Church of Christ and a wonderfully gifted songwriter and performer, had been invited to participate in the service. Later that evening she would be giving a concert of her music. Susan and Lynn, a former district superintendent from Maine, were in the middle of a discussion. Lynn was in charge of the service, and she had already determined where it would be appropriate for Susan to sing. She had asked Susan to do three of her songs. Lynn's problem was she couldn't get Susan pinned down on which songs she was going to sing. Every time Lynn asked, "What will you sing here?" Susan replied, "I'll know what fits in best when the time comes. I'll just follow the spirit of the evening." Lynn was beside herself and wanted something a little more concrete from Susan. Susan was calm and firm. I knew what Lynn was feeling. No minister wants to go into a service not knowing what will happen at every turn. I also empathized with Susan. I had heard her sing before, and I knew she would come up with the right music for each part of the service. Her music doesn't just come from her head; it comes from her heart and soul. She trusts life and its currents to carry her in ease, knowing that if she can relax and allow life to happen, it will be as it should be.

After dinner Priscilla, Susan Jarek-Glidden, Pat, and I returned to the ballroom. As I walked in, my breath was taken away by the transformation that had taken place. It was an enormous room, and in the front of it there was a stage set up from which the leaders of the service would speak. The other three sides were set up with enough chairs to accommodate the thousand women who would fill them in just over an hour. The theme of the week had been "Our Faith, a Wellspring of Hope," and following that theme, several women had designed a large and beautiful cascading fountain in the middle of the room, around which were hundreds of flowering plants. With the lights turned down, leaving just enough for people to see clearly, the ballroom had been transformed into a sanctuary of beauty and power.

The afternoon before, one of the women had made an announcement to the thousand. That same evening, Wednesday, any lesbian clergywomen who could trust that their identities would be protected were invited to gather in a designated room for a time of sharing and support. I am told more than thirty women attended that meeting. While they were together, they were asked to describe, in a short written paragraph, what each felt about being a lesbian and a United Methodist Minister. They were asked not to identify themselves in what they wrote. Their responses were collected, and with their approval, it was decided that what they had written would be read and shared at the closing service on Thursday evening. I was one of the four women who would read these responses.

The service began promptly at seven-thirty. At the designated time three other women and I took our places at the microphones at the four corners of the room. The lights were dimmed, and only the fountain, surrounded by the lovely growing plants and flowers, could be seen. A voice broke out in the dark silence: "We will be the voice of our lesbian sisters, who, because of the laws of the Church, cannot speak for themselves."

And then, taking turns, the four of us read the statements written by the women who had gathered in secret the night before. Our voices pierced the silence with their words of pain and hope.

"I am a woman who has been in ministry for twenty-three years. I acknowledged my lesbianism to myself twenty-three years ago. I ache to be free, to be creative in my wholeness. . . ."

"My congregation treats me like a princess. How kind I am. How sweet. How approachable. How pretty. Kids like me. Parents like me.

Grandparents adopt me. But nobody knows me. And when they do. . . ?"

"I am a lesbian with a beautiful, strong lover. When her mother found out about us, she confronted me and threatened my job and career. I celebrate the courage and strength and love that I claim in myself, for keeping on with my work and my relationship in the face of such threats. And I still have a good sense of humor!"

"I came to this consultation to gather my beloved friends, mentors, role models so that I can relinquish my orders in the context of support and love. They believe, and I believe, that I have a ministry, but I can no longer live a lie."

"I am an elder in the Midwest, serving my third appointment. I am a good pastor—and so far back in the closet that no one can see me."

"I am an elder in full connection serving an upper-middle-class congregation. I am mostly who I am; I am partly defined by my culture and my congregation. I am female and feminine; strong and capable. I function in a largely straight and mainstream community, but I am a lesbian. When my lover died of cancer, there was no one to tell, no one to grieve with me. When a subsequent relationship ended, there was no one to give support. Now I am growing older and I often wonder where and even if I will meet someone again. The closet is silent, dark, and lonely."

"Being thirty, lesbian, and single, serving in a rural area, has left me feeling alone and abandoned. I am choosing to leave to experience the support and care I need to feel whole again."

"My partner of four years dialogues with me when I'm preparing sermons, and we also meditate together. Yet when it comes time to give voice to my spirit with my congregation, the part of her that she shares with me is expressed with a deafening silence."

"I am beginning my fifth year in parish ministry. I feel blessed by the sustenance I have received from my partner of eight years and by the support and love I have felt from my lesbian clergy sisters and straight clergywomen and friends. I am sad about the pain that I and others have felt over being hated and shut out from God's Church. I know that I will eventually have to leave in order to maintain my own sense of personal wholeness."

The four of us read these and many other statements written by the lesbian clergywomen, and as we read, a heavy silence enveloped the room as each woman gathered in that place heard the cry of pain and loneliness from her sisters. And as we read each statement, pockets of women began to stand as a symbol of their solidarity with these sisters in pain. By the time we had finished our reading, almost every woman in the room was standing. Each was choosing to be a support for those who found themselves in pain, but no longer so alone.

When our reading was finished, three women came forward, carrying jugs over their shoulder. They were dressed in long, flowing skirts, and their feet were bare. Two of the women emptied the contents of their jug into the fountain. The third placed her jug, still full, at the foot of the fountain as the voice of one of the readers spoke out: "We cannot empty all of our pain into the Wellspring of Hope. The Church will not allow us to do this. But we have been nourished by our sharing this evening."

As the water poured from the two jugs mingled with the water already in the fountain, the streams of water cascading over the growing flowers and plants began to turn color until it was a clear and vibrant lavender, the adopted color of the gay/lesbian community. A deep common breath was taken in by every woman there at the sight of the stream of lavender water. Many were hugging one another and weeping. Slowly, at first very quietly, Susan Savell and her accompanist began the music. As the sound of the piano and Susan's humming became more audible, the women gathered began to take their seats. The sound of crying could still be heard as Susan, dressed in her white minister's robe and red stole, stood on center stage next to the fountain. The room was still darkened except for the spotlight that shone on Susan and the lavender fountain. Susan struggled to make her building emotions work for her, and her voice grew stronger and clearer as she hummed to the beat of the blues. Her hips swayed, even under the folds of the white alb, and her eyes sparkled when she broke out in her sweet, powerful voice. The spirit of the evening had guided her wisely, for the song that she had chosen to sing was one that would typically never fit into the order of a worship service, yet it was perfect for the moment. She was singing "Mean Old Woman Blues."

I've been a good girl all my life. Let me tell you, it's been boring, and I've paid the price never getting what I want for me. I've never really shown you just how mean I can be, but tonight there's no making nice in me, and darlin, I'm not just

> *askin, no, I'm tellin you, you listen carefully when I let you know what I want for me. I've got that mean, I'm gonna be a mean old woman blues.*

> *I'm gonna be a mean old woman someday before I die. I'm gonna be a mean old woman someday before I cry anymore. I'm gonna scream, shout, let the ugly out, and you're gonna feel what demanding's about, before I sing, I sing those mean old woman blues.*
>
> *Now I see how bad I've been treating myself. Let me tell you, it's been awful the way I've lost my health working hard to keep it all inside of me. I've been so sweet, and nice and understanding of everybody but myself. But look out darling, tonight I'm not just aching, no, I'm taking me home to California shores. Gonna get me some sunshine, and maybe more. I've got that mean, I'm gonna be a mean old woman blues.*

As Susan sang the words to her song, there was a shift in the mood of those gathered in the ballroom from pain and sadness to a joyful anger and power. Susan had taken our energy and transformed it. She had been the instrument of that transformation because she had been willing to go into the service blindly trusting that when the time came for her to sing, she would know what to do . . . and she did! Her voice—loud, clear, full of rhythm and life—had pierced what for some had been a first-time experience of knowing the pain and grief of what it is to live under the judgment and condemnation of the Church for being a lesbian. It had taken that raw pain of seeing injustice and had fired it up into righteous anger: anger for lesbians; anger for all women who have suffered at the hands of the powerful.

I had to leave before dawn the next morning in order to catch my plane back to Portland. I'm told that before the last service later that morning, before everyone left the conference, a young clergywoman approached her colleague who was scheduled to speak and asked for time to address her sister ministers. During the service this brave young woman announced that she was a lesbian and that because she could no longer live a closeted and persecuted life, she was going to relinquish her orders to her bishop. As her last official act as an ordained minister this young woman distributed communion to her sisters. And when the communion had been given to all, she removed her stole, the symbol of her ordination, and placed it at the foot of the Wellspring of Hope. That one simple, quiet act served as a witness to the Church gathered that morning—the act of a young woman who had discovered the depth and power of her own strength. There are many heroines and heroes, gay and straight, both inside and outside the Church. This young woman is one of them.

CHAPTER 13

August 24 grew near, and as it did, more reporters called to arrange for interviews: *Time, Newsweek, People, The New York Times,* Boston *Globe,* Boston *Herald,* Providence *Journal*. Everyone wanted the story now. There were phone calls from television studios wanting Winnie and me to be guests on talk shows. For two weeks before the trial there were reporters in our home from nine in the morning until late afternoon. It was an exhausting experience, yet it served two purposes: It kept me too busy to brood over the pending trial, and the reporters provided me with an outlet, a way to tell my story over and over again without boring close friends or Winnie. The cathartic experience actually helped me clarify my thoughts and reasons for bringing the issue to trial. The reporters did one other great service, for the gay/lesbian community: They helped us to tell our story, to let the world know that prejudice is still very much alive and that there are living, breathing people being hurt by that prejudice.

People magazine sent a young woman named Angela Blessing to cover the trial. She called a few days ahead to say she would be flying into Portland on the twenty-third and asked if we would give her an interview that afternoon. I arranged for her to come at one, after the TV newspeople were finished with their interview. She arrived right on time, and we spent an hour getting acquainted. Angela told us how she had been chosen for the assignment. I had told the media the trial would be closed to all but those who were members of the United Methodist Church. The Associated Press, United Press International, *Time, Newsweek*—all of them had been scurrying around trying to find reporters who could claim to be United Methodists. *People* magazine had chosen a rather novel way to handle the situation. Angela told us that two weeks prior, she had found a photocopied form with her paycheck which indicated she was to fill it out and hand it in to her supervisor. The form had one question: "Are you a member of the United Methodist Church?" Even though Angela was based in California, she was assigned to cover the story of the trial. She was a United Methodist!

Winnie and I had decided to drive to Dover, New Hampshire, on the afternoon of the twenty-third so we could relax before the trial, which was scheduled to begin at ten the next morning. We had already been told seating capacity was limited, and spectators would be seated on a first-come, first-served basis. We decided that Winnie and Angela should get to the church by eight on Monday morning.

We met Angela at the hotel at six-thirty Sunday evening. At dinner she told us that a photographer would be contacting us the next week to arrange for pictures and that we needed to be available for a few hours. It seems *People* likes to make it look as though the photographer has been following his or her subjects around for days when actually what happens is you are asked to change your clothes several times and drive to different locations in order to achieve that effect.

Angela asked us a lot of personal questions, but we were neither intimidated nor angered. We had grown accustomed to being asked personal questions by perfect strangers. We had discussed the matter months before and decided the only way the story could be heard was for us to be candid with reporters. It was the right decision for us.

John and Priscilla arrived at nine, and the four of us met in their room to go over last-minute details for the next day. John had brought a friend, his velveteen rabbit. The stuffed bunny was John's way of reminding himself that there is comedy, even in the absurd, that we humans often take ourselves and each other too seriously, and that there is a child in each of us needing to be nurtured and loved. John told us his little furry friend went everywhere with him: on camping trips in the mountains, on cruise ships to sunny islands, to clergy meetings and retreats, and yes, even to church trials! John is a very unassuming man who, on first sight, could easily be dismissed as ineffectual and harmless. He's short, about five feet six inches tall, and a bit round. He has an impish little grin most of the time, the sort of grin that lets you know that to John, life just isn't a series of life-and-death situations but is filled with humor as well. Two weeks before the trial he took to sending me a postcard every day. These postcards were funny, disarming, and just what I needed to keep perspective in my life. Every postcard had a different phrase printed on it, and each was priceless:

"Keep the Faith if you have any left."

"I don't know much about religion, but I know what I don't believe."

"Our rotten system is as good as anybody else's rotten system."

"Try not to despair. These are difficult times for God, too."

"Those who make it hardest to be a Christian in this world are the other Christians."

And my favorite: "If enough people knock their heads against a brick wall, the brick wall will fall down."

The four of us talked until late in the evening, and by midnight John and I felt sufficiently prepared for the next morning and we said good-night. Winnie and I spent a few minutes talking as we lay in bed, but before long we both drifted off to sleep.

Monday, August 24, 1987, dawned as a bright, cloudless summer day in Dover. It was the sort of day which would usually bring playful thoughts into my mind: ideas of going for a drive along the coast or of spending the afternoon with a good book under a shady tree. The agenda for this day, however, was not a playful one. As the veil of sleep began to slip away, and those first morning thoughts attempted to arrange themselves into working order, the seriousness and urgency of the day emerged into my consciousness.

Myriads of jumbled and uncensored concerns drifted in and out of focus: *Would the young neighbor we had hired to feed Smokey, our cat, remember that he liked to have warm water added to his canned food—served oatmeal style? God, I hope she remembers to clean the dish before she adds more food! I hope that John and Priscilla had a good night's sleep. Bless those two, they've been so good to Winnie and me. What would we ever have done without them? It will be comforting to have breakfast with them before going over to St. John's. I wonder who will be there. Will there be more friendly faces than unfriendly? What will we do if someone gets really nasty? I wonder if Winnie's doing as well with all this as she tries to make me think she is. Damn, I think we forgot to water the plants before we left yesterday!*

It's amazing, but when facing monumental and awesome events in my life, I start thinking about the most mundane things, like the well-being of my cat and plants or whether or not our friends had a good night's sleep. Maybe that's my way of keeping order and sanity in my life. Most of us have ways we use to protect and insulate ourselves from the craziness that is going on around us. One of my ways is to zero in on small and practical matters. Managing the small and practical helps me believe that I can also manage the big and nonsensical in life.

With my eyes still closed, I slid my hand over a few inches to find Winnie's shoulder. Her body felt warm and soft and reassuring next to mine. I rolled over onto my side and caressed her neck and face. She stirred and brought her arm around until her hand created a cradle for the small of my back. The alarm would ring soon, but for these few moments, for these few, sane, private moments, we needed to relax in the comfort of each other's gentle embrace.

We lay in each other's arms for a little while longer as we continued to offer one another touches of comfort and reassurance, and just before the alarm was due to invade the stillness of our time alone, Winnie pushed the sheets aside and swung her feet onto the carpeted hotel-room floor. In spite of everything that was different about this day for us, some things were still constant. Winnie would be the first to shower.

As I lay alone in the bed, I was grateful for the calm that had taken residence deep within my soul. The events of the past weeks, and even the anticipation of all that would take place on this day, seemed not to be real, as if they were happening to someone else and we were simply spectators watching the drama unfold. Yet they were very real, and we were aware of our participation in these events and at the same time felt removed from them.

Winnie emerged from the shower, and I reluctantly left the warm and secure womb of the bed. Our tea and coffee arrived from the hotel dining room, and I gratefully sipped the comforting brew before beginning my own morning rituals. We relished our time in the privacy of our motel room. There would be little enough once the proceedings had begun. Today promised to be very long.

When I was alone in the shower, my thoughts began to take an independent journey through uncharted territory: *We have about forty-five minutes before we're scheduled to meet John and Priscilla for breakfast. I need to go over the line of questioning with John one more time. I wonder how George and I will react when we see each other today.* As the warm beads of water washed over my body, the last vestiges of sleep reluctantly gave way to wakefulness and clearer thinking. I came out of shower feeling prepared to meet the demands of the day.

I had chosen very carefully the dress I would wear. It was purple, my symbol of defiance and pride for an occasion meant to strip me of all sense of self-worth and goodness. Since taking a leave of absence from parish ministry more than two years earlier, my style of dress had changed drastically. It had become more free and self-expressive, but today's outfit, referred to as my "minister's dress," was chosen to reflect a sedate and proper manner befitting a clergywoman in the United Methodist Church. I slipped an amethyst crystal, suspended from a purple cord, over my head. It glistened in the morning light filtering through the window, and I was aware of the love represented in this precious gift given to me by Priscilla and Susan at the Women Clergy Conference in New Jersey the week before. Finally, I pinned a small pink triangle to the front of my jacket. During World War II known homosexuals were forced to wear this badge of identification in the concentration camps of Germany. In more recent times this symbol of degradation has been adopted by the gay/lesbian community as a symbol of honor and pride. On this day I would wear the pink triangle as a reminder that even though I wore it with pride, there were those who would want me to be ashamed of my lesbianism. There were those who, even though they would not think of exterminating me in an oven, were nonetheless choosing a less evil but just as effective form of degradation and persecution. In all this I saw my purpose as being one of refusing to be degraded and of turning the trial, the Church's form of persecution, into a triumph, both for myself and for the gay/lesbian community.

As I looked at my reflection in the mirror, I was fully aware that what would happen on this day, regardless of the outcome, was bigger than Winnie and I were, bigger than George Bashore, bigger than Dover, New Hampshire, bigger than this one isolated event. The results of this day would affect the lives of thousands, not only those in the United Methodist Church but people representative of all religious bodies. With this realization came a deep awareness of my own frailty. Yet, in my recognition of the seriousness of the day, as well as the implications that it carried for the lives of others, was the knowledge that I would have to see this drama through to completion.

There was a knock on the door. It was John and Priscilla. John handed us a cardboard box and said: "This is a little something we picked up that we thought would be a good memento of the occasion." We peeled back the tape, and I reached in and pulled out a glass. The box contained five more just like it. Each glass had the same inscription:

"Living well is the best revenge." John and Priscilla were right. Living well, being proud of ourselves, challenging the Church in the way we were—that was our revenge.

The four of us had breakfast together, and then Winnie and I left for the church. Already the parking lot was occupied by more than a dozen cars, and two of my male colleagues were pacing the asphalt, waiting to direct new arrivals into the appropriate parking spaces. Several representatives of the media had also arrived at this early hour, and they were huddled together by the entrance to the Christian education wing. Winnie and I exchanged a few words of comfort and reassurance and then gave each other a kiss. Angela had also arrived early. Knowing that she was there to keep Winnie company eased my mind considerably as I headed back to the motel for a final briefing with John.

Back in the dining room, John and I turned to putting the finishing touches on our preparations. John, once again and with great patience, went over the line of questioning he would use when I was on the witness stand. We had gone over it repeatedly, but doing it now seemed to steady our nerves and help us feel we were using the time to some good purpose. Finally we were ready to leave, and the three of us piled into John's Volvo.

This second trip to the church seemed endless. I needed to see Winnie again, to reassure her and to find comfort in her reassurance. I needed the ballast she seemed to provide in my life, especially over the past months that had led to this day. When we arrived at St. John's, the parking lot had filled; but spaces had been reserved for the principal participants of the day, and we were guided to a space close to the building.

St. John's United Methodist Church is not an easy place to locate unless one is familiar with the local area. It appears to be nestled in what was perhaps once a pasture. Green, sloping hills lead from the road to the church property, which is expansive. The church building is not visible from the road, and one must take care to watch for the sign indicating the entrance. Once off the road and onto the grounds of St. John's, one is immediately struck by the gentle pastoral scene. The church building, which is at the far end of the property, is surrounded by well-kept lawns spotted by large old trees that testify to the grace and beauty of the setting and to the decades during which the land was left to grow unaided by human wisdom. Those who had planned for the structure which would be named St. John's had had respect for the land's natural beauty and had designed a building that would acclimate itself to its surroundings rather than try to modify the land in order to accommodate it to modern devices. How strange, I thought, that such a naturally sacred space carved out by the universe would be chosen as the site for such profanity as would happen today.

As John, Priscilla, and I walked the few yards from the car to the paved area in front of the church, I tried to assess the situation. Thirty or more media people were gathered under a large maple tree in front of the sanctuary, and they appeared to be holding an interview with George Bashore. Two of their large mobile units were parked along the edge of the lot, and long electrical wires, which led from the units, snaked their way along the lawn. Huge satellite disks were mounted atop these roving news station clones, which made them look like something out of a Steven Spielberg movie. Half the media people had notepads in their hands and were hastily alternating between writing and asking questions. The other half were shouldering cameras of varying shapes and sizes while elbowing for better positions from which to take pictures.

As I took it all in, I was torn between wanting to run away in flight and wanting to stand there with my hands on my hips and bellowing out a great big hearty laugh. In spite of the seriousness of the occasion, there was a circuslike quality in what I saw, and it reminded me of one of the postcards John had sent to me the week before: "I disagree with what you say, but I respect your right to be punished for saying it."

John squeezed my hand, and Priscilla put her arm around me. The three of us headed toward Winnie and Angela, who were sitting at a picnic bench on the other side of the lawn. Winnie and I hugged as cameramen scurried to catch our embrace on film. John, Winnie, and I then hurried into the church before any of the reporters could get to us. We wanted to get a feel for the room in which the trial would be held. Winnie was full of news about the hour and a half she had already spent at the church. Apparently Sherwood Treadwell had been placed in charge of seating as well as checking people's United Methodist's affiliations as they signed in at the table in the hall. He had been at the church when Winnie first arrived and had informed her that seating at the trial would be given on a lottery basis. People who wanted to attend would register, and the names would be written on a slip of paper. The names of twenty journalists and thirty spectators would then be drawn at random. From what she told us, Winnie had let Sherwood know, in no uncertain terms, that she was going to get a seat at the trial no matter what methods he was using to determine who got in. After Winnie's little talk with Sherwood, he decided to go ahead with the original plan of seating on a first-come, first-served basis.

The all-purpose room had been set up to resemble a courtroom. It was long and narrow, and at one end were thirteen folding chairs facing the center. They were for the jury members. Front and center was the table where Bishop Irons would sit. Next to it were a chair and small card table from which witnesses would testify. Three feet over was another long table at which the court recorder sat with her notepad and electrical recording machine. It would be her responsibility to take the official court transcript of the proceedings. Two long tables stood next to each other about three feet apart in front of the judge's table. The table to the left was for George Bashore, the conference chancellor, and the minister who would be serving as counsel for the bishop. The table to the right was for John, Elizabeth, and me. Behind us were rows of seats for spectators, and already they were beginning to be occupied by those who had registered early enough to be admitted.

In our preparations for the trial, John, Elizabeth, and I had agreed we needed to be sure expert witnesses were called. We decided we needed three: a biblical scholar, a theologian, and a scholar in the field of Christian ethics. It was my responsibility to choose and invite these three people. John and Elizabeth were thrilled with what I was able to do. Dr. Burton Throckmorton, a Bangor Theological Seminary professor and noted author and authority in the area of New Testament studies, had agreed to write a statement and serve as a witness at the trial. Dr. Marvin Ellison, chair of the ethic department at Bangor Seminary, submitted a written statement concerning the Christian ethics of homosexuality and was also present. Dr. Virginia Ramey Mollenkott, coauthor of *Is the Homosexual My Neighbor?*, wrote a paper and was also available at the trial to testify to the Christian theological perspective of homosexuality. When we were told, two weeks before the trial, that these three authorities would not be allowed to give their testimony, Winnie ran off a hundred copies of each of their statements, and we included them in a media packet distributed to all reporters at the trial. We also rented a meeting room at the motel and scheduled a press conference to be held during the dinner break on the day of the trial. We made it clear to everyone that Burt Throckmorton, Marvin Ellison, and Virginia Mollenkott would not be allowed to give their testimony at the trial because Bishop Irons had ruled their statements were irrelevant. It seemed to us what Bishop Irons was saying by his ruling was what the Christian Scriptures, theology, or ethics had to say on the matter of homosexuality was of no consequence. What mattered was the law of the Church and whether or not I had violated that law. Burt, Marvin, and Virginia were not allowed to give their testimony, and because none of them is a member of the United Methodist Church, they were not allowed to be spectators. The three of them did come to the trial, though, and throughout the whole day they waited on the lawns outside the church building along with the others who were not granted entrance.

Elizabeth arrived about forty-five minutes before the trial was scheduled to begin. She had sent her family ahead on vacation and was planning to join them as soon as the trial was over. She had a few last-minute words of counsel for John, and the two of them huddled together at the table assigned to us. John put his briefcase on the tabletop and opened it to take out the United Methodist *Book of Discipline*, the list of questions he was planning to ask those called to the witness stand, and a stack of notes. His velveteen rabbit occupied a large corner in the briefcase, and John gave his little furry friend a warm stroke before closing the lid.

I was feeling restless and wanted a cigarette. There were no provisions made for smokers inside the building. I needed to be with Winnie, smoke my cigarette, and calm down a bit without having to talk with reporters. We went into the kitchen just behind the courtroom and approached one of the women who was making coffee. She greeted us warmly and ushered us to the back side of the building, where we were out of the sight of reporters and could relax for a few moments.

Ten o'clock came, and the trial did not begin. John was called to a room downstairs, where Bishop Irons reminded him of the parameters he would be allowed in his line of question. He was told he could not ask questions of me concerning my theology, my understanding of Christian Scriptures or ethics. He was warned that his trying to do so would not be tolerated. When he returned, John told Elizabeth how his hands had been tied. Bishop Irons had guessed John was planning to use me to give Burt's, Marvin's, and Virginia's statements. In fact, I had memorized them just for the occasion. John and Elizabeth sat next to each other at the table, huddled over papers and *The Book of Discipline*, and whispering in hurried tones. Finally John came over to where Winnie and I were standing.

"OK, Rose Mary. I can't ask you a lot of questions. Bishop Irons will stop them before they are even out of my mouth. So I'm going to ask you one question. That will be the signal for you to take the ball and run with it. You get as much out from those three statements as you can. Wander as far from the question I've asked as possible. Bishop Irons probably won't try to stop you. If he does, at least you will have tried, and everyone in the courtroom, including the reporters, will have seen it happening. I'm going to try to ask you other questions. He'll stop me. But the reporters will have seen that, too. They have to know that he has put this gag order on me."

I told John I understood. For the first time in our relationship, John could see I was in no mood to chat or to plot and plan. I felt like, and was behaving like, a lion in a cage. All I wanted to do was pace. Winnie and I headed back outside—this time through the front door. We needed to give the media what they deserved from us after so many weeks of working on this story. We took deep breaths, pasted smiled on our faces, and walked out into the sunshine holding hands.

CHAPTER 14

The trial was convened nearly an hour later than scheduled. There was tension building in the room as Sherwood Treadwell announced the rules to which the spectators were being asked to conform. No pictures were allowed to be taken during the trial proceedings, and no mechanical recording devices were allowed to be used by anyone except the official court recorder. The jurors were then ushered into the courtroom. After they had taken their seats, Bishop Irons entered from a side door.

My hunch is that few of us had ever been in a court setting before, and the only knowledge we brought about such proceedings was what we had been able to glean from Perry Mason. As Bishop Irons came through the door, everyone in the room began to look around nervously. Some began to stand; after all, that's what's done on television. I also began to stand, and as I did, I glanced over at the jurors. They all had remained seated, and one of the jury members indicated with a subtle shaking of the head that I should stay seated as well. It was clear this juror was trying to give me the message I should not even try to lend dignity to an occasion that had none.

Bishop Irons called the trial to order and then asked if either counsel "had any objections to the regularity of the proceedings and/or the form and substance of the charge and specifications." After both counsels had approached the bench, a recess was called so that Bishop Irons and the two counsels could meet. John and Elizabeth had drafted three objections:

1. We objected to the fact that Bishop Irons, upon receiving a list of witnesses from both counsels two weeks before the

trial, had overruled John's calling Dr. Virginia Ramey Mollenkott, Dr. Marvin Ellison, and Dr. Burton Throckmorton on the basis that "the evidence which was proposed to be offered through their testimony is not relevant to the issue of the trial."

2. Our second objection was that trial was not undertaken as the last resort, as prescribed by *The Book of Discipline*. John reminded Bishop Irons that it seemed that Bishop Bashore, the Joint Review Committee, and the Committee on Investigation had not considered or sought any alternative but to ask that my ordination be rescinded. Bishop Irons reminded John it was I who had asked for the trial. John responded by saying: ". . . I think it's inappropriate to task her with requiring a trial. It's the only real alternative and it could hardly be called reconciliation. Also, I don't believe the option of extending her leave of absence was seriously discussed. . . ." Bishop Irons overruled this second objection as well.

3. John's third and final objection was that there had been communications on pretrial matters which included Bishop Irons, Bishop Bashore, and Church counsel but which excluded John. *The Book of Discipline* states that all pretrial discussions must include the presiding officer and both counsels. This objection was also overruled, and shortly after the trial was called back to order.

The counsel for the church, the Reverend Stephen Mott, was first to make an opening statement in which I was accused of being a self-avowed practicing homosexual.

BISHOP IRONS: How does the accused plead? Guilty or not guilty?
REVEREND MACDOUGALL: The accused respectfully declines to enter a plea.
BISHOP IRONS: The court, in the absence of a plea by the accused, will enter into the record, that the plea is not guilty and we will proceed then, to try the case. . . . The trial court is bound by the 1984 discipline of the United Methodist

> Church, to make judgement on the charge and only the charge presented to it, by way of the Committee on Investigation of the New Hampshire Annual Conference. Attached to the charge are the specifications, time, places and specifics of events alleged to have taken place. In the matter of the case of The Church versus the Reverend Rose Mary Denman, the charge is that she has committed an offense, to wit, a practice declared by the United Methodist Church to be incompatible with Christian teachings. The specifications make clear that the practice on which the accused is charged is contained in paragraph 402.2 of the 1984 United Methodist Church discipline which states: Since the practice of homosexuality is incompatible with Christian teaching, self-avowed practicing homosexuals are not to be accepted as candidates, ordained as ministers, or appointed to serve in the United Methodist Church. Therefore the trial court may consider only this charge. Your function, as members of the trial court, or in effect jurors, is to consider the evidence presented and then determine whether Reverend Denman is guilty or not guilty of the charge. In that connection, I want to point out that the issue for your consideration will not be the wisdom of the church's statement on homosexuality, or ordained ministry, or whether one agrees with it, but rather whether the accused has been guilty of the offense charged, namely a practice declared by the United Methodist Church to be incompatible with Christian teaching, and if you ultimately find the accused guilty of the offense, it will be your responsibility to fix the penalty in accordance with paragraph 2624.1.(h). . . .

The Church counsel worked very hard to make one point very clear: Bishop Bashore had no choice but to bring charges against me.

> In the fall of 1986, she [Rev. Denman] wrote to Bishop Bashore, informing him of her intention to transfer to the Unitarian Universalist Association. Last March, Reverend Denman requested her leave of absence be continued, until transfer to the Unitarian Universalist Association could be affected. Bishop Bashore, with the request for transfer before him, was in the position of having to declare to the body re-

ceiving the transfer, that the ministerial member involved was in good standing, which he could not do.

According to Reverend Mott, Bishop Bashore, in order to maintain the integrity of The United Methodist Church, as well as his own, had no choice but to deny my request for transfer.

Following the opening statement, the trial proceeded with the questioning of witnesses. The first witness to be called to the stand was the Reverend Ann Partner, the chair of the Board of Ordained Ministry. Reverend Mott followed a line of questioning which sought to outline the chronological order of events which led to the trial, including letters sent back and forth between Bishop Bashore and me. These are the same letters that I have quoted earlier in this account, and during her testimony Reverend Partner was asked to read all or portions of several of them.

John followed with his line of questioning, during which he attempted to establish there had been some cover-up within the Board of Ordained Ministry in regard to the nature of my leaving the denomination. Minutes of the April meeting had originally indicated that a letter I had written to Bishop Bashore, stating that I was withdrawing to unite with another denomination had been read. A revised copy of these minutes indicated that the district superintendent had merely referred to this letter. In fact, there had never been such a letter. All the letters I had written to the bishop were clear on my request: that I be granted an extension of my leave of absence in order to complete the transfer process into another denomination. Yet John and others had, over the weeks previous to the May meeting of the Annual Conference and my announcement that I was seeking trial, heard I had written a letter of withdrawal from ministry in the denomination, that in fact, I had quit. When I did not fulfill this prophecy, the bishop brought charges against me, hoping the charges would frighten me into withdrawal rather than allow myself to be dragged through a church trial. Again I surprised them all by not responding as they had predicted. By the time the trial became a reality from which the Church could not escape, thanks to the help of the media, there were only two alternatives: to tell the truth or to attempt to cover up their lies and game plans that had backfired. They chose the latter and in many ways were exposed through their own trial process.

In his questioning of Ann, John also established that originally the bishop had filed several charges against me: The first was I was a self-avowed lesbian, while the others were charges I had already, in essence, left the denomination when I requested to be dropped from the conference mailing list. What the bishop's charges failed to include was the fact that the letter I had written to him requesting that my name be dropped from the conference mailing list made clear that the reason for the request was my anger at receiving circular mail while my letters to him regarding my standing with the denomination were ignored. The Board of Ordained Ministry upheld the bishop's complaints and charges, and it was upon these the board recommended I not be granted continuation of my leave of absence. Later the bishop withdrew all the complaints except the one referring to my lesbian life-style. The board never reviewed its vote. John's last question to Ann gathered all the above information: "So, then, what we have in the way of minutes is either a letter or a report of a letter of resignation. What we don't have is a vote, but what you're saying is that there was no letter of resignation that you saw and there was a vote."

Ann said, "That's correct."

Later, in his cross-examination of Ann Partner, Reverend Mott tried to indicate that what the minutes actually said was: "A report of a letter from Rose Mary Denman to Bishop Bashore, indicating her desire to withdraw her conference membership to unite with another denomination was shared by the District Superintendent. . . ." This felt like a last-ditch effort to pull the Church out of its own quicksand. There isn't a whole lot of difference between resignation and withdrawal, and in any case I did neither. Had I been at a point in my process with the Unitarian Universalist Association to withdraw, I would have done so and would not have needed the United Methodist Church's permission to do it.

Following Reverend Mott's cross-examination of Ann Partner, John was allowed to give his opening statement. It was quite lengthy. Therefore, I will quote it only in part:

> . . . We were stuck, you might have noticed, on how to plea. We're still putting our heads together. And it's a close call, because you could say she should plead guilty in that she is not contesting being a homosexual. She is not contesting the fact that she is in a loving, covenant relationship with another woman. She is not contesting homosexual practice. . . . But I

> also said it's legitimate to plead not-guilty, because if you believe that the practice of homosexuality is not something that you're guilty of, in a sense that it is not wrong in the eyes of God . . . (then how can you plead guilty?). . . . Reference is made to the paragraph in The Discipline, about celibacy in singleness and fidelity in marriage, which sounds like a wonderful standard, that I think we'd all say we could uphold at first glance. The difficulty comes for gay and lesbian people in that the church does not permit them to get married, and so it seems to them to be a Catch 22. In my not entirely illustrious career, so far, I have blessed motorcycles, packs of dogs, a time capsule, mobile homes, insulation and even a toilet, but were I to bless the union of two Christian people (who were gay or lesbian), it would be an offense, chargeable before a trial such as this, so that option isn't open to me. And so what sounds like a wonderful, fine moral standard, is actually a trap for gay and lesbian people. . . . Her actual request was for an extension of the leave of absence, so that she might apply to the Unitarian Universalist Association. Of course it's up to them if she gets in too, but she wanted the opportunity to apply this fall, but the chance is not hers because this trial date came today. And so she must answer the charge. Much has been made of the fact that she has requested this trial, and in the most narrow sense, that's true. She has requested it, but it's a very short menu to pick from: "Would you like to withdraw under complaint? Would you like to stand silent or sit silently while the Annual Conference votes on a motion to terminate you, or would you request a trial?" If you wish to say that you are not guilty, in the sight of God, withdrawing under complaint doesn't make it. Being silent while people vote you out doesn't make it either. So this is the only forum in which she can say that she is not guilty in God's sight. . . .

John's speech was moving, but it was easy to see he was nervous. As a minister who was looking to stay in the system yet at the same time was acting as counsel in opposition to the bishop—his boss—he had every right to be nervous. As I sat at the defendant's table next to Elizabeth, it was difficult to recognize all the emotions within me. I had grown to love John and Priscilla and to have a great deal of respect and admiration for them and Elizabeth. They had given of themselves in such costly and concrete ways that they were beginning to look like giants to me. John possesses one of the most brilliant minds in the denomination. He is quick-witted and has an uncanny ability to turn a phrase in such a way that it is immediately quotable. Yet he is also a very vulnerable man, and as quick as he is to demonstrate his wit and intelligence, he is also the first to let you know he is involved in his own personal struggles. The combination of quick mind and gentle soul would seem to be the very qualities that would make John an invaluable asset to the New Hampshire Conference of the United Methodist Church, to the whole denomination. However, John does not possess one characteristic highly valued in United Methodism or any other institutional religion: He is not easily molded into a manageable follower. This has caused the conference no amount of frustration when dealing with John, and as he often likes to remind both himself and others, it somehow places him in the precarious position of being one of the few members of the clergy who are "downwardly mobile."

When John completed his opening statement, he called Bishop Bashore to the stand. He and Elizabeth had long since stopped telling me how John would question the bishop. When we had discussed it in the past, I told them they could not ask the bishop the questions they were planning. I was still seeking to protect George Bashore, even if it meant losing points for myself at the trial.

Bishop Bashore was noticeably nervous and flustered as he sat in the witness chair. The room was silent as John cleared his throat and began his line of questioning. Two major points were made during the time the bishop was on the witness stand. Both were shocking, to me as well as to those gathered in the room, especially the other clergy.

The first point John was able to establish was that from the very beginning of my communications with George Bashore in the summer of 1985, he had not considered my letters to him confidential and had, in fact, discussed them with the cabinet. (The bishop and the district superintendents form the cabinet in each conference.) As John questioned the bishop further, it became increasingly clear this was a normal course of action.

> JOHN: . . . The 1985 letters are the initial letters from Reverend Denman talking about her sexuality. Were they held in confidence?

BISHOP BASHORE: No, that became a matter of discussion in the Cabinet.
JOHN: Can you tell us anything about the discussion?
BISHOP BASHORE: Well, that's a matter of common practice. Whenever there is a minister in any one of the Annual Conference, whether it's a matter that's confessional to a District Superintendent or to myself, this is a matter that's discussed frequently in the Cabinet, in terms of talking about what kinds of deliberations should be made, since we carry responsibility for on-going appointments of clergy.

There was a noticeable shift in the room as every clergyperson present began to understand the ramifications of what had just been said. From the time a person begins to make application for the ordination process in the United Methodist Church, he or she is encouraged to understand that the bishops' and especially the district superintendents' function, in part, is to be pastors to the pastors. We are encouraged to approach our relationships with these persons as we would ask our parishioners to approach us. Many ministers, when in personal or professional crisis, turn to their bishops or district superintendents for support and advice. Because we have been taught that what members of our congregation tell us as their pastors is confidential, we have always assumed the same code of ethics holds true in our relationship with our bishops and district superintendents. What Bishop Bashore said on the witness stand helped everyone present to see that no minister can make such an assumption. In essence, ministers have no one to serve as their pastors, knowing that what is revealed between them will be kept in confidence. Any part, or all, of what is said to a bishop or district superintendent may be discussed by the cabinet and can have a great deal of bearing upon the kind of church a minister is appointed to serve. For ministers, it would appear that there is no outlet for conversation which is confessional in nature and to be shared in confidence.

The second point John was able to make clear through his line of questioning Bishop Bashore was that in essence, the choice to bring charges against me in an attempt to bar me from transferring into the Unitarian Universalist Association was arbitrary and unnecessary. Previously Bishop Bashore had indicated to me, in a letter, that one of the options open to me was to take voluntary location—in other words, to resign from ministry. This choice has no negative connotations and is most often chosen by those ministers who discover, after some time in parish ministry, that they want to work in another career. There are other instances in which ministers who have committed offenses choose voluntary location rather than disciplinary action. In some ways this measure seems to be abused by the church as a quiet way to get rid of those ministers viewed as undesirable. The minister is gone; no fuss, no muss. This was an option held out to me. When I refused it and again requested an extension of my leave of absence in order to have the time needed to join with another denomination, charges were filed against me by my bishop.

The key point here was that in reality, both voluntary location and withdrawing to unite with another denomination require that a minister be in good standing. The bishop had refused to allow me to withdraw to unite with another denomination because he could not consider me a minister in good standing, yet at the same time he was offering to allow me to choose voluntary location. Had his reasoning for not allowing withdrawal in order to unite with another denomination been to uphold the integrity of the Church, then, for the same reason, he should not have been offering voluntary location. Also, in his letter to the president of the Unitarian Universalist Association, Bishop Bashore had already made it clear that even though I was an ordained minister in the United Methodist Church, he could not consider me in good standing because of my lesbian life-style. That alone should have eased his need to maintain his own, and the Church's, integrity. For the first time since the wheels toward trial had been set into motion, I understood that it was all so unnecessary . . . or was it?

By the time John had completed his questioning of Bishop Bashore I was close to tears. My hunch is that Bishop Irons was also aware of the ramifications of Bishop Bashore's testimony and how it was affecting the clergy in the courtroom. As soon as Bishop Bashore stepped down from the witness stand, Bishop Irons called for a half hour recess. Winnie knew I was shaken by what I had heard, and she immediately came over to me and asked if I would like to go outside.

There was a rush of reporters and photographers as Winnie and I walked out the front door. They had been waiting outside for hours with no idea of what was taking place in the trial proceedings. They were eager for comments. Winnie and I stood just outside the door facing the cameras and microphones. She had her arm around me in support as I tried to hold back the tears. I was able to answer only one question before my eyes began to fill and my throat tightened to the point I couldn't keep my voice from shaking. The reporters noticed how desperately I was fighting to remain composed, and one of them held his microphone close to me and asked: "Rose Mary, what are you feeling right now?"

My reply was a much as I could get out: "I need to be alone for a few minutes."

I will never forget what happened next. It was a response no one would ever expect from the press. In one quick moment, without hesitation, every camera was brought down and every microphone was taken away from my face. The thirty or more media people in front of us parted like the Red Sea to make room for me to pass, and not one of them asked another question. Winnie and I made our way through them and walked around to the side of the building. Not one of the reporters or photographers tried to follow us, even though we could be seen from where they stood. They honored my need to be alone with Winnie, and I will always be grateful for their sensitivity to that need.

For the first time since spring, when I had decided to take the issue to trial, I cried. Winnie wrapped her arms around me as I buried my face against her breasts and wept. Marvin Ellison approached to ask if there was anything he could do, and I turned to him and cried in his arms as well. None of it, not the decision to go to trial, not standing before my peers at the Executive Session of the Annual Conference to give my address, not even the meetings with the Joint Review Committee or the Committee on Investigation, had felt like a betrayal. All along I had maintained that George Bashore was acting out of his sense of integrity, just as I was acting out of mine. I argued with John, Elizabeth, Winnie, and everyone else that if I wanted George to respect my right to be who I was and to act out of my convictions, then I needed to respect his right to be who he was and to act out of his convictions. I had not studied *The Book of Discipline* as closely as John and Elizabeth in their preparation for trial. Until John questioned the bishop, I had no idea there had indeed been other options open to him, that he had chosen to play a power game, and that the game had gone out of his control. It was sitting in the courtroom listening to all this come out that brought me to the point of breaking. George had been my bishop, and I had loved and honored him. I had also trusted him, right to the very last, and he had betrayed that trust. I am grateful for one thing in all this: I didn't discover any of the lies until it was too late, until we were in the courtroom.

Believing George was living out of his center had encouraged me to do the same. I was never out to beat him. Had I known earlier he had betrayed my trust, I'm afraid I, too, would have given up my own center of truth and chosen to fight to win, no matter what the cost to my own integrity. John and Elizabeth were right to keep what they had discovered from me until the day of the trial.

I'm also grateful friends did not tell me about another event that happened on the day of the trial until weeks later, when I was in a better frame of mind to absorb it. Before John and I had arrived at St. John's on the day of the trial, the media had been interviewing Bishop Bashore under an old oak tree just outside the church building. One of the reporters asked the bishop if, aside from the fact I was a lesbian, I had been a good pastor. I'm told the bishop's response was that because I had been in Conway for only one year, I had not been there long enough for him to be able to assess my abilities adequately. Unfortunately the reporters did not pick up on the fact that even though I had been in Conway for only one year, Bishop Bashore had ordained me in 1981, and I had served under him in other churches for five years. He had visited one of my congregations in Howland, Maine, while I was pastor there, and I had been to his home to visit with him and his family for weekends on two occasions. During those years George Bashore had made it clear to me he thought I was a good pastor. It hurt me to know he couldn't verbalize the affirmation to the reporters on the day of the trial.

By the time the half hour recess was over I had managed to get my emotions under control enough to go back into the courtroom. I knew John was planning to call me to the witness stand next. My heart was pounding heavily as I took my place before the jury and observers. I was nervous; I was petrified. I knew I had only one chance to say what needed to be said. There would be no other opportunities like this one, and I had to make it count, not only for me but for others as well, like the young clergywoman at the women's conference the week earlier who had placed her stole at the foot of the Wellspring of Hope as a symbol of her willingness to leave the ministry rather than live a life of lies. John asked me several questions, and I answered them. I wasn't brilliant. In fact, as I reread the transcript, I realize that at times I hardly made sense at all. With John's help, I was able to say I believed God had created me to be a lesbian, just as God had created me to be a woman. I testified to the fact that I did not reach this discovery, or the decision to live my life fully as a lesbian, until I had first done a great deal of soul-searching, reading, and praying. When John asked me his final question—what I wanted from the Church as represented by the clergy who were serving as the trial court—my response was clear. I looked over at the rows of clergy serving as jury and said: "You've asked me to think about that for two weeks, and I still don't have an answer. I guess what I want from the jury and from the Church is the courage to look beyond the law to see what is right and not necessarily assume that the law is right because it is the law."

Following my testimony, both counsels were given the opportunity to make closing statements. John's was eloquent, and I will quote it in part.

> The charge says "Committed an offense." And I think the reality is that Reverend Denman IS an offense to the church, rather than having committed one, and once it was known that she is a lesbian and is open and is in a covenant relationship with another woman, the decision was made very early that she's got to go and preferably quietly, so as to not give scandal in the body of Christ. And my position is that the scandal is the decision to make her go away quietly, not who she is.
>
> . . . [T]his is a very sad occasion for me, because I think our opportunities for reconciliation have gone past. We have a duty to the law of the church to uphold it. We have a duty to the will of God, to always be open to what that will is, and my fear is that in confronting a tough issue, like human sexuality and all its mystery and unknownness, we will fall back on what's familiar and go with the rule. . . . And the risk of that is that our Discipline, which initially started as a guide for Christian living and a document that would bring joy and fullness to Christian lives, if it becomes just the rules, and we forget the theological task, and we forget the covenant community, and we forget the call to love one another, even when we don't understand, instead of being something that enhances our Christian life, becomes the world's longest suicide note for the church, in which we get bogged down in the legalism.

After John had finished his closing remarks, Reverend Mott gave his, a basic outline of the Church law prohibiting clergy members to be in active homosexual relationships. His argument was in view of the fact that I had fully admitted to being in an active homosexual relationship with Winnie, I was in direct violation of the Church law and must therefore be found guilty.

Following Reverend Mott's closing remarks, Bishop Irons addressed the jury of ministers, reminding them, as had Reverend Mott, that their only task was to determine whether or not I was in violation of Church law. The jury was then instructed to retire to the jury room until it had reached a verdict.

The jury indicated it was not ready to make a deliberation, and Bishop Irons agreed to entertain questions. One, in particular, raised quite a stir.

> JURY MEMBER: I thought I heard it said, at the beginning, that we would have the opportunity to ask questions.
>
> ANOTHER JURY MEMBER: Yes, it was.
>
> BISHOP IRONS: That was true and I never saw a hand raised at the end of each witness that was there, and I think we're now past the time. The instruction was . . . let's not have comments out there, please. . . . The instruction was you had a right to raise that at the end of the witness. Now, we're at the point where the only thing that is before you are the two matters we have dealt with. . . .

In fact, however, the instruction was that the members of the jury would have the opportunity to ask questions. It was never made clear when they were to pose those questions. None of them thought to raise a hand immediately following a line of questioning, and so the opportunity was lost, and the jury was instructed, once again, to retire to the provided room in order to make its decision.

CHAPTER 15

It took nearly an hour for the jurors to arrive at a verdict. I studied their faces as they filed to their seats, trying to discern what their decision might be. Bishop Irons addressed the jury foreperson.

> BISHOP IRONS: Reverend Smith-Rushton, how does the jury find?
> REVEREND SMITH-RUSHTON: We find the Reverend Rose Mary Denman in violation of The Discipline of the United Methodist Church, paragraph 2621.1B.
> BISHOP IRONS: You find her guilty?
> REVEREND SMITH-RUSHTON: That is correct.

It did not go unnoticed that the jury foreperson did not use the word "guilty" in her reading of the jury decision. The next morning, over breakfast with two of the jury members, they told us it had indeed been an intentional act. The jury members knew that in view of the fact that their only choice was to decide whether or not I had broken Church law, they would make their verdict reflect just that. They did not want to imply they saw me as a guilty person. I was grateful for their sensitivity and their courage.

Following the reading and recording of the verdict, which came as a vote of 11 to 2, with two abstentions, Bishop Irons instructed the counsels to speak to the jury concerning the penalty which they would require. John, the first to speak, quite simply asked that the jury see fit to give to me what I had been asking for all along: an extension of my leave of absence so I would have the time needed to transfer into another denomination.

The counsel for the Church then gave his message to the jury. It, too, was clear and simple: that I be sentenced to involuntary termination, nothing less than being thrown out, or given a dishonorable discharge, if you like.

Bishop Irons then proceeded to outline the task at hand for the jury. Several members of the jury had questions about the parameters they were allowed in making a decision about sentence. Bishop Irons clearly stated that they had three choices:

1. Suspension of ordination, which would prohibit the exercise of all functions of the office of ministry.
2. Involuntary termination, which would strip me of my ministerial office completely.
3. Expulsion from the church, which would include stripping me not only of my ministerial office but of my membership in the denomination as well. In effect, expulsion is the same as excommunication.

One of the jury members then posed another question: "The defense has made a request for a leave of absence. Would that fit under the category of suspension?"

Bishop Irons said: ". . . the category of leave of absence is not appropriate, because in leave of absence, the pastor has the right to practice ministry in the charge to which she or he is appointed. Therefore, the categories that are here, do not offer that as an option to the trial court. . . ."

To the three of us sitting at the defense table, as well as to many of the observers present, Bishop Irons had just tied the jurors' hands. He had provided them with a very limited menu from which they must decide my fate. When the jury had retired from the courtroom, we were told we were in recess until such time as it was ready to bring its sentence to the court. It was after 10:00 P.M., three hours later, that we were told the jury had reached its decision.

The jury foreperson was visibly shaking as she stood to read the sentence. She approached the podium and positioned it so it was facing the defense table and those who were present as observers. The other members of the jury stood surrounding her as a symbol of solidarity as she began to read from a prepared statement:

> We affirm the social principles of the 1984 Book of Discipline, which states, "Homosexual persons, no less than heterosexual persons, are individuals of sacred worth, who need the ministry and guidance of the church in their struggles for human fulfillment, as well as the spiritual and emotional care of a fellowship which enables reconciling relationships with God, with others and with self." It is not clear to us that the Reverend Rose Mary Denman has received the adequate spiritual and emotional care of such a reconciling fellowship within the United Methodist Church.
>
> We now seek the spirit of such a reconciling relation, by recommending that the Reverend Rose Mary Denman be suspended from the exercise of the ministerial office until the next regularly scheduled executive session of the New Hampshire Annual Conference, scheduled for June, 1988. We wish to have it recorded that our vote was 12 to 1. [There was one abstention.]

I had been holding John's hand throughout the reading of the sentence, and I could feel his hand closing more tightly around mine as the foreperson read the jury's decision. By sheer force of will, and with the guidance of a spirit more generous than that of the Church, the jury had found a way to allow me to keep my credentials intact until I could be accepted into the Unitarian Universalist Association. The suspension would be in effect for nearly a full year. I was scheduled to meet with the Fellowship Committee of the Unitarian Universalist Association in three months. If all went well, I would receive ministerial fellowship in the UUA long before the next executive session of the New Hampshire Conference of the United Methodist Church.

To John, Elizabeth, and me and to many of those who were present that night, the meaning of the sentence was clear: The jury had made its decision in such a way that I was truly vindicated. I had not been practicing ministry for more than two years. I had not requested to be appointed to active ministry but had asked only for my credentials to be kept intact until I could receive ministerial fellowship in the UUA. The bishop had refused my request. The Board of Ordained Ministry had refused my request. It was a jury of my peers, in a church trial designed to strip me of all dignity, that stood beside me and found a way for me to leave the ministry in the United Methodist Church with integrity as well as loving support.

Later, when the trial was ended, Bishop Bashore was to tell reporters the decision of the jury was a victory for the Church. Yet, to those present that night, who witnessed George Bashore slump over the table with his head in his hands as the sentence was being read, it was clear there was no victory for the Church on August 24, 1987, in Dover, New Hampshire. For the first time in my life I had witnessed and experienced the politics of the Church. This was also the first time in my life I had been strong enough to live by the truth as I knew it, regardless of the consequence. That night, and for months after, one phrase continued to play itself in my mind: "And the truth shall set you free."

In early September I received a letter from George Bashore which included three items:

1. A reminder that I was not to practice any form of ministry while under suspension and that if, and when, I was received into ministerial fellowship in the UUA, I was to submit my ministerial credentials to the district superintendent.
2. An outline of the ruling concerning the release of church court transcripts which dictates that in this case, both Bishop Irons and I would need to give written permission for the transcript records to be released to any other parties.
3. A request that I sign a release granting him permission to secure a copy of the transcript of the trial.

In October I wrote the following letter to Bishop Bashore:

Dear George,

I've taken this long to respond to your letter after the church trial because I wanted to be able to have had the time to put these past months into perspective. I also wanted to be able to speak out of my heart and the pain that is there rather than out of the anger that, for a time, was serving as a mask for my pain. I hope these months have served to help you in the same way.

Please know my choice to seek trial was made because I had truly come to a place where to do otherwise would have been, for me, lacking in courage and truth. For the first time in my life I was given the responsibility, mission and grace to confront the institutional church. It is difficult for me to, even now, think in terms of the word, yet I do truly believe that, in this instance, I was called out to be a prophet. I accepted the call with full knowledge of the pain and judgment that typically and historically befalls those who accept it. The pain and judgment have, at times, weighed very heavily upon me, yet through it all, I have remained clear about my belief it was both necessary and right for me to have taken the stand I did. This conviction has been a centering place for me—a strength.

The one source of pain I had never considered in all of this was you, George. Perhaps that is why, as I reflect back upon the proceedings of these past six months, I realize that of all the elements involved, I remained most vulnerable to you throughout. Right to the trial, I maintained that you, too, came to your place in all of it with a deep sense of truth and integrity. Perhaps that is why what you have done has caused me as much pain as it has. As awkward as I feel calling myself a prophet in all of this, I feel equally as awkward confronting your lies. I love you, and even in the pain you have caused, it causes me more pain to write such an accusation to you. I have tried to stop loving you and caring about what I have so often seen as the tenderness of your soul. It would have been so much easier for me if I could have stopped loving you. Perhaps you were able to cause me so much pain because I never stopped loving you. There is so much in you that is good. It is the acknowledging of your goodness, while still needing to acknowledge your lies that eases my disappointment and pain. It only helps me to realize none of us is ever totally pure or totally evil. We are, each of us, a crazy, baffling mixture of each, and perhaps the answer lies in accepting and embracing all the parts of ourselves and each other. Perhaps this is how the process toward healing and wholeness begins and continues.

Your testimony was so painful to witness. Until you spoke,

I never realized the duplicity of your choices and actions in refusing leave of absence in order to complete my transfer process into the U.U.A., yet allowing for voluntary withdrawal. If both required that I be a "minister in good standing," how could you refuse one while at the same time pursue the other? It was at that moment I began to realize none of it had been necessary. Somehow that seemed to cause me the most pain, while at the same time it helped me to see Providence at work.

Perhaps the most painful moment came when I was told that while being interviewed by the press and asked to comment on the effectiveness and quality of my ministry, you lied by saying because I had only been in Conway for one year, you could not reflect upon such a short-term ministry. Had you acknowledged you had ordained me over six years ago, had a clear understanding of my ministry, and had personal experience of my ministry, you would have maintained your own integrity, increased the credibility of your stand with the press, and won an even higher respect from the clergy and laity for whom you are bishop.

Finally, and perhaps most painful was this last letter from you addressed to me as "Ms.," with no acknowledgment of the fact that although I have been suspended, I remain a full member of the Annual Conference, and therefore, entitled to the title "Rev."

Please allow what has happened, as well as what I have written in this letter, to heal your soul and open your heart to the pain the church, and you as its instrument, inflict every time legalism is chosen as the course of action.

Warmly,
Rose Mary

On November 12, 1987, I met with the Ministerial Fellowship Committee and was granted ministerial fellowship in the Unitarian Universalist Association.

CHAPTER 16

More than a year has passed since the trial, and much has taken place in that time. Winnie and I have flown all over the country in response to invitations to be guests on various television talk shows. I have also received many invitations to speak before congregations, including United Methodist, about our experience of the trial. We have made valuable new friends among the extended gay/lesbian community as I have responded to requests to hold seminars, give talks, and perform Sacred Union services for gay and lesbian couples wanting to make life commitments to one another. The Unitarian Universalist Association recognizes the validity and rightness of such unions and encourages both its ministers and members to nurture the wholeness of gay men and lesbians as we seek to make rituals that will honor our lives and choices.

The experiences of, and surrounding, the trial have, in a very real sense, enriched Winnie's and my life, as individuals and as a couple. Yet it has not been without its pain, confusion, and price. In spite of the fact that we took every precaution possible to protect ourselves and each other, our lives did not go untouched.

One of the most concrete ways in which we sought to nurture ourselves and our relationship was to choose to seek the help of a counselor. Dr. Laura Gordon was, and continues to be, a great source of support and insight. She has helped us grow, as individuals and as a couple, as she has sought to help us to identify our pain and be healed toward wholeness. She has also helped us see the strength within us, and we have grown through that strength.

My parents spiraled back into a place of nonacceptance of me as a lesbian, and of us as a couple, when I told them about my decision to take the issue of my ordination to trial. They were ashamed of me and the publicity I sought. They felt I had humiliated them before our extended family and their friends. My father and I were not able to reach reconciliation before his death in March 1988. Because of our limited financial resources, I flew to his funeral in Arizona alone. Aunts, uncles, cousins, my sister and her husband, their three daughters, my son, and mother, as well as many of their friends in the area, were at the calling hours, the funeral, and my parents' home for much of those three days. I was surrounded by family, yet the isolation I experienced was overwhelming. At times I wondered if I was invisible as conversations went on all around me yet never included me. It was only the daily phone calls to Winnie and one conversation with Laura that helped me get through those three days. My cousin Gerry talked with me about what was happening. He was witnessing my experience as an outcast in my own family, and he saw my pain. My son, who has always accepted my relationship with Winnie, even in his youth and awkwardness, made attempts to reach out, yet he was experiencing his own private pain and confusion over his grandfather's death. It was a time when I felt very much alone.

On the afternoon before the funeral my mother and I had a rare few moments alone, and I seized the opportunity to reach out to her. I cried as I sat across from her in the living room: "Mom, don't let what happened between Dad and me happen to us. Don't die before we can learn to love each other again. You're the only mother I have. I can't go to the store and pick out another mom. I love you, and I need for you to love me."

"I do love you, Rose Mary. Of course I do, you're my daughter."

"Don't just love me, Mom. Accept me, accept me and Winnie, because that's who I am."

That was all we said to each other about the subject. I know that this past year has been a real struggle for Mom in many ways. She and my father were married for more than forty years, and they shared a very special relationship that was good for both of them. Mom has grieved, mostly alone with her own thoughts and memories, yet somehow, during the time since my father's death, she has also found the strength within herself to begin to accept my relationship with Winnie. This past Christmas, for the first time, she sent each of us a gift. She is coming to understand that Winnie is an important part of my life and that I love

Winnie much in the same way she loved my father. For me, the Christmas gifts were my mother's way of saying: "I don't understand, and I may not like it very much; but I am beginning to accept you for who you are." That is more special a gift than anything that could ever be purchased in a store.

As I have experienced the pain of rejection from family members, I am keenly aware that my story is not unique to the gay/lesbian community. So often parents, upon discovering that their son or daughter is a homosexual, are thrown into such a state of confusion and guilt that they lash out at the very person who needs their love the most—their child. If we are to take the most recent studies of homosexuality seriously, then we must begin to believe that parents do not condition their children to be gay or lesbian by how they raise them. If we could only begin to see that homosexuality is simply another alternative to loving, perhaps we can stop trying to find a person or an event to blame. There is no blame. There is no guilt. The only guilt, if there is any to be had, is in throwing away relationships which might have been: relationships between parents and children; relationships between siblings; relationships between friends. Homosexuality is not a disease to be cured or a sin to be healed. It is a life to be lived and celebrated, no less than heterosexuality.

I remember the night of May 20, 1987, when I stood before my ministerial colleagues at the Executive Session of the Annual Conference. There was so much anger in that room. If I could have the opportunity to address those in this body again, I would remind them of the statistics that tell us at least 10 percent of the population is gay or lesbian. Statistics also tell us that among the helping professions, ministry included, the ratio of gay men and lesbians is even higher. There were nearly one hundred people gathered in the room that evening. Did my colleagues in ministry really believe that I was the only homosexual in the room? And if among us we had three hundred children, then we were the parents of at least thirty more gay men and lesbians. If my colleagues express their anger and condemnation of homosexuals to their families as strongly as they did on that night, then how can they ever expect their children will trust that their parents' love is unconditional? Why is it most parents assume it is other people's children who are gay or lesbian? Can we ever begin to realize that whenever we condemn the masses, we may very well be condemning our children, our parents, our friends, possibly even ourselves?

I came to the discovery of my own lesbian identity out of a stance of strong condemnation of those who were homosexual. I had been conditioned to judge those who loved another of the same gender. It was not a God-given awareness that those who were homosexual or bisexual were sinful and somehow less than heterosexuals. I was taught to judge, and that is really another form of hate. One must be "very carefully taught to hate."

In the Christian Church, God is most often addressed as "Father." There are those who have also begun to verbalize that God, being neither male nor female, can also be thought of as "Mother." In either case, the Church attempts to help its members to understand that God loves us like a parent and that we can turn to God for love, support, understanding, and guidance in much the same way as we do our earthly parents. The Church also teaches us if we really want to know how to be good parents, we can study Scriptures and model our love for our children after the love we receive from our heavenly "Father." It's hard to tell which came first, but somewhere along the line many people have come to the belief that yes, God loves us, but only if we are good, only if we fit the mold of whatever it is we think is the norm, only if we obey God's word as interpreted by the Church. As children, even as adult children, we often experience this same pattern in our relationship with our parents. We begin to experience rejection or withdrawal of our parents' love whenever we do or say something that does not meet with their approval. We begin to experience our parents' love as a qualifying commodity, as something that can't always be counted on but that can be given or withdrawn at their will. So, which did come first? Do we fashion our behavior toward our children upon our understanding of our relationship with God? Do we withdraw our love and support from our children when we don't approve of their words and actions because we believe that is what God does to us? Or have we fashioned God into our own image? Have we assumed that because our own ability to love is fragile, and sometimes limited, God's love must be the same? I don't have an answer, and I certainly don't have a way to prove my hunch, but I strongly suspect we have, somewhere along the line, chosen to cast God in our own image. Somehow we have come to believe that God just can't be more loving, more tolerant, or less judgmental than we.

The judgment of homosexuals reaches far beyond the boundaries of family and friends. It is oftentimes internalized by gay men and lesbians who reach a point of hating themselves. This self-hatred is acted out in many ways: alcoholism, eating disorders, overwork, drugs, ghettoizing, and promiscuity. For years the only safe place for gay men and lesbians to be together was in the gay bars where alcohol and, unfortunately, drugs were easily accessible. New sex partners could be found with relative ease. When a person hates and judges him/herself, having anonymous sex is easier than establishing a relationship. Relationships mean knowing yourself and knowing the other person. Who wants to know more deeply that which is hated, judged, and rejected?

There are many who will point to the promiscuous history of the gay/lesbian community and tell us we have caused their judgment to fall upon ourselves. Yet gay or straight, we all know relationships take a lot of work. They also need a great deal of support. Straight people sometimes have a difficult time seeing how much built-in support heterosexual relationships have, and how little homosexual relationships are given. The straight community has joint tax returns, marriage certificates, joint ownership, wedding celebrations, and anniversaries. There are marriage counselors, marriage enrichment weekends, and couples encounters. Families and friends of a straight couple in trouble will, often to the detriment of the individuals involved, encourage the couple to "work things out," to "save the marriage." The surviving spouse in a straight relationship openly mourns the death of a mate, and the family, Church, and social community support that mourning process. Gay and lesbian couples typically get none of this support. The state does not recognize our unions with one another. The Church, for the most part, will not honor us with weddings. We pay double for health insurance because we do not qualify for the "family plan." We must file individual income tax returns, even though we share the same housing and pool our combined incomes. Our families usually do not even know, let alone recognize, our anniversary dates. Often, because of their lack of tolerance and understanding of our relationships, family members will do all in their power to break us up, and many around us will tell us that it's for our own good when they are successful. And it is all too common an event for the surviving spouse in a gay/lesbian relationship to be locked out of any plans for, or attendance at, the funeral of the deceased. Often the dead person's family will go so far as to ransack the couple's home and take furniture and treasured mementos with them, leaving the surviving spouse broken and homeless. Yet we are told that it is we who are guilty of being promiscuous, that we are sick, and that our inability to maintain a stable relationship with one person is proof of our sickness.

Fortunately, for many of us there has been some shifting of attitude in and toward the gay/lesbian community over recent years. We are realizing a growing pride in who we are. We are learning to lend dignity to our lives, even when no one else will. We are learning to create our own rituals of commitment. We are discovering ways to become family to one another when our own families will not support and be with us. We are finding ways to strengthen and nurture our own relationships and to celebrate our lives together. With the help of those in our community who are trained lawyers, we are learning how to protect ourselves and each other with powers of attorney that give our spouses the right to make decisions for us in the event we cannot make them for ourselves; with living wills that will empower our spouses to make the decisions about our funerals and burials; and with wills to assure us our partners will not be left homeless after we have died. With the help of both gay and straight professionals in the fields of ministry and counseling, we are learning new ways to celebrate and nurture our unions with one another.

Winnie and I have been fortunate to find Dr. Laura Gordon. She honors our union and seeks to help us find new and better ways of communicating with each other and nurturing each other. There was a time, not too long ago, when those in the field of counseling saw their task as helping the homosexual adjust to living the life of the heterosexual. How far we have come! Here in Portland, Maine, we have been blessed by a friendship with a minister and his wife who are trained in the area of leading marriage enrichment weekends. Last year they agreed to tailor the program and lead a weekend for gay/lesbian couples. It was a wonderful experience for all of us, and the minister and his wife were surprised by just how much gay and lesbian couples have in common with straight couples. We share the same struggles and joys in seeking to grow as does anyone else. We will be experiencing another couples' weekend with these friends in the spring of this year. They have agreed to train Winnie and me, and another couple, to be weekend facilitators so that we can bring this program to the gay/lesbian community. With the help of these two straight friends, we can get the tools necessary to help other gay/lesbian couples work toward strengthening their relationships. Now that's progress!

During the fall following the trial, Dick Harding, the pastor of the United Methodist church in Wellesley, Massachusetts, invited me to give a sermon to his congregation. We chose the first Sunday of the month for my visit. The first Sunday of the month is typically Communion Sunday in many United Methodist churches. Dick and I had agreed that in spite of the fact that my right to practice ministry had been suspended by the United Methodist Church, I would assist him in consecrating and distributing the communion elements to his congregation. Two weeks before the service I received a phone call from the chairperson of the pastor/parish relations committee. He explained that Dick was being pressed by members of his congregation who did not want me to come at all, but especially on Communion Sunday. It had nothing to do with our "disobedience" of the court ruling but with their fear of AIDS. These people were afraid that because I am a lesbian, they would be in danger of contracting AIDS by receiving communion from my hands. I was asked, rather reluctantly, if I would come two Sundays later. I was angry but agreed to the change of dates. Before the service Winnie and I met with the adult Sunday school, which was attended by thirty or more persons. We addressed the issue of AIDS and tried, to the best of our ability, to answer the questions posed to us. At one point in the morning I decided to go for broke: "There are those in this congregation, some of whom may be in this room right now, who are afraid that Winnie and I, because we are lesbians, might expose you to AIDS. Besides the fact that AIDS cannot be contracted through casual contact, I need to tell you that lesbians who are in monogamous relationships, who do not use drugs, and are not hemophiliacs are at lower risk of having AIDS than any other segment of the population. Heterosexuals are at an even higher risk than lesbians. With this in mind, and using your rationale about casual contact, perhaps Winnie and I need to leave for our own protection. Otherwise we might run the risk of contracting AIDS from one of you!"

This rather strong comment seemed to break the ice. The rest of our time with the class, and later with the whole congregation, went considerably well. It was weeks later that I came to realize that our presence with the people of Dick's church might have benefited them in a concrete way. It seems the week following Winnie's and my visit with the Wellesley congregation, an older man, who had been a member for most of his adult life, found the strength and courage to share an experience with the adult Sunday school class which had taken place two years previous. He and his wife had watched their son die of AIDS. No one in the congregation, nor any of their friends, knew the pain and sorrow these two people shared as they had nursed their dying son. They had been too ashamed to seek help and support from their friends or the members of their church. They knew, from comments people had made in conversation, there was already too much judgment of those unknown, faceless, nameless dying people. They could not bear having the son they loved loathed by their friends and neighbors. As this man shared his grief, he also shared the fact that it was his son's friends, mostly other gay men, who had been the support he and his wife had so desperately needed. It was these gay men who came to their home to help them to nurse their son, to sit with him during the lonely hours of the night as he wasted away. It was these gay men who buried their son with them and who mourned with them after their son had died. It was these gay men who continued to visit this man and his wife for months after the funeral, who brought comforting stories of vibrant and happy times spent with their child, and who in turn listened to the parents of their friend tell their stories and memories. These gay men, these outcasts of society, had, like the good Samaritan, bound the wounds of the sick, buried the dead, and brought comfort to the living.

From what Dick told me, the courage of this man to share his story with the members of his church brought a new sense of relief and freedom to him and his wife. It was also just the kind of gentle yet disarming confrontation the people of the Church needed to help them to see how much their blindness and judgmentalness had cost others—not nameless, faceless others, but one from among them. We can only hope the learning and softening will continue.

When I am asked to lead worship services and to speak to congregations around the country, I am usually given the freedom to design the service and to choose the music that will be used. Shortly after the trial I rewrote the words to an old, familiar hymn: "Joyful, Joyful, We Adore Thee." It is a song which celebrates *inclusion* rather than *exclusion*.

Black and white and red and yellow searching for equality.
We work that this common vision will become reality.
With the passing of each moment, we grow closer to our goal.
Hope within us springs eternal, pouring forth from every soul.

Men and women asking questions, power struggles hurt and maim.
Yet we seek to find the answers to the fears we cannot name.
We are different, yet we are equal, each having her or his own dream.
Let the love that lives within us pour forth like a cleansing stream.

Hear the cry of poor and hungry, as they struggle to survive.
Some are wealthy, others scrambling just to keep themselves alive.
Can we share what has been provided for all the earth's humanity?
Living, loving one another, guided by God's charity.

Sexuality in question seems to bring out all our fears.
Threatening to undo our peace and bringing some of us to tears.
If we really all are equal, how can this division be?
Let's lift up our ways of loving, celebrating you and me.

Counting all the ways we're different only brings us to divide.
Color, gender, loving issues break into a roaring tide.
We can let the storms within us clash, and rumble, and destroy,
Or become a wonder fabric, gifts from God for our employ.

My message is clear. The voice of the gay/lesbian community is clear. To those of you who hate us, before you even know us: See our faces, hear our stories, know our hearts. To those of you who would turn your backs upon us, your children, your brother or sister, your neighbor, your friend: Remember, like you, we need to live fully and to love another. We need your love, your support, and your acceptance of our way of living and loving. To those of you in the Church who lock your doors to us, telling us we are unworthy sinners I shout: LET MY PEOPLE IN!

INDEX

Index